"From student activist ⸺
guished career with the UN, Rob Work has been a ʙ⸺⸺⸺⸺
thought leader as well as a practitioner of social transformation
in the interest of progress for peace and sustainability. Through
this remarkable collection of essays, Work shares spiritual as
well as pragmatic concepts that enable individuals and societies to adapt to new challenges and evolve. It is a fascinating
read and a valuable road map for both personal and societal
transformation."

—Charles F. "Chic" Dambach,
President Emeritus,
National Peace Corps Association

"This is a most generous offering of a life poured out in tireless
service, humble gratitude, and honest self-reflection. Anyone who
has led a life of self-inquiry, social and organizational analysis and
development, and conscious care for self/planet during this time
will find in Rob's essays a kindred spirit, a comrade in arms, a wise
elder. In these complex times of great transformation, it is good
and necessary to step back and see from where we have come
and ask the perennial questions of humanness: Who am I? What
do I do with this one precious life? How do I endure and make
sense of the suffering? In these essays, Rob beckons us to join him
on the dance floor of life and evolutionary development of consciousness. This is a treasure trove of creative and analytical writings that arises from the heart and dances off the pages of history
in a delightful variety of styles and expressions. Living a conscious
life is not for the faint of heart, and we come away feeling encour-
aged, humbled, moved, and challenged by the emotional honesty,
the intellectual discipline, the "miracle of communication" that is
shared so generously through these essays.

"I like the way Rob revels in the art of writing and becoming conscious of his knowing, being, and doing. I reread the essay on 'Organizational Energy' twice as it was so in depth, comprehensive, mind extending, intellectually challenging, and so important as a context for the whole series of essays. I so appreciate his invitations to the reader to reflect on our own personal experience with the inclusion of reflective questions in many of the pieces. With that, he creates a conversation, a learning environment for the reader. I also appreciated his use of gender neutral terms and advocacy for women in a number of the essays. I was quite touched to read his journey around his wife Mary's passing, moving through his grief, embracing the future. Two favorites are 'The Christology of Pierre Teilhard de Chardin', and 'There is Only the Dance.' I also very much appreciated his reflections on the 9/11 tragedy. The structure and flow of the essays are wonderful. Very readable. The stream of consciousness writing, I read out loud like a rap song. The variety of writing styles made the reading very interesting. Thanks to Rob so much for the generosity of this work and for his ongoing dedication to seeking and articulating truth and wisdom on behalf of the greater collective. There is so much richness and beauty in these works that I know I will return to them to gain more insight and understanding and encouragement for the ongoing journey."

—Tina Spencer,
yoga instructor,
former ICA staff member,
Australia

"This book is a special gift from Robertson Work to the rest of us for two reasons. The first reason is that it is a treasure trove of case studies from which we can learn the essential lessons of what it means to be working out of kindness and courage for the benefit of others. The particulars are interesting certainly but the distilled values and attitudes that show up with consistency throughout the narratives are the most valuable to know. They are the things that can be taken to different places, at different times for different people, and still prove to be applicable and essential. They are the things that can be passed on to future generations to aid in their own responses to life's challenges.

"The second reason is that the sense of purpose and dedication to the work embodied by Rob across a variety of settings, through time, makes explicit what Reinhold Niebuhr (1892-1971) advised us: 'Nothing that is worth doing can be achieved in our lifetime; therefore we must be saved by hope. Nothing which is true or beautiful or good makes complete sense in any immediate context of history; therefore we must be saved by faith. Nothing we do, however virtuous, can be accomplished alone; therefore we are saved by love.' (*The Irony of American History*, 1957)

"Rob shows what that means in reality through his enduring witnessing of challenges, setbacks, and successes facilitating human striving for a better life."

—Harold Nelson,
PhD, professor and consultant of
systemic design and whole systems design

"I found this book to be full of different concepts, theories, and reflections that can be a vital guide to address social, spiritual, and self transformation. It takes courage and vulnerability for a writer to share their thoughts and ideas with the world. Courage encourages us to challenge ourselves and the world around us. The author gives practical reflection questions to guide readers to teach, and ideas to counter the global rise in political extremism, economic inequity, and misunderstanding of cultural differences. I highly recommend this book to educators, activists, organizers – especially interfaith organizers – therapists, theologians, and counselors."

—Elsa Javines Batica,
retired facilitator,
trainer, and consultant

"In his essays, Robertson Work has shared with us a lifetime of his growth in knowledge, experience, and spirituality. What a gift. We may feast on his journeys in service of the poor, women, organizations, and students. And his academic essays, including the demythologization of Christ, clarification of the context of the Bible, interpreting the writings of St. John, Pierre Teilhard de Chardin and others, are extraordinary! My brain and my heart have been on overload! I will read and reread his writings on Life and Death, so eloquently offered. And I will be inspired to dance and make music, as I try in the remainder of my life to care for all beings, as we face crises such as climate change and pandemic."

—Kathleen Callahan,
former Deputy Regional Administrator,
Environmental Protection Agency (EPA),
and Deputy-Director of Research Management at
Lamont-Doherty Earth Observatory of
Columbia University

Society, Spirit & Self

Also by Robertson Work

Book author
*The Critical Decade 2020 – 2029: Calls for Ecological,
Compassionate Leadership*
Earthling Love: Living Poems 1965 - 2020
Serving People & Planet: In Mystery, Love, and Gratitude
*A Compassionate Civilization: The Urgency of Sustainable
Development and Mindful Activism – Reflections and
Recommendations*

Chapter author
Changing Lives, Changing Societies
Decentralization and Power-Shift
Engaging Civil Society
*Life Lessons for Loving the Way You Live
(Chicken Soup for the Soul)*
New Regional Development Paradigms: Vol. 3
Reinventing Government for the 21st Century

General editor and contributor
Participatory Local Governance
Pro-Poor Urban Governance: Lessons from LIFE 1992-2005

Contributor
Cities, People and Poverty: UNDP Urban Strategy
Re-conceptualizing Governance
The Urban Environment

Society, Spirit & Self

Essays on the One Dance
1966 – 2021

Robertson Work

ISBN: 9780578977003

Library of Congress Control Number: 2021917383

C2P – Compassionate Civilization Press
146 Woodburn Drive
Swannanoa, North Carolina
28778 USA

Front cover image of Sufi whirling dervish is from Shutterstock
Cover design by Amnet Systems

This book is dedicated to
my brother
James Duncan Work, *M.A.*
and my friend and colleague
Cosmas Gitta, *Ph.D.*
and to
you
my dear reader;
may each of us and all beings everywhere realize peace,
happiness, understanding, and compassion.

Contents

Foreword

As you read *Society, Spirit & Self: Essays on the One Dance* by Robertson Work, be prepared for a creative and unpredictable journey. This book is a combination of leading edge intellectual frameworks for understanding human development in global society, a deep dive into profound explorations of spiritual development in our time, and a heart changing, intimate look into how Rob has been transformed again and again over many decades in his journey of empathy for individuals and local communities. These essays take you on a reflective journey of passionate engagement in global development around the world.

I knew Rob well when we studied at Chicago Theological Seminary in the late 1960s. As a writer and a thoughtful conversationalist, he was blessed with the ability to analyze and articulate the social and spiritual thought leaders and movements of our time. We experienced the impact of the assassination of Dr. Martin Luther King Jr. in 1968 while engaged in the ICA's 5th City community development project on the westside of Chicago. However, those times were just the beginning.

Robertson's essays were written in response to his growing social, spiritual, and cultural awareness over the last fifty-five years. Rob began his service leading development programs around the world with the Institute of Cultural Affairs (ICA) before joining the United Nations Development

Program (UNDP) as policy advisor. Later he taught at New York University (NYU) in the Wagner Graduate School of Public Service. He has travelled the globe, always empowering communities, cities, and even nations in developing plans to care for and actively engage all people in building the future. Throughout his responsibilities and projects, Rob remains humble, funny, and grateful for every moment of his life lived in service.

These collections of essays are not linear autobiographical snapshots of Rob's life and thoughts but organized as three collections and nine themes that recur repeatedly over the years. Insights in one essay reverberate in other essays and deepen meanings that develop into profound understandings. I often found myself going back and forth after seeing connections between the essays. Rob refers in his introduction to various ways to read the book. Take his advice and discover which approach is best for you. Find the essay that truly speaks to you and re-read it. For example, the essay on Teilhard de Chardin opened up for me the spiritual foundations of whole-systems thinking. The essay on "Truth, Power and Lifestyle" at the beginning of the collection on self transformations is so relevant to the economic and political polarization prevalent around the world today.

Robertson Work is a public intellectual, which is evident as you read his growing list of challenging and compassionate books. Yet, I would add to that description a service worker and friend who seeks peace, reconciliation, and the very best for each of his colleagues and readers. His has been a life of projects, a life of prayer, and a life of practices. In that way, we can all be inspired by his insights. If you get a chance to meet him or write to him, he will honor you for your service and life direction. Lasting change for our communities and nations requires our collective cooperation. He refers to this effort as a movement of movements (MOM) and invites us all to join in creating the future.

—David D. Elliott,
international educator,
Hanoi, Vietnam,
15 July 2021

Introduction

It is summer 2021. The climate crisis pounds the world daily with super heat, fires, and floods and is met with continued denial, empty targets, and inaction. The COVID-19 pandemic worsens with new variants, many in the West refusing to be vaccinated or to wear masks, overcrowded hospitals, exhausted medical staff, and most of the world unvaccinated. Efforts to disenfranchise voters are growing through new laws of voter suppression and gerrymandering. White supremacists, religious fundamentalists, and many of the superrich and their corporations are doing everything in their power to sow doubt, falsehood, anger, and conspiracy theories. Systemic income inequality is growing with the rich rapidly increasing their wealth, the middleclass in decline, and the poor unable to pay for rent. The US federal administration is attempting to turn a new page through legislation. Will it happen? Will it be sufficient? What about a Green New Deal? What should be happening in local communities? What can I do? What can mindful activists around the world do to make a difference?

Could the essays in this book be of any help in reinventing society, touching truth, and empowering compassionate action for self and others?

You are at the doorway of an exhibition of essays saved, selected, collected, and curated over fifty-six years. Now at seventy-seven, I am sharing these with you in the hope that they might intrigue or even inspire you.

I hope that you will experience these essays as offering useful perspectives, models, meanings, methods, directions, challenges, and guidance. There are sixty-five reflections in this book written from 1966 to 2021, from age twenty to seventy-six. I decided that they should be published for you in 2021 at the beginning of this critical decade and century of crisis and opportunity. May life on Earth, including humanity, thrive and evolve.

All my life, I have been concerned with societal, spiritual, and self reinvention and transformation. I have tried to help people improve their communities, organizations, cities, and nations. I have worked with people to become more awake, aware, understanding, empathic, and compassionate. And, I have engaged with my own life through reflection-in-action.

For ease of reading this book, I organized my writings into three collections and nine themes. The collections are societal transformations, spiritual transformations, and self transformations. The essays promote societal responsibility, perceptions of ultimate reality, and practices of personal relatedness. In these encounters, you may see how you might further engage in reinvention and transformation of society-spirituality-self that is the One Dance.

Each collection contains elements of the other two, and many essays combine aspects of two or even three of the collections' perspectives as there is a natural intermingling of views and topics.

The societal transformations collection is about how to create a better community, nation, and world. The three thematic groupings are whole systems change, sustainable human development, and visionary social activism. Some of the individual reflections were written in 1990 – 2001, and others in 2017 – 2020.

The whole systems change essays deal with organizational energy in a whole system transition of self, society, and planet, development epistemology, capacity building, and being a reflective practitioner. The sustainable human development essays concern human development and urbanization, urban development, values and principles, and democratic governance and the HIV/

AIDS pandemic. And, the visionary social activism essays focus on post 9/11 new directions, the urgency of climate chaos, the movement of movements (MoM), defending democracy, overcoming authoritarianism, transformational thinking, and caring for all people in the COVID-19 pandemic.

The spiritual transformations collection concerns how to know what is true, good, wise, and loving. The three themes include demythologized Christianity, progressive Buddhism, and worldly spirituality. Half of them were written in 1966 – 1967, and the rest in 1987 – 2004, with one in 2013.

The demythologized Christianity essays are about the thinking of Rudolph Bultmann, Pierre Teilhard de Chardin, and the Gospel of John. The progressive Buddhism pieces deal with the Buddha-event, the great perfection, the middle way, and practicing compassion and wisdom. And the worldly spirituality essays concern the movement from separation to unification, Norman O. Brown's *Life Against Death*, and social artistry.

The self transformations collection is about how to live your calling, your authenticity, and your unique power. It has three themes including my mission and vocation, awareness and identity, and being and presence. These were written in 1986 – 1989, 1994 – 2008, and in 2018 – 2021.

The mission and vocation essays focus on a new vision of reality, transformation of the Institute of Cultural Affairs (ICA), transformational seminar designs, celebrating the ICA's thirtieth anniversary, and creativity, grief, and gratitude in the COVID-19 lockdown. The theme of awareness and identity includes essays of my reflections on the Landmark Forum, the first two gates of Angeles Arrien's book on the second half of life, intimacy, and a playful, philosophical stream of consciousness. And finally, the being and presence essays include a reflection on my love of the dance, confessions of a reflective bureaucrat, peace and war, gratitude, turning sixty, the shift from red knight to hermit monk, and my life-long spiritual journey.

The earliest essays in the book were written in 1966 – 1967 in Stillwater, Oklahoma, and Chicago, Illinois. I was twenty and twenty-one years old, attending my senior year of undergraduate school in English at Oklahoma State University (OSU) and then starting graduate school at Chicago Theological Seminary. The essays in this first period are theological reflections on the nature of reality, human perception, and social change. I was raised a Christian and was a college activist for civil rights, women's rights, and peace and nonviolence. In 1965, I was awakened to being accepted just as I am with a global calling to help create communities and a world in which every person could realize her/his/their full potential.

Then, there was an essay-gap from 1968 to 1985. In those eighteen years, I was deeply engaged in Chicago, Malaysia, South Korea, Oklahoma, and Jamaica, creating a family, trying to awaken the historical Church to its role of service to the least, the lost, and the last, conducting community development demonstration projects in poor rural and urban communities, and teaching and training in leadership methods, and participatory planning. I wrote a few poems in that period but do not have any prose pieces. I guess I was too busy "saving the world" to stop and write my reflections.

Then, the second phase of essay writing began in Caracas, Venezuela, in 1986 – 1989. This was a creative, volatile time of several missional, intellectual, and spiritual changes in my life and within the structures of the nonprofit organization that I was part of since 1968 – the Institute of Cultural Affairs (ICA). In this period, I was introduced to meditation, Buddhism, integral and whole systems theory, a new vision of reality, and the transformative work of Jean Houston, PhD. And importantly, the staff association of the ICA – the Order Ecumenical – was being dissolved.

The third set of essays was written in 1990 – 1997 in New York (New York City, Larchmont, and Peekskill) during the period when I was decentralized governance policy advisor with the United Nations Development Program (UNDP). Here my mind was full of concepts of sustainable human development, urbanization, local governance, environmental initiatives, capacity building, and being a UN bureaucrat.

In 2001 – 2008, the fourth group of essays was written in Garrison and Cold Spring, New York, before and after the death from cancer of my beloved wife of thirty-five years, my grief, and my unanticipated marriage to a most wonderful person who is a writer and Zen priest. My reflections in this time were about 9/11, grieving, aging, falling in love, UN retirement, and Zen Buddhism.

Then, the book has an eight-year gap 2009 – 2016 without any essays with one exception. In that period, I was busy teaching at New York University (NYU) Wagner Graduate School of Public Service, giving talks to UN and other conferences around the world, launching my blog and writing many posts, and preparing to publish my first book in which appear many of my talks, posts, reflections, and recommendations.

Next, I wrote several essays in a fifth and final period of 2017 – 2021 in Swannanoa, North Carolina. These pieces are on the urgency of social activism, the COVID-19 pandemic, and my personal spiritual reflections. During that time, I also published four books (see below).

Within each of the nine thematic groupings, the essays are arranged chronologically. The pieces range in length from one to thirty-five pages.

The book begins with three essays – one from each collection – that were among the favorites of the prepublication reviewers. A reader may then wish to focus initially on a particular collection, or even a specific theme (see Contents). Or the book can be read from beginning to end starting with a broad societal context, plunging into spiritual reflection, and concluding with thoughts concerning the author's life experience. Or a reader can jump around, moving in and out, taking time between readings for reflection and perhaps writing.

Also as mentioned above, during the fifth time frame, in 2017 and 2020, I published four books. These include a manifesto/handbook – *A Compassionate Civilization: The Urgency of Sustainable Development and Mindful Activism*; an autobiography – *Serving People and Planet: In Mystery, Love, and Gratitude*; a book of poetry – *Earthling Love: Living Poems 1965 – 2020*; and a collection of my conference talks given around the world in 2010 – 2019 – *The Critical Decade 2020 – 2029: Calls to Ecological, Compassionate Leadership*. With one exception, the essays in this current book have not been published before. Nor do they include, again with one exception, any of my professional papers written for UNDP.

In this book, I am sharing some of my mind's body of work of a long journey of action, reflection, and writing. This is the fifth volume of my legacy series comprised of a manifesto, autobiography, poetry, talks, and now, essays. I realize that one of my accomplishments is to have lived my life as a self conscious being who has left a trail of actions and words on this beautiful Earth. This is in fact what every human does and leaves without exception. One thing that is unique about my life is that I am leaving these five books reporting on my actions, observations, reflections, interpretations, and recommendations.

In addition, there are eleven other books containing my chapters or other contributions related to my professional endeavors promoting decentralized governance and innovative leadership.

I hope that you enjoy these essays and find yourself empowered, your thoughts provoked, and your life energized.

—15 August 2021,
Chickadee Cottage,
Swannanoa,
North Carolina, USA

Writing: A beginning

(16 October 2003, Garrison, New York)

Writer's block. What to say? What to write about? Write to whom? Why even try to write? Am I even a writer? What is a writer? What are words anyway? Do they make a difference? Isn't the important thing ACTION? Are words a form of action? Of being, doing, and knowing, where do words reside? Are they not part of all three?

We BE within language; words give us a meaning to be; words articulate the Ground of Being. We DO with words; words shake the world; words create history. We KNOW with words; words are our mode of thinking; we put our thoughts into words.

How can my words give comfort? How can they love others? How can they sustain others? How can they clarify, give meaning to others? How can they encourage, affirm others? How can they challenge others? How can they make others happy? Through my words I reach out into the world and love.

In the beginning was the Word and the Word was with God and the Word was God. The primal act of creation. Let there be Light. And there was Light. Calling all things into being, naming all things, giving identity to each and everything.

Without words where would we be? Who would we be? Would we be at all? Are they not the defining act of being, doing and knowing?

But then again, what is the relationship of words to experience? Is experience not the primal source? Is experience not closer to the truth, the Truth Itself? Is experience not our very nature, to experience?

But is not our awareness even more primal? To be aware of our experience even before we give it expression in words? Is not awareness closer to the truth, the Truth Itself? To be sentient, is this not our nature, our ultimate nature, our Buddha nature?

THREE FAVORITES

Before the three collections and nine themes, here are three essays, one from each collection. These were among the favorites of pre-publication readers. You may of course have different favorites.

From the collection on societal transformations, theme of visionary social activism: Post 9/11 Reflections

From the collection on spiritual transformations, theme of demythologized Christianity : The Christology of Pierre Teilhard de Chardin

And from the collection on self transformations, theme of being and presence: There Is Only the Dance

And please remember, you can read the essays in the book in any sequence that you like.

Post 9/11 Impressions, Reflections, Interpretations, and New Directions,

(11 – 17 September 2001, New York)

This essay is from the collection on societal transformations, part of the visionary social activism theme. It was written immediately following the 9/11 tragedy. Some of it was later published in the Oklahoma State University Arts and Sciences magazine.

An Impression: 12 September 2001

All of us are deeply saddened and shocked by the tragedy of yesterday. Our family is safe, but so many families are in mourning.

Yesterday morning, my son Benjamin was driving his mother Mary into Manhattan for her chemotherapy treatment but turned back when they saw smoke in the distance and heard the news. I took the morning train into Manhattan. When I arrived in Grand Central, I noticed something strange. Almost every other person was using their cell phone. When I reached the newsstand, around one hundred people were watching the TV monitor that showed two towers on fire. I was deeply shocked and kept saying "how sad, how sad."

When I got to my office at the UN, colleagues were gathered around a radio and asked if I had heard that the Trade Center had been hit by two planes. I said yes, then I went into my office and cried for those who were losing their lives and being harmed. My son Christopher had left me a voicemail asking me to call him at work. When I called him, I broke down again. A colleague then said that the Pentagon had been hit. We heard that other planes were still in the air and that the UN was being evacuated.

Another colleague who has an apartment near the UN invited several of us to stay with her until further notice. From her apartment, we saw billowing smoke coming from southern Manhattan and in the space where the twih towers had stood, we saw a smoke-filled void. Later, some of us were able to get back to Grand Central and catch a train north to Westchester County. I got off at Fleetwood where Benjamin had brought Mary and where our children live. After I greeted them, I broke down a third time while repeating "there is so much suffering in the world; how can we relieve this suffering?" We then drove back to Garrison in Putnam County.

An era of world history has ended. What happens now depends on the response of each of us. My prayer is that this tragedy will be more than a wakeup call to terrorism requiring retaliation but will be a profound wakeup call to the suffering, confusion, anger, and hatred around the planet that calls for our compassion for our fellow human beings and all living beings. Over a billion people live in poverty. The natural environment is imperiled. HIV/AIDS is devastating whole nations. People are victims of racism, ethnic cleansing, religious persecution, economic and cultural marginalization, and gender violence. People are trapped in ideologies that justify greed, fear, and violence. The wealthy want to protect their privileged lifestyle. The downtrodden cry out for justice and a chance to live.

May all sentient beings everywhere experience happiness, peace, compassion, and wisdom.

A Reflection: 13 September

As a human being, a UN staff member, and an American citizen, I would like to share some of my reflections. As human beings, we are all grief-stricken by the events of the week. Grief has several stages. It begins as shock, then denial, numbness, disorientation, remorse, pain, and overwhelming loss. Grief is always an occasion for personal transformation. Grief breaks our heart. Out of this wounding, we can either become more compassionate or more fearful, angry, or embittered. Grief-work is especially important. We must take the time needed, pay attention to ourselves and others, accept what is happening and be careful that we move toward compassion rather than anger and hate.

Compassion does not mean weakness. It does not mean letting other people continue to provoke terrible innocent suffering. It means coming into a space of acceptance and love out of which cool decisions can be made. It means creating the circumstances for the protection of innocent peoples everywhere. It means restraining and holding accountable those who have violated others' rights of life and happiness. It means going to the very source of human confusion and ignorance to transform the wellsprings of hatred and violence within each one of us.

As a staff member of the UN, I believe that we must use the tremendous energy generated by this tragic event to catalyze an explosion of global, human development. Just as the tragedy of World War II gave birth to the United Nations, this unprecedented event in and of itself must be interpreted and transformed into a controlled chain reaction of energy and emotion – the difference between a nuclear power plant providing electricity to light peoples' homes and a nuclear holocaust.

We must expand the world's attention from the singular nature of this tragedy to other tragedies of similar or even greater magnitude – massive, extreme poverty of over one billion people, an imperiled natural and built environment, the devastation of entire countries by HIV/AIDS, natural disasters and civil wars, and the victimization of people by racism, religious persecution, ethnic cleansing, economic and cultural marginalization, and gender violence. We must transform the very nature of "globalization" from economic and military might to global human development.

As an American citizen, I pray that this tragedy will be for my country a profound wakeup call and moment of reflection on deeply held human values of life, liberty, and the pursuit of happiness. I pray that we will take our time in grief-work, care for those who mourn and need support, immediately increase human security for people everywhere, immediately set in motion constraints on all forms of violence against innocent people, set in motion the international processes of justice to bring to accountability those who are so filled with self righteousness and hatred that they believe that their analysis of reality and history justifies the intentional suffering and destruction of their fellow human beings.

My prayer is that we remember that no one, none of us, has clean hands. We must remember Nagasaki and Hiroshima. We must take responsibility for the consequences of the violent interventions made in other lands and of the people and movements we have supported and the people who have lost their lives. The self-righteous always have God on their side – both sides, on all sides. Perhaps this belief is the most dangerous of all – that our view of reality, my view of reality, is sufficient justification to harm and destroy other human beings and other forms of life.

This is a moment when we must be kind to ourselves and our neighbors. We must do our grief-work. We must take immediate action to protect innocent people and to restrain and hold accountable those who would harm others. We must channel our rekindled passion and love of life into small and surprising and massive and shocking acts of good will around

the planet. As the great paleontologist, philosopher, and priest
Pierre Teilhard de Chardin once said,

> *The task before us now,*
> *If we would not perish,*
> *Is to shake off our ancient prejudices,*
> *And to build the Earth*

May all sentient beings everywhere know compassion and wisdom, peace and happiness, and be about the business of building this Earth.

Interpretations and New Directions: 17 September
Some of our most treasured and trusted categories and assumptions have been blown apart along with the lives of thousands of precious persons and several beautiful buildings. It would be a grave mistake to interpret last week's tragic events and the prospects of the years ahead relying on the conceptual frameworks of previous centuries. If ever we needed new categories with which to think, analyze and strategize, it is now.

In this rapidly globalizing world, there is no North and South, no East and West, no developing and developed world, there is only one small planet. Sixty-two nationalities worked in the WTC. New York City can now identify with cities in other parts of the world such as Lebanon and Sri Lanka. Each country has its rich and poor. All countries face common challenges such as ozone depletion and HIV/AIDS.

Nation-states can no longer guarantee the security of their citizens. Armies cannot protect us, nor can missiles or missile-shields. Mass murder by a handful of people is not warfare in any historical sense of army against army, nation-state against nation-state, battlefields, victors, and vanquished.

Technology has been exposed as value neutral – equally powerful for creation or destruction. A sophisticated jet airplane taking people to vacations, family visits, returning to home or office is also a weapon of mass destruction.

Inequalities that were possible in previous centuries – billionaires eating at the same table as the malnourished – are no longer tolerable. We are too intimate in time and space. We cannot hide our wealth or hide from others' impoverishment.

Good versus evil has been laid bare as an oversimplification in a world of mind-boggling complexity, with six billion people each with 10 billion brain cells and only "six degrees of separation." At any moment on the planet for every act of hurt, there are a billion acts of kindness.

We must think beyond dualism – us or them, black or white, win or lose. We must learn to tolerate subtlety and complexity of analysis and strategy. We must look at the whole system in its interconnectedness and its mutual causality not only at discrete, mechanistic pieces. Reality is a whole system with dimensions of interior and exterior and individual and collective.

We must look *within* for solutions not expecting our external technologies alone to save us. Where within ourselves do we find confusion and ignorance, anger, and hatred? When and how have we harmed other people and other forms of life? How has this affected us? What is of ultimate value to us in this life? Do our emotions and ideas control us, or do we control and direct them?

We must talk to our neighbors and our enemies. They are human beings just like us with bodies, emotions, and minds. What are their hopes and fears? What are their values and assumptions? What are their worldviews? What are their analyses of reality and history? Without continuous dialogue, human relations and trust break down.

Human behavior is a manifestation of the human mind and heart. What a person thinks and feels determine their sense of what is real. To change a person's images, ideas, and emotions is to change their worldview and subsequently their behavior both individual and institutional.

All people have seeds of anger, hatred, and violence in the soil of their minds. For some people, these seeds are watered by experiences, feelings and ideas, sprout and grow, becoming strong plants. Each of us must take care not to allow these seeds to be nurtured and cultivated. We must instead nourish seeds of compassion, kindness, and love. In fact, these are not only seeds but also the fundamental nature of mind itself that has become obscured and must be realized.

A global network of like-minded people, whether they be filled with love or hate, cannot be bombed out of existence. If ignorance and hatred have gained control, their minds and hearts must be changed. They must gain self-restraint. Until this happens their ability to manifest and exercise their ideas and feelings must be curtailed. This can be done by inhibiting their access to information, capital, communication, transportation, weapons, and opportunities of acting out their intentions.

Power must be decentralized throughout a society. In this way, no attack on one building, one city, or one group can result in societal paralysis and chaos. Power must reside throughout networks of self-generating nodes of intelligence each with the capabilities to decide and act.

It is becoming dramatically clear that ultimately there can be no guarantee of individual or national security, prosperity, or happiness unless these exist in some measure throughout global society – community by community. If only a few people have comfort and convenience and most of their neighbors struggle for survival in squalor and hopelessness, the causes and conditions exist for jealousy, pride, greed, conflict, fear, hatred, and violence. If for no other reason than self-interest, setting aside the motivation of compassion and love, it would benefit the rich and powerful, the well-off and comfortable if they provide opportunities for their brothers and sisters in need wherever they are.

What if we lived as one human family? What if we could create heaven on earth? What if the source of true happiness were found in helping others? What if compassion and wisdom rather than violence and confusion were the fundamental nature of the human being and could be realized person by person? What if we saw the world as one of abundance rather than scarcity and that the challenges facing us were ones of distribution of opportunity and access rather than hoarding and competition? What if we discovered that idealism and the "vision-thing" were the most practical, pragmatic, and transformative ways of viewing and dealing with reality and change?

What actions could be taken?

- Commit $1 trillion to eradicating global poverty in memory of the 3,000 people who died on 11 September.
- Invite the world community to join in a Millennium Project of Building the Earth.
- Establish a global electronic network of dialogue and reconciliation.
- Hold a series of regional and global conferences of dialogue and reconciliation with representatives of all perspectives and backgrounds.
- Have a day of amnesty and forgiveness for all those who have committed violent crimes.
- Establish programs of individual and organizational transformation with an array of tested, effective methods from different traditions.
- Transform prisons into schools of transformation.
- Teach transformative methods and approaches in all schools.

More than anything else, what is needed at this time is a response to our own suffering that is shocking and unexpected – a massive act of good will toward our enemies and those who suffer around the world. This response, rather than a rain of missiles killing thousands of innocent people, would set the stage for a new era of world history rather than the mindless perpetuation of centuries of violence and needless suffering.

Death is not the enemy. Death is a natural part of life and is the basis of our compassion for each other. The fiercest enemies we face are our own ignorance, mistrust, anger, hatred, pride, and intolerance.

Let us then herald the onset of a thousand years of global human development – community by community, person by person. May all people everywhere realize the cessation of suffering in perfect joy and happiness.

The Christology of Pierre Teilhard de Chardin

(1967, Chicago, Illinois)

This essay is from the collection on spiritual transformations, part of the theme of demythologized Christianity. The thinking of Fr. Pierre Teilhard de Chardin (1881-1955) has influenced me for the past fifty-four years. Here is my first attempt to capture some of the basics of his thought. It appears that he was driven to merge his scientific observations with a theological interpretation.

A Christological formulation is central and paramount to the whole of de Chardin's meta-scientific cosmology. To witness to this centrality, de Chardin's Christology will be placed within the context of his cosmogenesis (the evolution of the cosmos.) First, his doctrine of God as Creator will be briefly dealt with; then his theory of the creation of the cosmos as beginning and continuing process through the stages of matter, Life, Thought, and Hyper-Consciousness will be discussed; then his eschatology, and finally the ethics implied in this schema.

De Chardin's Christology (although almost always discussed in non-traditionally-theological language) will be seen as present and active throughout every aspect and process involved in his theory of cosmogenesis, a theory which he did not presume to call metaphysics, ontology, or speculative philosophy, much less theology, but rather spoke of as a "hyper-physics," or even simply as "an attempt to see and to make others see what happens to man and what conclusions are forced upon us, when he is placed fairly and squarely within the framework of phenomenon and appearance." (*The Phenomenon of Man*, p. 31) In other words, he writes as one humbly observing the facts (however humbling his observations are for his reader), and he respectfully leaves the task of academic philosophical discourse (whether metaphysics, ontology, or whatever) on and about his vision to others. This is not to say, however, that de Chardin did not at times (was not forced to) elaborate his thought "philosophically" because, as a self-conscious pioneer-visionary, the man was forced to go beyond the purely "scientifically orthodox" terminology and formulations, and into the highly speculative and oft times poetic realms of discourse. Even so, his thought is notably marked by a rigorous logic which sometimes leads to amazing conclusions and syntheses but is nevertheless coherent and necessary – at least in appearance. It is precisely here as well as in following through on the rich implications of his thought that the work of others who come after de Chardin lies in untangling and reassembling his well-informed outline of "the phenomenon of man."

Before de Chardin's cosmogenesis as such is analyzed, let us attempt to gain a very generalized appreciation for his whole theoretical effort.

The life work of de Chardin appears very much to be of one stuff – not only in the sense that his being was an integrated union of the two main functions of the paleontologist and the religious visionary, but also his intellectual life suffered no duality. This is grasped best, perhaps, if we see de Chardin working as a self-avowed naturalist who saw the universe as one self-enclosed Process. For de Chardin there was no realm of the natural along side of the supernatural; thus, his cosmology does not contain the essential dualism between matter and spirit that we would rightly expect from

Thomism. But rather for de Chardin, matter and spirit are two aspects of the same uni-verse: "related variables" of the same nature.

What de Chardin has in fact written is a natural history of the universe in process which includes past, present, future, and that which is beyond all space-time. What his research has shown him is that by extrapolating from the actuality of the most recent phenomenon in the cosmos—human consciousness—we can become informed of the process that has led up to this new creation and the process that can be projected by extending the "graph" of evolutionary movement into the far distant future.

De Chardin's primary emphasis is very decisively upon the nature of human consciousness, and from that nature he is informed of the nature of cosmogenesis itself. He describes this consciousness in the following terms which will be dealt with later: reflection; individualization; centeredness; the within of things; personalization; involution; convergence; loving. From these few statements, we shall move immediately into de Chardin's "system."

For de Chardin the universe was and is being created by God. By this, he means that the world is the work of God, that all things depend freely upon God, that creation itself is good. God, then, is the First Cause, the Prime Mover (and as we shall see, Cause itself, for there is no moment when God creates and a moment when second causes develop.) Because creation is a transcendent act, one can never place it on the same level as phenomenon nor can it be conceived as intervening and breaking the chain of phenomena; God makes things make themselves. We must not, therefore, limit our vision of creative activity to the beginning of things because the beginning of things is not a phenomenon. From the phenomenal point of view, the beginning of time cannot be grasped. As Pierre Smulders writes, "Because pure non-being is not a reality and outside of the world there is no time, there is then not a 'moment' when no creature existed." (*The Vision of Teilhard de Chardin*, p. 67) Thus God "creates and shapes us through the process of evolution." (*The Future of Man*, p.79) The creative action of God does not suppress the laws that exist in creatures. In fact, the creative action of God lies hidden in the very actions of creatures themselves. In this way we see that all of creation is utterly dependent upon God. Creation is coextensive with the totality of duration and hence it is a transformation of phenomena. This is a view of creative transformation of phenomena, i.e., an act in which the created pre-existent grows into a totally new being.

Anything much beyond this description of God's action can only be got from a description of evolution itself: that is to say, a description of the new emergent being that has and will come about through cosmogenesis. In other words, for de Chardin, God is finally known as He has been, can be, and will be seen within human space-time history and even beyond it.

The movement of this history can be depicted as a spiral with its coils moving upwards to a single point. The entire spiral has a common axis or pole, just as each successive circle has a common center. This model represents the movement in the universe toward increased unification and complexification as these are directed and energized by a common pole or center. The process broadly speaking can be described as the transformation of matter into spirit with the central, energizing force for this transformation the self-same force in which human love participates, i.e., the attraction of centers for one another.

For de Chardin, this "centration" of all phenomena of the cosmos is of crucial importance. Just as in the centered atom, the natural granule of simple, elemental matter, it is this "being centered on itself" aspect of all things that makes for the process of involution, or matter moving back onto itself. This is to say that because of a closed chemistry (a circumscribed arena for limited chemical interaction) and the play of large numbers in space and time, Life was created on this planet.

Thus, geogenesis (the evolution of the earth) became biogenesis (evolution of life) because of the very curvature of the earth: the planet is round and, therefore, centered and thus all its processes move in on themselves without escape.

With the creation of Life, there developed an interiorization of matter centered in organisms which constituted the "within" of the universe – for here there was freedom, a selective responsiveness to the "without of things" which was determined. Thus, a metamorphosis had taken place in the creation of complexity within a living organism out of the diversity and simplicity of matter.

Because of the curved layer of the biosphere on the planet and the natural forces at work in biogenesis, Thought developed within living organisms. This Thought became reflection when organic consciousness acquired the power to turn in on itself; for the first time Life was thoroughly individuated as a "center in the form of a point at which all the impressions and experiences knit themselves together and fused into a unity that is conscious of its own organization." (T P of M, p. 165) Thus the noosphere (the layer of self-consciousness on the planet) was created and centered as part of geogenesis and biogenesis.

The gradual perfection of this consciousness (hominization) develops through human socialization, civilization. This is because knowledge is the natural object of conscious reflection. To be conscious is to know and to know that you know. Because of this, knowledge implodes upon itself to unite mankind. "Object and subject marry and mutually transform each other in the act of knowledge; and from now on man willy-nilly finds his own image stamped on all he looks at." (T P of M, p. 32) In the centered consciousness, the person, and the universe, come into being as a unity. From this, we see that cosmogenesis is both Personal and Universal. Thus in "thinking the world" we confer upon the world a unity it would otherwise be without. Human knowledge is the conquest of matter put to the service of mind; therefore, increased knowledge is increased power which is increased action which is increased being.

The Evolution of the Cosmos is now taking place within human consciousness. Because the noosphere is a whole which is closed and centered, individual consciousness is being brought by this super-concentration into association with all the other centers surrounding it. In this way, humankind will inevitably converge in a Hyper-Personal Collectivity of consciousness which will include all the individual centers of consciousness in complete harmony and unity with one another (while maintaining their "personality.") This unity will be held together necessarily by another center of the entire Collection. This center de Chardin calls the Omega point, and it is here that his theory reaches "the end of the world." Here beyond space-time, all the Universe will be completely Personalized. This is what he points to as the Christian Parousia. At this stage beyond all the other stages that lead to it, the personal consciousnesses of mankind will be utterly fulfilled (totally differentiated while in total union.)

De Chardin gives the Omega four primary attributes: its autonomy; its actuality in the present moment; its irreversibility; and its transcendence. It is the second aspect, its present actuality, which will now concern us.

Omega is not simply a hypothetical concept which de Chardin places at the end of cosmogenesis to tie everything up neatly – far from it. It is rather one with God as Creator and one with the animating, guiding force that directs cosmogenesis. This bring us back to our initial statement that for de Chardin "Christological formulation is central and paramount" to the whole of his cosmology. Omega is Christ, and cosmogenesis is Christogenesis. And because the creation is continuing within the universe at this very moment, Christ is present.

If the world is convergent and if Christ occupies its center, then the Christogenesis of St. Paul and St. John is nothing else than the extension, both awaited and unhoped for, of that noogenesis in which cosmogenesis – as regards our experience – culminates. Christ invests himself organically with the very majesty of his creation. And it is in no way metaphorical to say that humans find themselves capable of experiencing and discovering this God in the whole length, breadth, and depth of the world in movement. To be able to say literally to God that one loves him, not only with all one's body, all one's heart and all one's soul, but with every fiber of the unifying universe – that is a prayer that can only be made in space-time. (T P of M, p. 297)

Omega, then, is the Prime Mover Ahead calling all to Himself – the Good Shepherd. Christ is the All in All, He is the final fulfilment of that which is presently fulfilling: The Personalization of the Universe.

It is with a concluding discussion of the third aspect of Omega, its irreversibility, that we will move into ethical considerations, especially the nature of human freedom in relation to cosmogenesis.

To repeat, what de Chardin has developed is a necessary and inevitable cosmogenesis which is in fact already a fact. The Christian has evidence of this reality: "For a Christian believer it is interesting to note that the final success of hominization (and thus cosmic involution) is positively guaranteed by the 'redeeming virtue' of the God incarnate in his creation." (T P of M, p. 307)

Now that humanity has become conscious of the movement which carries it onwards, it has more and more need of finding, above and beyond itself, an infinite objective, an infinite issue, to which to dedicate itself.

And what is this infinity? "The effect of twenty centuries of mystical travail has been precisely to show us that the Baby of Bethlehem, the Man on the Cross, is also the Principle of all movement and the unifying Center of the world; how then can we fail to identify this God not merely of the old cosmos but also of the new cosmogenesis, this God so greatly sought after by our generation, with you, Lord Jesus, you who make him visible to our eyes and bring him close to us?" (*The Hymn of the Universe,* p. 138)

Here we have in prayerful, confessional form de Chardin's own affirmation of the unity of person of the Christ of the Cross and the motivating power of all Evolution. Nowhere in his writings does he attempt any kind of establishment (by

proof-texts or any other means) of the continuity between
these two Persons, but it is beyond question that he understood
his own work as "one who attempts to see" the whole phenomenon of man as critically informed by the "living reality" of his
speculative model, i.e., the Christ of the Christian dogma. "In
one manner or the other it still remains true that, even in the
view of the mere biologist, the human epic resembles nothing
so much as a way of the Cross." (T P of M, p. 311)

But what we ought here to be more concerned about is the
nature of a human being's free capacity to choose for or against
the Omega. De Chardin himself is not entirely clear on the
meaning of the inevitability and "irreversibility" of the Omega.
At one point in reference to movement toward Omega, he says
without qualification: "Assuming success – which is the only
acceptable assumption – under what form and along what lines
can we imagine progress developing during this period?" (T
P of M, p. 277) And later in the Postscript he says: "As regards
the chances of cosmogenesis, my contention is that it in no way
follows from the position taken up here that the final success
of hominization is necessary, inevitable, and certain." (T P of
M, p. 306) The most economical way of reconciling these two
statements seems to be to suppose that inherent in the first is
the assumption that only by assuming the success of Omega
can we then theorize about its nature; and in the second the
not so well hidden implication that it is only by way of Christian
revelation that a man can finally know that Omega is certain,
never with phenomenological descriptions of evolutionary ten-
dencies. Surely this must be considered as one manifestation
of a hidden evangelism for the Gospel that runs through all de
Chardin's writings.

Given this understanding it can be said that human freedom in relation to Omega is of the same nature as that of the
decision for or against the Christ in the New Testament: a man
either decides with eternity or against it. For de Chardin, if
he decides for Omega, he will work for the increase of human
consciousness on this planet. His ethic will be one grounded

in an ultimacy of the nature of the "last things" (eschatology.) With this final resolution of his relationship to the cosmos, the believer is free to unite with his neighbor in love and to work in the transformation of the spiritualized matter of the earth into pure spirit. In this way, man participates in the universe of process in its own reflective-self-recreation.

There Is Only the Dance

(4 April 1994, Larchmont, New York)

This essay is from the collection on self transformations, under the theme of being and presence.

Yesterday, I sprained a toe while practicing ballet. Now at forty-nine, I am doing something which I have longed to do for the past forty years. This minor injury will keep me from practicing for a week or two. Why do I so enjoy learning ballet, dancing ballet, watching ballet, as well as all other dance forms for that matter?

Ballet is the quintessential European art form, tracing its lineage back to the 17th Century French court. Its grace and elegance are a code of courtly etiquette. Ballet embodies the Western longing for transcendence of earthly existence, of escaping the limitations of gravity, for conquering nature. To master this artform requires supreme control and discipline. Ballet is a never-ending quest for the perfection of an idealized form of human bearing and movement. It is also the basic vocabulary for all Western dance. Modern dance may make use of ballet technique or may depart from it or rebel against it, but modern dance cannot ignore ballet.

As a boy growing up in a small Oklahoma town, I was fascinated and attracted by the images of princes and princesses, of knights and castles in my story books. I drew pictures of princes, played with my toy castle and knight set and dressed up like a prince. Somehow this identification with European royalty and nobility transported me from my mundane existence to a realm of beauty and splendor, of true ladies and real gentlemen. Sometimes I thought that I should have been born a few centuries earlier in courtly Europe.

I was a tall slender boy and could do the splits. I was shy and felt that I was not an attractive person. My mother was always telling me to stand up straight and not to stand pigeon-toed. I had to wear glasses at a young age and later got my teeth straightened. It seemed that everything was wrong with my young body and that it had to be corrected, to be made acceptable. I now see that the ideal of perfection was being instilled in my child's mind.

At university, I remember watching a friend practicing with a group of students for a performance of West Side Story. How I wanted to join them. But I was too shy and uncertain of myself.

I will never forget the thrill of seeing, for the first time, Rudolph Nureyev, and Margot Fonteyn, both now dead, dance Romeo and Juliet in a Chicago performance in the 60s. Nureyev in his powerful jete was pure elegance and grandeur. He seemed to stay airborne forever. Ms. Fonteyn was pure grace and lightness. Together they were poetry in motion.

Over the years, I have been enthralled by dance performances I have witnessed in many parts of the world – Javanese courtly dance, classical Thai dancing, ancient Indian dances, Kenyan tribal dancing, Filipino folk dancing, Egyptian belly dancing, American Indian circle dancing, Hawaiian dancing, Mexican folk dancing, Chinese acrobatic dance, and classical Korean dancing. Each of these communicated vast dimensions of meaning to me about their cultures. I have enjoyed beautiful ballets by some of the world's great companies including the New York City Ballet, the American Ballet Theater, the Dance Theater of Harlem, and the Joffrey Ballet.

I have been challenged and energized as a spectator by the creativity of modern dance companies such as the Alvin Ailey American Dance Theater, the National Theater Dance Company of Jamaica, Feld Ballets, Garth Fagen Dance, Nikolais and Murray Louis Dance, SUNY Purchase Dance Corps, Sardono Dance Theater, Paul Taylor Dance Company, Martha Graham Dance Company, Trisha Brown Dance Company, The Parsons Dance Co., Erick Hawkins Dance. Co., Ralph Lemon Dance, Philobolus, White Oak Dance Project, and the Bill T. Jones/Arnie Zane Dance Company.

I have also danced – Jamaican reggae, Venezuelan joropo, the waltz, sacred dance, square dance, American popular dance, American Indian circle dance, improvisational dancing and now ballet. When I am dancing, I feel more alive. Music flows through me and sets my body in motion. While I am dancing, I am connected to myself, others, and the ground of being.

The rediscovery of my love of dance and dancing happened in 1986 during a seminar on "Sacred Psychology" with Jean Houston in Chicago at an ICA summer program. One of the psycho-physical exercises involved dancing in an expressive mode. I found myself moving in ways I never dreamed. I was released to express myself in motion and movement as never before. I remember seeing a poster at the seminar on which was written, "There is only the Dance!" I realized that for me, dance was a grand metaphor for the dynamic movement of the cosmos, the Earth, and the human.

Everything is in motion! Electrons, photons, molecules, cells are in constant vibration. The stars, the planets, the galaxies are in continuous movement. The evolving earth rearranges her continents and seas, plants and animals, air and rivers over and over again. The human species has emerged and moved and evolved and transformed repeatedly. Civilizations rise, flourish, and transform or disappear. Everything participates in the Great Dance of the Universe! The Hindu God Shiva dances both creation and destruction. There is only the Dance!

As I reflect on my life I see that I have approached my work with NGOs and the UNDP as a choreographer and a dancer. I have choreographed human development projects in rural villages and urban slums, in corporations, and NGOs, in over forty countries around the world. I have tried to bring artistry and grace into social relationships. I have brought people together in surprising movements which changed the way they viewed each other. I have danced from West to East, from wealthy communities to poor, from cities to villages, from listening to teaching, from crying to laughter, from death to life, from ecstasy to despair, and from stillness to action.

At forty-nine, it is not easy to study ballet. The proper age to begin is around nine. Over the past three years, I had often thought about taking ballet lessons. Four months ago, I began dieting and exercising. I got up my nerve and visited the Alvin Ailey American School for Dance and observed a ballet lesson. I bought some black tights and ballet slippers. Finally, three months ago, I took the plunge and joined a class at SUNY Purchase. I was so nervous and timid that my wife kindly drove me to the first class.

Nevertheless, study I do. I am awkward. I cannot remember my ballet teacher's instructions. I cannot execute all the steps. My back is stiff. My "turn out" is not very turned out. I sweat. My muscles give out. But onward I go. For my twice weekly lessons, I am fortunate to have a wonderful teacher who has danced in the Ballet Russe de Monte Carlo. I am her worst student but one of her most devoted. I practice by myself every weekend. I am reading a book on classical technique. I attend dance performances as often as possible.

And after I have studied ballet for a year or so, I may transfer to modern dance. I hope to learn to express myself more fully and to choreograph dances, to express the truth about life in motion, the ecstatic dance of matter and of spirit.

Heal quickly little toe!

COLLECTION
Societal Transformations

This collection contains essays on whole systems change, sustainable human development, and visionary social activism.

THEME

Whole Systems Change

The terms whole systems change, transition, transformation, and design are all used in this theme as well as elsewhere in the book. These essays are filled with conceptual frameworks from ICA, Jean Houston, Ken Wilber, Nigel Calder, Edward Hall, Harold Nelson, UNDP, and others related to systemic approaches to societal change.

Orchestrating Organizational Energy within a Whole System Transition of Self, Society, and Planet

(April 1991, New York)

This essay is based on a two-day seminar that the author designed and conducted for a firm in Caracas, Venezuela. The first three sections explore personal development within a new experience of reality, and the final two deal with releasing creative energy to increase effectiveness in any organization. It contains mind expanding frameworks and models of whole system transition helpful in personal, organizational, and societal development. It also contains questions and activities in which a reader can engage. Time frames and data are from 1991. This essay is relevant for 2021 as there is still a need to expand our understanding of time, consciousness, culture, energy, and management in this critical decade of chaos and creativity. At the end of the essay is a bibliography of the books referenced throughout. At thirty-five pages, in five sections, this is the longest essay in the book. You might enjoy savoring one or two sections at a time, interspersed with reflection or other essays, or you may wish take it all in at one reading.

In this essay, we will cover a lot of ground. As you read, you will co-create, experience, and explore. You may find this paper interesting, challenging, provocative, or stirring. To gain the most from reading, you are asked to suspend your assumptions and judgements until the end. You are invited to be inquisitive, to observe yourself, your reactions, and your responses. I have selected materials, including several models and exercises, which I believe you will find fascinating. Together, we will make the connections between the theories we will be discussing and their applications in our lives, especially in your life and work and in your society. First, we will focus on a new experience of reality and personal development. Initially, we will ask the question: Where am I? We will situate ourselves in the micro-macro context of space-time. Next, we will ask the questions: How did we get here? and What time is it? Here, we will situate ourselves in the multidimensionality of space-time, its various states of interiority. Next, we will raise other questions: What and who am I? We will situate ourselves in our humanity, the essence of which is consciousness of consciousness of consciousness.

Then, we will focus on the implications of this New Paradigm or modelling of reality for our participation in the life of our nation and organization. In both cases, we will focus on culture, and we will focus on energy. We will be interested to bring our thinking down to the ground so that we may answer the questions of: What can I/we do to increase the effectiveness and satisfaction of our fellow citizens? What can I/we do to better manage our culture to release its unique genius to higher levels of effectiveness and integration?

We must go through all of this to get to the next question, because the transition in which we human beings find ourselves in this decade on our planet is so foundational to our own understanding of ourselves as human beings, that we much "stop our world", and ask the fundamental questions of our existence. And only then, do we have a chance of understanding and intelligently managing the chaotic forces in which we find ourselves.

1. The Macro-Micro Context of Space-Time.

Now, we will enter the macro-micro context of space-time, in response to the question of: Where are we? We will explore eleven nested realities, each of which is a whole system, and which together constitute a whole system. But first, let us check our own mental imaging.

When I ask you the question, "Where are we?", what mental picture comes to your mind? What are the largest features of your picture? What are the smallest details of your picture? What difference does it make whether your picture is very expansive or incredibly detailed? What difference does it make to a manager if he/she operates out of an expansive context or a highly detailed context? Well, that tells us where we are in our current mental imaging.

Eleven Nested Realities

Let us review these eleven nested realities.

The particle field is nested in the atom, which is nested in the molecule, which is nested in the cell, which is nested in the organ, which is nested in the organism, which is nested in the social environment (including family, community, organization, nation, etc.), which is nested in the Earth's physical environment (including plants and animals, water, land, and air, from the local, to the continental, to the planetary), which is nested in the Solar System, which is nested in the Milky Way galaxy, which is nested in the Universe. Our individual existence is halfway between the sub-atomic level (-5) and the universe level (+5). What is the significance for us that we are composed of these five micro levels, and that we are projected into these five macro levels? We find ourselves midway between the infinitely small and the infinitely huge. Each one of us as an individual organism is a whole self-organizing system, nested between other whole systems, that both include us and constitute us in the vastness of macro and micro space-time. This awareness strikes me with awe and fascination, shatters my complacency, shakes me out of my routine, makes me feel my connectedness, of being part of all that is, of being at-home, utterly one with all other realities. How does it make you feel? What difference does this awareness make for you?

At the sub-atomic level, particles which are fields of energy come into being and go out of being in infinitesimal bits of time. Most of the atom is vast empty space, the creative void, charged with energy. The physicist David Bohm speaks about the implicate and explicate order at the subatomic level, the enfolded and unfolded dimensions of reality. Manifest being is constantly unfolding and enfolding. Every particle knows where every other particle is. This is system-wide information, not faster-than light signaling.

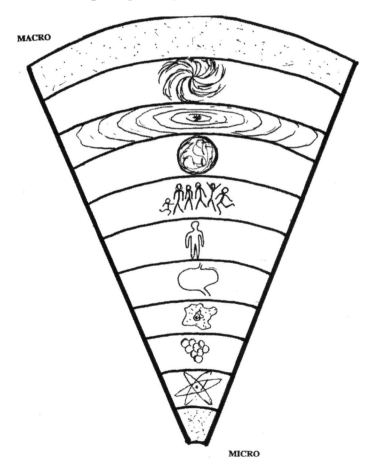

The atom is a steady state energy field which does not spiral down. It maintains its level of energy in a steady state. Perhaps, the energy field of the atom meshes perfectly within the field of the universe or even goes in and out of being (on and off) as the inventor Isaac Bentov writes.

Atoms come together and constitute molecules, some inorganic, and some formed by carbon chains, or organic molecules. Since carbon atoms can form alone or together with many other kinds of atoms, an unlimited number of chains different in size, branching, folding, and composition, the morphologic and chemical diversity of the organic molecules is, in principle, infinite.

Molecules come together to form cellular structures membrane, intra-cellular components, and nucleus. If a cell interacts with a molecule and incorporates it in its processes what takes place because of this interaction is determined not by the properties of the molecule but by the way in which that molecule is "seen" or taken by the cell as it incorporates the molecule in its autopoietic dynamics.

Cells form tissues of organs. Organs form organisms. Organisms form societies. Societies are part of the Earth as a living system. The Earth is the third planet from its star, as part of the solar system. One of millions of stars comprising the Milky Way galaxy, our sun is situated in a rather peripheral position of about eight kiloparsecs (one kiloparsec equals 3,260 light years) from the center of the galaxy. Our galaxy is one of a cluster of galaxies as part of the universe entire. Isaac Bentov presents us with a picture of the cosmos looking very much like a squashed jelly donut, with a white hole and a black hole at the center. However, you wish to picture the universe, it is vast beyond imagining and mysterious beyond comprehension.

And so, here we are, halfway between unimaginable smallness, and unimaginable largeness. How did we get here? What time is it? And, what and who are we? These are questions which we will raise and explore later. First, I would like you to do an exercise which will allow more of your mind and body to explore our located-ness.

A Micro-Macro Journey

To benefit from this exercise, you need to relax and concentrate. We will use some techniques which allow for both. First, close your eyes. Breath in and out slowly several times. You are becoming relaxed. Become aware of your feet. Relax your feet. Relax your ankles. Relax your thighs. Relax your buttocks. Relax your pelvis. Relax your stomach. Your chest. Your heart. Relax your throat. Your face. Your forehead. The top of your head. You are totally relaxed and gently aware of your whole body.

Now, we will begin to concentrate and take a journey. Become aware of one of your organs. How does it feel? What is going on with it? What is it telling you? Take your consciousness within the organ to the cellular level. What do you see? What is happening? Now go into the molecular level. What is this like? What do you hear? Now enter an individual atom. What is the energy like? What does it taste like? Now enter the field of an electron. You are traveling at mind boggling speeds. You are aware of every other electron in the universe. What do you know?

Now travel back to the atom, the molecule, the cell, the organ, to your total body seated in your chair. You are now ready to take the journey outward into space. You see yourself sitting in your chair from above your body. Now, you see the whole room, the building you are in, the community, up you go until you can see your nation, continuing, you see your continent, and finally the entire planet in its blue-white-green swirling colors. Out you go past Mars, and on to Jupiter, to Saturn with its great rings, and to Uranus, Neptune, and finally past Pluto, you leave our solar system. You are now traveling through our galaxy, past millions of stars. And now you are leaving our galaxy. You see other galaxies which constitute our cluster of galaxies. And on you travel to the source of the Cosmos itself. There you rest and commune. What do you hear? What do you see? What do you know deep within? After you have finished your deep conversation, you are ready to return. You travel through vast space, past millions of clusters of galaxies, until you arrive at our cluster of galaxies. You travel to the Milky Way galaxy and on the edge of one of the spirals you see the Sun-star. You re-enter the solar system. You race past the other planets, until you see once again our exquisitely beautiful planet, Earth, hanging in the void, looking so fragile and small. You enter the Earth's atmosphere and race through the clouds until you see land and water, you come closer, and you see forests, plains, rivers, then you see your community, you see the building where you are sitting, you re-enter this room, and you re-enter your body. You have traveled to the farthest reaches of space, but you return refreshed, invigorated, awake. Now open your eyes, and look around. What do you see? How do you feel? What do you wish to say? What happened to you? How does knowing and experiencing our place in the universe affect us? What difference does it make? How does it affect our human relationships in our family, community, and organizations?

2. The Multi-dimensionality of Space-Time: How did we get here? And what time is it?

We just explored the macro-micro context of space-time. We were dealing with outwardness or externality. Now, we will turn our attention to inwardness or interiority. We will explore the multi dimensionality of space-time. We will first read and reflect on a story about how we got here. And then, we will try to determine what time it is. What we will discover is that it is many times – that there are wrinkles, loops, and many dimensions of time, that time is culture, that time is an aspect of consciousness. Soon, we will focus on this consciousness as it manifests in the system of the self, in the system of society, and in the planetary system.

The Universe Story (*Timescale*, Nigel Calder)

First a story. Relax and read: Sometime around 13.5 billion years ago, there was no time; there was no space; there was no matter; there was no energy. Then at some point in this mysterious cosmic vacuum, there appeared a ripple, ever so slight. And out of this perturbation of nothingness, came the Big Bang, an explosion so catastrophic that astrophysicists tell us that we can still hear its echo in the universe today. And out of this white-hot primeval explosion came matter, energy, space, and time. This was the creation of the universe. In the first second of this unimaginable burst, quarks, electrons, protons, photons, and other particle-fields formed. In the first 300,000 years these particles came together to make atoms. After one million years, galaxies and quasars began to form, where elements began to be made. Our sun and its system of planets including our planet which we call Earth was formed around 4.5 billion years ago. Life emerged on Earth around 4 billion years ago. The continents began forming 2.8 billion years ago. 1.8 billion years ago there was an oxygen revolution. 1.7 billion years ago proto animals began to form. Plants appeared 1.3 billion years ago. Sex was invented 1 billion years ago. The ice ages began 950 million years ago. 620 million years ago, worms appeared. Vertebrate animals appeared 510 million years ago. Life on the land appeared 425 million years ago. Insects appeared 395 million years ago. Amphibians and trees 370 million years ago. Reptiles 313 million years ago. Dinosaurs and flowers appeared 235 million years ago. Petroleum-making took place around 170 million years ago. Birds appeared around 150 million years ago. Marsupial mammals emerged around 125 million years ago. Pre-primates appeared 95 million years ago. Dinosaurs became extinct around 67 million years ago. Early horses emerged around 55 million years ago. Early cats and dogs and new world monkeys show up 35 million years ago. Whales evolved about 25 million years ago. Grass appears 24 million years ago. Apes and monkeys split 21 million years ago. Elephants appear 7 million years ago. Modern dogs 6 million years ago. Apes and ape men split 5 million years ago. Modern camels, bears, and pigs evolve 4 million years ago. Early cattle appear 3.5 million years ago. Stone tools are used 2.4 million years ago. Robust ape-men appear 2.2 million years ago. Hunting cultures evolve 1.9 million years ago. Fire-making happens 1.4 million years ago. The mammalians peak 1 million years ago. Emphatic icing begins 800,000 years ago. Brown bears appear 700,000 years ago and wolves 650,000 years ago. Homo sapiens evolve 600,000 years ago. The ice ages continue. Fishing culture is 420,000 years ago. Tools are used 160,000 years ago. Neanderthals appear 120,000 years ago. Proto-modern humans and ritual burials evolve 100,000 years ago. Herbal medicine is practiced 60,000 years ago. The cave-bear cult is active 47,000 years ago. 45,000 years ago, there was a mental revolution: the necessary mutations occurred to allow for speech. Modern humans begin appearing in different areas of the planet 40,000 years ago. The first calendars were used 35,000 years ago. Trading began 30,000 years ago. The first communities larger than family bands began 29,000 years ago. Tailored clothing was invented 25,000 years ago. The bow and arrow were invented 20,000 years ago. The Americas were peopled 19,000 years ago. Cultivation and animal herds were formed 18,000 years ago. Dogs were tamed 12,000 years ago. Accountancy was first established 10,700 years ago: by this time, the herdsmen in the hills of Iran were sufficiently proprietorial about their animals (goats and sheep) to count them and pledge them, using the oldest known system of accountancy. The world's first town arose at Jericho around 10,600 BC, and the burghers built a wall around it, four meters high to protect their stockpile of grain from herdsmen who might sooner steal than trade for it. Finally, the ice age ended in 10,300. Rice is cultivated, and water buffalo and pigs are tamed 9,500 ago. The first city of Catalhoyuk flourished in Anatolia 8,800 to 8,000 years ago. Weaving began in 8,500. Irrigation in 8,000. Stone buildings in 6,500. The political lineaments of the modern world began to appear 5,600 years ago in Mesopotamia, with the first tax demands issued by parceling up the clay accountancy tokens in clay envelopes marked with official seals. Some bright clerk then thought of dispensing with the tokens and envelopes and making his marks on flat clay tablets. Writing thereby originated, 5,500 years ago. We see warrior kings in 5,300, pack animals in 5,000, horsemen in 4,900, the first empires in 4,400, chariots in 4,100, the first alphabet in 3,800, Chinese writing in 3,500, the rise of the Mayas in 2,750, Greek science in 2,600. The Iron Age brought religious ferment to Asia, with Taoism, Confucianism, Jainism, Buddhism, Zoroastrianism, and Judaism all being articulated 2,550 to 2,500 years ago. Paper was invented 1,900 years ago. The abacus was invented in Eurasia around 1,500. Printing began 1,300 years ago. The first managed economy appeared 930 years ago in China. The Aztec empire rose 700 years ago. Guns were first used in warfare 650 years ago. The first printing press was invented 540 years ago. The breakout of the European navigators can best be dated from 1492, when a westbound Spanish flotilla stumbled upon the Americas, mistaking them for Asia. The slave-and-sugar trade began 450 years ago. The European imperial companies were formed 400 years ago. The first astronomical telescope was invented 390 years ago. Science was formalized 330 years ago. Steam energy was invented 290 years ago. Oxygen was discovered 230 years ago. The French revolution took place 210 years ago. Marxism was formulated 130 years ago. The telephone was invented 120 years ago. The automobile 110 years ago. Radioactivity was discovered 100 years ago. The first aircraft was invented 100 years ago. Electronics were invented 95 years ago. Radio broadcasting became widespread 77 years ago. The global population boom began 70 years ago. Arabian oil was found 59 years ago. Antibiotics were created 50 years ago. Nuclear energy and the first computer were created 48 years ago. The A-bomb 46 years ago. The television boom happened 41 years ago. The structure of genes was discovered 38 years ago. The first spacecraft was launched 34 years ago. Men first set foot on the moon 22 years ago. Gene splicing began 18 years ago. Space vehicles landed on Mars 15 years ago. Nine years ago, the inhabitants of the Earth found out where they stood in space and time because of discoveries in physics and evolution. And today (1991), the Japanese are the longest living humans, have the highest human development index, and provide more foreign aid than any other nation. This is story of how we got here.

What struck you? What do you recall? What was amazing? How did you feel?

And where are we headed? How might humanity continue to evolve? I like Jean Houston's vision of the next few centuries. She says that we are going through a whole system transition and are in the first few years of a Type I High-Level civilization, which has never existed before. "That means that on the sensory level, we become responsible for biological governance, for the governance of the world ecology, and that requires psychologically that we grow in kind, that we do have access to many more frames of mind to be able to deal with this kind of complexity. It also means that the nature of friendships and relationships and partnerships between people is going to change radically and deeply. I think there is a great future for marriage, but I think it is changing radically in our time, and that is why it is so difficult for couples right now, to know how to treat each other as women come to full partnership with men, and all the old expectations are banished. I think mythically it means that we are moving into a planetary myth with Gaia at the center; and spiritually, I think it is coming to mean a daily life as spiritual exercise. And I believe that during this Type I High Level civilization, which certainly will last for the next few hundred years, we will have as our tasks going to other planets, making them habitable, or in space colonies; and those (which is most of us) who remain will have to be creating a viable ecology and, a world which we mutually nourish, and which nourishes us to the fullest of our capacities.

"I think that at some point in the future there might be Type II High-Level Civilizations in which we become responsible on the sensory level for the orchestration of the resources of the solar system. And we will have an increase in our utilization of our psychological selves; for instance, we will no longer be schizophrenic, but we will be poly-phrenic; and we will have access to the enormous archetypal contents of ourselves as well as the many selves of our selves. We will mythically, probably, also be coming close to in some way incarnating the archetypes. One will be the laughter, the laughing, and the laughed; the thinker, the thinking, and the thought; the creator, the creation and the creating. And then, I think that at some point there will also be Type III High Level Civilization which will be galactic, and in which we will become co-responsible for the orchestration of even larger resources. We will join the galactic milieu and become the creators of worlds, capable of Genesis".

Is Jean right about the next several hundred years? Of course, no one knows. But our vision of the future affects what action we take in the present. For example, if I believe that things will continue along lines like the present, I will try to continue to do the same things which I know now. If I believe that the world is going to end in disaster and conflagration, I will act in despair and cynicism, and simply take care of myself. Or if I have a vision such as Jean's vision of the future, I will be open to new technologies, new ideas, new lifestyles, new types of organizations and new business ventures. I will risk new actions. I will create the new.

So here we are, somewhere between 13 billion years of past evolution and facing hundreds, thousands, millions, billions of years of future evolution. What and who are we amidst this? This is the question we will explore next. But first, I want to share with you a Map of Time, which I think you will enjoy. What time is it? Well, it depends upon which dimension of time you are in.

In modern industrial society, time has become monochronic. We have often lost our sense of polychronic time. In fact, cancer is the disease of compressed, stressed time: chrono pathology. But in fact, time is not something linear, unchanging, and constant. In 1904, Einstein discovered that time was relative to the location of the observer and his/her speed and direction of movement. Time is a cluster of concepts, events, and rhythms covering an extremely wide range of phenomena. As people do quite different activities (write books, play, schedule activities, travel, get hungry, sleep, dream, meditate, and perform ceremonies), they are unconsciously and sometimes consciously expressing and participating in different categories of time. I want to share with you a Map of Time (which was developed by Edward T. Hall, an expert on culture.) In this model, there are nine types of time: biological time, personal time, physical time, metaphysical time, micro time, sync time, sacred time, profane time, and meta-time (the time of all the other times). As responsible people, we must know what time it is.

The Map of Time (Edward T. Hall)
Biological Time. Before life appeared on the earth, the light and dark cycles, occasioned by the rotation of our tiny planet as it exposed first one side and then the other side to the sun made up an important part of the environment in which life evolved. The ebb and flow of the tides, the swelling and shrinking of the atmosphere, and the seasoned rhythms established by the travel of the earth in orbit around the sun formed the basis for other sets of clocks as life began. It was these rhythmic changes from light to dark, from hot to cold, and from wet to dry that forced upon early living forms the very qualities that set the stage for later forms of life. As life evolved, the external cycles became internalized and took on lives of their own. In humans, there are hourly shifts in the hormonal levels of the blood. Internal timing mechanisms are at work in the young man who has not discovered girls yet, who wakes up one morning feeling a new stirring in his blood (as happened to my son Christopher) and is amazed at how pretty the girl next door has suddenly become. Anyone who has traveled east to west or west to east for more than three hours on a jet airplane and who has suffered jetlag has firsthand experience in how our body rhythms are set according to the 24-hour cycle of the planet. On the behavioral side, the Japanese have been experimenting with biorhythms and keeping track of the periodicity of highs

and lows in human energy, intellectual activity, and sociability. They report a reduced accident rate when their bus drivers drive more carefully during a "critical" phase.

Personal Time. Personal time has as its primary focus the experience of the flow of time in different contexts, settings, and emotional, and psychological states. Sometimes, we experience that time is "crawling" or other times we experience that time is "flying". Personal time is more subjective than biological time which is relatively fixed. It is the right hemisphere of the brain that is affecting our sense of time. Environmental and physiological factors also help explain these great shifts in the way in which time is experienced. The slowing down of brain waves and the heart and respiratory rate during meditation have produced instances where people reported that "time stood still".

Physical Time. Sitting in our sealed office buildings, it is difficult to be aware of the sun in its annual pilgrimage from south to north and back. In pre-industrial societies, people became highly conscious of the movement of the sun and based planting, harvesting, and ceremonies on these dates. Establishing the longest and shortest days and seeing the pattern that repeats itself, gave people a sense of the orderliness of the universe and laid the foundations for modern science. Newton treated time as absolute, but Einstein proved him wrong. He argued that a fast moving astronaut could leave this earth and return a century later to find every-one he knew had died, while he himself had aged only a few years. Astronomers studied the shift toward red in the spectra of receding galaxies and dated the universe around 13.5 billion years old. To reduce this to a human scale is impossible. Likewise at the other end of the physical scale, time can be measured by clocks to trillionths of a second, but we cannot experience this amount of time. So absolute time prevails in our daily lives. We can only experience a small part of the spectrum of time, just as our eyes can only see a small part of the spectrum of light. Even more astounding then the 13.5-billion-year reach of time is that physicists now believe that time can move either forward or backward at the sub-atomic level. There is not a clue as to what this will mean in the future – reversal of aging, for example?

Metaphysical Time. All cultures report on the experience of this extraordinary dimension. Individuals report experiences of transcending time and space. Most people have had a brush with "deja vu" (I have been there before). People have experiences of pre-cognition and clairvoyance. These experiences are difficult if not impossible to explain, but nevertheless people have them. These experiences may have to do with time waves, resonances, the nested reality of time or infinite fractal waves in motion. We should investigate chaos theory for some help, perhaps.

Micro Time. Micro time is unique to each culture. Monochronic and polychronic times are examples of major patterns of this time. Monochronic time is that shared by most North European countries and cultures. Time is up front. If you have an appointment at 10 am and you arrive at 10:01 am you are late. In polychronic time, time reveals itself. In some cultures, if you are invited to a party on next Wednesday and you arrive on Thursday you are not late. There can also be simultaneity of time. In some cultures, many different things can legitimately happen at once. With computers we are all moving into poly-chronic time.

Sync Time. The term to be in sync is derived from the media and dates to the beginning of talking pictures. Since then, frame-by-frame analysis of motion picture film taken during normal transactions of daily life reveal that when people interact, they synchronize their motions in a truly remarkable way. This is what happens when people fall in love. Charismatic leaders entrain others by their voice and motions. Rock bands entrain the people listening and dancing. A baby synchronizes its movement to the human voice. People who are out of sync with a group are disruptive and do not fit in. Different people move to different beats. Each culture has its own beat. A little later, we will explore the beat of your culture.

Sacred Time. Modern American-European people have some difficulty understanding sacred or mythic time, because this type of time is imaginary – one is in the time. This kind of time is like a story. When American Indian people participate in ceremonies, they are in the ceremony and in the ceremony's time. They cease to exist in ordinary time. By putting themselves in sacred time, people subconsciously reaffirm and acknowledge their own divinity, but by raising consciousness they are acknowledging the divine in life. This is the rhythm of grace, the strain of eternity.

Profane Time. In the Western world, profane time marks minutes and hours, the days of the week, months of the year, decades, centuries – the entire explicit, taken-for-granted system which our civilization has elaborated. This is everyday time of our watches and calendars. People are attached to and controlled by this kind of time. We are entrained by our schedules. They "itify" us. Cancer is a rage against that entrainment, that time-stress.

Meta Time. Meta time is made up of all those things that philosophers, anthropologists, psychologists, physicists, businesses leaders, and others have said and written about time. It is not a different time in the true sense but an abstraction from different temporal events. It allows us to acknowledge each of the eight experiences of time for what it truly is and to live in each of them.

John Wheeler, the Princeton physicist, says that space-time is made of quantum foam. Perhaps all events are connected in and by and through this quantum foam. With our consciousness, we can enter the quantum foam and affect events. We can co-create the future and re-create the past.

In any case, this map makes it possible to categorize different historical periods and cultures. The Hopi Indians, for example, traditionally lived almost entirely in a world of sacred time. Awareness of sync time is more developed in Black Africa than in American-European cultures. One gets the impression that in the subcontinent of India, the metaphysical and the sacred are fused into one. In the USA, we make few distinctions between profane time and micro time. It appears that if one culture emphasizes a particular segment while another emphasizes a different one, the results can be extraordinarily significant.

Choose one of the eight types of time. What are examples of this type of time in your culture and society? Examples in your community or organization? Personal examples? What is the struggle to be in this time? What are ways of helping people live in this time? What other type of time conflicts with this time? Draw a picture of this time type.

3. Exploration of a Holistic Consciousness of Self, Society, and Planet

Earlier, we asked the question Where are we? We discovered that we are halfway between the micro-dimension of the electron and the macro-dimension of the Cosmos. We experienced the awe and fascination of our place in space. Next, we asked the question of How did we get here and What time is it? We discovered that it has taken 13.5 billion years to bring us to this moment, and that we are poised to enter a future radically different from anything we have ever known. We also experienced that time is multi-dimensional and relative to many external and subjective factors. We discovered that in each of our cultures, we have our own rhythms of time.

Now, we are exploring the question of What and Who are we as human beings? In this section, we will focus on the nature of consciousness and in particular the consciousness of consciousness of consciousness. Søren Kierkegaard, the Danish philosopher, put it this way: "the self is a set of relationships, that relates itself to those relationships; and in willing to be the self that is its relationship to those relationships, grounds itself transparently in the power that posits it."

Willis Harman, President of the Institute of Noetic Sciences, and former Stanford University professor of electrical engineering and Senior Social Scientist of futures studies at the Stanford Research Institute, talks about the causal reality of consciousness as he describes three types of metaphysics, M1, M2, and M3. This can be oversimplified as follows. M1, he calls Materialistic Monism. This is the perspective that the basic stuff of the universe is matter-energy. We learn about reality from studying the measurable world. Whatever consciousness is, it emerges out of matter (that is the brain) when the evolutionary process has progressed sufficiently far. Matter gives rise to mind. M2, he calls Dualism. In this perspective, there is matter plus mind. There are two fundamentally different kinds of basic stuff in the universe, matter-energy stuff, and mind-spirit stuff. Matter-energy stuff is studied with the present tools of science; mind-spirit stuff must be explored in other ways more appropriate to it (such as inner subjective exploration).

The M-3 perspective he calls Transcendental Monism. The ultimate stuff of the universe is consciousness. Mind or consciousness is primary, and matter-energy arises in some sense out of Consciousness. (What was before the Big Bang? What is the quantum foam? What is creativity, and how do inventions happen? How do cognition and perception create the world?) Ultimately the reality behind the phenomenal world is contacted, not through the physical senses, but through deep intuition. Consciousness is not the product of material evolution; rather, consciousness was here first! Mind gives rise to matter.

He goes on to suggest that in Western society there is shift going on from M-1 to M-3. At first, this seems as outrageous to us as the proposition that the earth revolved around the sun did to seventeenth-century Europe. Nevertheless, he asks us to explore this possibility as possible.

Three Systems: Self, Society, Planet

In looking at holistic consciousness, I want us to get inside the reality and the inter-relationships of three systems: self, society, and the planet.

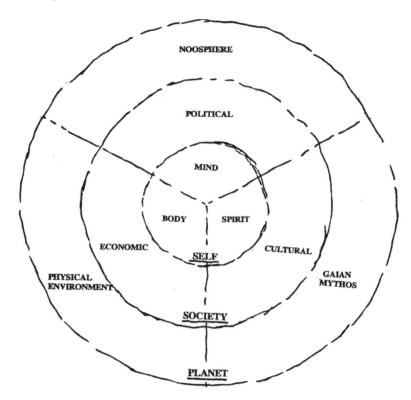

HOLISTIC, ECOLOGICAL CONSCIOUSNESS

In the center is the self or the individual as a system of body, mind, spirit. The next system is the society which can be viewed being composed of the dynamics of the economic, the political, and the cultural. The third and final system which we will explore is the planetary, with the dimensions of the physical environment of the Earth, the noosphere, and the Gaian Mythos. As you see each of the dynamics on the lower left are of a similar nature: the body, the economic, and the physical environment. In the same way, the mind, the political, and noosphere are closely related. And finally, the spirit, cultural, and the Gaian mythos are related. This model helps us see the inter-relationships of three nested or interlocking systems, each one reflecting the other. What we will be concerned with as we analyze each of these and their interrelationships is the crisis which we experience when these systems are out of phase with one another and the real possibility of their moving into harmony or sync with one another.

The Individual System

Ken Wilber has developed a comprehensive model of consciousness. The first stage of consciousness of the self is that of the body. This is the pre rational or sub-conscious realm and includes the archaic, magic, and the mythic. The second stage of consciousness is that of the mind. This is rational and self-conscious. The third and final stage of consciousness is that of the spirit. This is transrational or superconscious and includes the psychic, the subtle, and the causal. Let us go through the model again at more depth and in more detail.

The Self as Body. Archaic consciousness includes the material body, sensations, perceptions, and emotions. Magic consciousness includes simple images, symbols, and the first rudimentary concepts. Mythic consciousness includes concrete operational thinking, conformist behavior, and a sense of belonging.

The Self as Mind. Rational consciousness includes formal operational thinking, and propositional or hypothetico-deductive reasoning.

The Self as Spirit. Psychic consciousness includes the merging of the psychological and physical, the psyche, vision logic, integrative logic, and self-actualization. Subtle consciousness includes the archetypal level, the level of the "illumined mind", a truly trans-rational structure, intuition in its highest and most sober sense, Platonic forms, and self transcendence. And finally, causal consciousness includes the unmanifest ground and suchness of all levels, the limit of growth and development,

Spirit in the highest sense, the Ground of Being (Tillich), Eternal Substance (Spinoza), and Geist (Hegel). Elsewhere, Wilber outlines additional sub-structures. What is important is not whether there is this or that structure but that the human self is seen as a complex system of evolving and inter related dimensions. In our modern industrial society, we acknowledge that we have a body (rather than that we are our body) which we must keep under control, and that we ought to be rational (rather than that that is our very nature to be realized). And there we stop. In a secularized society, there is no acknowledgment of the self as spirit. This is relegated to the specialized and separate realm of formal religion.

The self is a body-mind-spirit system. What we see and experience is that often these three dynamics conflict with each other. We also see and experience that our societies are often not structured to acknowledge and develop the fullest manifestation of the self in each person. In fact, we have defined and structured our societies and our organizations to exclude the full participation of every person in his or her own self development. We have assumed that the economic pie is too small to share with everyone, that the political structures are too unresponsive and unaccountable, and that the cultural milieu is too negative to honor and celebrate the unique gift that each person is within the society. This brings us to the next system in which the self in nested – the societal.

The Societal System
Social process can be seen as being comprised of three interlocking dynamics: economic commonality, political commonality, and cultural commonality. This model is well known, but the one to which I am referring was developed by the Institute of Cultural Affairs (ICA) in 1971 in an international research conference.

Social phenomena are a result of what Humberto Maturana and Francisco Varela, two Chileno biologists, have called "third-order structural couplings". This means that human society is not simply a collection of organisms with individual nervous systems, or even simply the structural coupling of these organisms, but that because of the recurrent, mutual, and reciprocal nature of these interactions a third-order structural coupling occurs. This phenomenon is experienced in the realm of culture, through the creation of language and the consequent behavioral coordination through communication. This sets up transgenerational stability of behavioral patterns acquired in the communicative dynamics of a social environment. This takes place because as we have seen the very essence of the human phenomenon is consciousness. We not only know, but we know that we know, and we can know how and what we know. In addition, we manifest will, volition, and vision which together operate on the material world through our actions and our technology, which is an extension of our body and mind.

Economic processes are the foundation or body of society. Here, we have the dynamics of resources, production, and trade. The economy feeds and nourishes the society. The economic processes are found in the natural, technological, and human resource identification and development, industry, manufacturing, product development, marketing, financial institutions, and trade.

Political processes are the organizational or mental aspects of society. Here, we have structures and processes of order, justice, and welfare. Political processes organize the functioning of the society. The political dynamics are found in the courts, the police, the hospitals, the governmental structures of society.

Cultural processes are the meaning giving or spiritual aspects of society. Culture has to do with the symbols, the rites, and the myths or stories of the society which make transparent the significance of the activities of the society. Cultural processes illuminate the profound or universal dimension of being a human society. The cultural dynamics are found in the family, the educational structures, the arts, and in religious and spiritual activities.

Usually, a society is in imbalance, that one of the three dynamics is overpowering the others. It is possible to re-balance a society by strengthening and growing up the weaker dynamics. Also, often a society is not in harmony with the nature of the individual selves that constitute the society. People's bodies, minds, and spirits are not nurtured and developed adequately by the structures of society. In fact, people are often crushed or left out altogether in many of the social processes. It is possible to create increased harmony between the essential nature of the individual and the essential nature of sociality.

The Planetary System
The next larger system in which human society finds itself is the planetary system. This can be seen as the physical environment, the noosphere, and the Gaian mythos.

The Physical Environment. The physical environment is constituted by the crust and atmosphere of our planet, that is the land, water, plants, animals, and the air of our planet. This is the skin of the body of the planet. We are all growing increasingly conscious of how human activity can damage this skin and thereby damage the biosphere which sustains human life. There are many new efforts which must be intensified to care for the environment, to make for sustainable development. This means that aspects of industrial society which are destroying our physical habitat must be substituted for with alternative activities.

The Noosphere. This word comes to us from the French priest/ paleontologist, Pierre Teilhard de Chardin. The noosphere is the thin envelope of consciousness that covers the planet as the atmosphere does. This has included culture and language, and now it includes the electronic technologies of mass communication and transportation – satellites, tv, radio, fax, computer networks, jet airplanes, space shuttles, etc. that are linking the entire human race in one global city. This film of consciousness acts as a global brain for the Earth. I recommend that you watch the film "The Global Brain" to explore this further: (https://www.youtube.com/watch?v=B1sr9x263LM). This is related to the political dynamic of society and the mental dynamic of the individual, but on a planetary level.

The Gaian Mythos. The Gaia hypothesis was developed a few years ago by James Lovelock and Lynn Margulis. This hypothesis is that the Earth is alive as a single organism. This understanding is transforming our understanding of the role and place of humans on this planet. The video I mentioned talks more about this. All I will say is that this global myth or story that is emerging is corelated with the cultural dynamic of society and with the spiritual dynamic of the individual. Of course, there are many competing stories about our planet. We used to think that the Earth was flat. The photograph of the Earth from space has forever changed the way we see and think and feel about our planet. More and more, we do not say we live in a world but on a planet. This is a fundamental shift from being bound in a social reality to being part of a cosmic reality, for the word planet makes us think of the sun, which is a star and of our galaxy, the Milky Way, and eventually of the entire Cosmos. This new story provides a profound connection with the history of the cosmos, the history of planet Earth, and the history of life on this planet. We are a star's way of looking at a star. Constituted of atoms and elements which were created in stary furnaces, we are now self reflective consciousness which sees and knows who and what we are. These three nested systems constitute our consciousness, our essence. The more we can create harmony between and among these three systems, the more fulfilling human life will be. This is our destiny. This is our possibility.

The video I mentioned is based on a book by the Englishman Peter Russell by the same name. The URL is above. If you watch the video, be aware of your reactions – physical and emotional. What are they telling you about yourself? What do you remember? Images? Words? What did you feel? Emotions? Confusion? Anger? Fear? Excitement? What did this remind you of? What other stories came to mind? How would you tell this story in your own words? What is the significance of this story? For the world? For your country? For your organization? For you person-ally? What does this video make you want to do? What do you need to do? What do you want to do but do not know how? Now, recall a photo of the Earth from space. Relax. Breathe deeply. What do you think of? How do you feel? What comes to you?

4. Releasing Creative Energy to Increase Effectiveness

Your Country's Energy Assets

Now, let us shift our focus from personal development within a new experience of reality to releasing creative energy to increase effectiveness. First, you will explore your country's greatest energy resource. Next, we will conclude this essay by gaining clarity on how to orchestrate organizational energy within your country's unique culture.

What is your country's greatest source of energy? It is not the solar or wind. It is the third-order structural coupling of its human consciousnesses that live on this part of Earth's skin. We will raise the question of: how are we this people? But first, we need to put your experience of being a people into a context of the planetary ecology of cultures.

Three Source-Images

When we look at our species, we notice dramatic differences in the way people come at life in different parts of the planet. I want to share with you a model of cultures which the ICA began working on 25 years ago. As I have experienced and reflected on different cultures around the world, I have continued to elaborate this model. We can distinguish three source level images below the level of culture: those that emerged from a deep sense of unity; those that developed from dualism; and those that developed from a tri-polarity.

In the East, there are two great cultural source-images, one from the Chinese and the other from India. The UR or source-image of the Yellow People is that of corporateness. The UR or source-image of the Brown People is that of transcendence.

Both are closely related to the human spirit. They are based in unity consciousness and intuition.

MODEL OF SOURCE IMAGES

OF HUMAN CULTURE

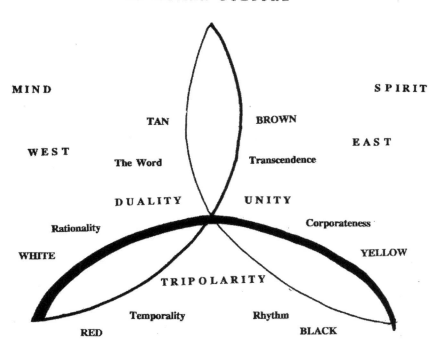

MIND   SPIRIT

TAN   BROWN

EAST

WEST

The Word   Transcendence

DUALITY   UNITY

Rationality   Corporateness

WHITE   YELLOW

TRIPOLARITY

Temporality   Rhythm

RED   BLACK

SOUTH

BODY

In the West, there are two great cultural source-images (or URs), one from the Greco-Roman-European experience and another from the Middle East. The UR of the White People is that of Rationality. The UR of the Tan People is that of the Word. These are closely related to the human mind. They are based in dualistic consciousness.

In the South, there are also two powerful cultural source images, one from Africa and the other from the Indigenous of North and South America. The UR of the Black People is that of rhythm. The UR of the Red people is that of temporality. Both are closely related to the energy of the human body and its place in Nature. They are based in trinitarian consciousness of space-time and energy.

Now of course, this is a great oversimplification and indeed may or may not be universally accepted. That is not the point. The point is that there are dramatic differences in the ways humans evolved around our planet, and this is one way of looking at that evolution of human cultures as emphasizing deep structures of human consciousness as it emerged within its geographic and natural setting on the Earth's surface.

For example, here in the New World, the Americas, what do we find? For the past 500 years, a new mixture of cultures has been coming to these land masses. The Americas have as their root cultural image that of the Red People, temporality, the pattern of the Aztec calendar, the rhythm of siesta and fiesta, the day after dayness, and then the wild explosion of carnival. But on top of this root image has been poured vitality, energy, and rhythm from Africa, the rationality from Europe, the corporateness of China, the spirituality of India, and the commitment to your word and the Word from the Middle East. We are the world. We are totally mixed up. We are a rainbow of colors and cultural images, values, assumptions, and lifestyles.

Now add to this mix the onslaught of the revolutions of the 20th Century: urbanization, secularization, and the scientific technological revolution. Then turn up the heat with the current global economic crisis of the open market and the coming apart of the great political ideologies and empires. Now who are we? How do we continue to create a pluralistic society? The Koreans and Japanese have it easy. All Koreans, for example, have a common 5,000-year-old history, speak the same language, have the same culture, are of the same race. It was relatively straight forward to align people to create an economic miracle. People were already more or less in alignment. Now of course the Koreans have their problems and tensions. But these have to do with too much familiarity, self knowledge, and internal conflicts. In the New World, this is not the case. Our common histories are at the longest 100 to 500 years old. We speak many different languages. We are of many different races. We have different cultural values and assumptions. Yet, we are thrown together into nations and are admonished that we should behave and become productive and compete with the rest of the world. While in effect, we are a microcosm of the world. Everyone has come here to live and make their own way. How do we cope?

We have been looking at the planetary level and now at the level of the Americas, but what about your country? What is the unique culture of your country, which if understood, affirmed, and orchestrated, could release tremendous energy?

Cultures are not only constituted by their source-images, but by fundamental tensions within them which spin them into orbit. There are foundational polarities at the heart of every culture. This is the yin and the yang which together create a whole, dynamic culture. At a deep level of these polarities, cultures manifest what I will call their "depth spirit problem" which tends to block them from moving forward and realizing their profound gift or genius which is their contribution to the planetary ecology of cultures. It is energetic tension of these two which activate the culture.

Venezuela Society

Take Venezuelan society, for example; I have been told about and have experienced the following polarities in dynamic tension: political parties vs civil society; citizen vs community; individual need vs ethical behavior; modern economy vs informal economy; male vs female; public interest vs private interest; entrepreneurs vs workers; man vs nature; statism vs private initiative; productive society vs leisure society; ancient myth vs new myth; sexual energy vs mental energy; and order vs chaos.

I have been told and have experienced that the profound gift or genius of Venezuela is its human-centered energy. I believe that this energy arises out of a deep love and empathy for each other after generations of suffering and difficulty. Everyone assumes that everyone should have his or her share of the oil bonanza, his house in the barrio, her hook up to electricity.

I have been told and have experienced that the depth spirit problem of Venezuela is *desconfianza* (mistrust.) There is mistrust at every level and between every sector and person. Everyone assumes that everyone is going to *aprovechar* (take advantage) just as they intend to *aprovechar.* I believe that this mistrust arises out of a reduced context within which to exercise responsibility.

Venezuela, in my opinion, as a system is "typhonic becoming membership, on its way to egoic" to use Ken Wilber's categories. It is an energetic, people-centered society rather than a rational, mental, legalistic system such as the USA. Venezuela values humans and human relations more than law-and-order. Unlike in the USA, there are very few homeless people in Venezuela. The government allows people to build small houses on land which does not belong to them, and then connects them with the basic services of electricity, water, garbage disposal, etc. There is a common sense about socialist distribution; everyone should benefit from the oil wealth of the nation. The family is more important than the community. There is a basic goodness, almost an innocence, permeating the society underneath the corruption and violence which are manifestations of a reduced context of responsibility. Members of the elite in Venezuela have set in motion reforms of the political and economic systems which are altering basic assumptions and values. The people at the local and state levels who were elected in December 1989 are now exposed to the accountability before the public rather than the party for the first time. But at the moment of creating a new system, it is important that Venezuela does not create a system of overkill of legalism and consumerism.

People are asking, what next after our charismatic President? Will people be ready for a managerial president or turn out of fear back to a military government? How can wise people be nurtured in every sector, community, and organization such as Ramona Pacheco in Marcelo, Barlovento? The changes are not just political and economic, but more fundamentally, they are cultural. Everyone is more aware and reflective due to the collapse of the previous system which had been built on oil wealth, buying people into the system and mistrust between every sector. Now is the time to engender systemic thinking within the population. This moment of openness will not last forever. Something will happen next. What it is depends upon what people think, do and be now. A Portuguese fruit vendor last year hired a professional head-hunter to find him a marketing manager to export fruit in response to the open, global market without subsidies and protectionism. People are changing their ways of thinking and action which will constitute a new way of being.

Now for the questions. What do you think about the above? What are the tensions within your own country, within its culture or cultures? What are some of the positive and negative aspects of your country's culture? What is the role of the private sector? The government? The NGOs? The grassroots? How can these sectors work in partnership? How do you release the creative energies of your society to the globe?

What did you learn about your culture? About yourself?

5. The Dance of Musical Management: How be us?
Previously, we contemplated the big picture, the ever unfolding of space-time, which eventually created human consciousness and culture, which as self-reflective can look outward to the Cosmos and inward to the sub-atomic level, backward at its great journey of evolution, forward into the centuries and the millennia, and inward into its own subjectivity and Source-levels. Next, let us look at the here and now in your country, your community, and your organization. Earlier, you explored

your country's cultural dynamics within a global context. Now, let us conclude by looking at organizational energy within the context of human energy; we will ask the question: how do we in our country be ourselves to our highest degree of effectiveness and satisfaction within our organizations and communities, as part of our national and world community? How be us?

Human Energy (Mary Work)

Before looking at organizational energy, I would like for you to consider a model of human energy developed by Mary Elizabeth Avery Work, my wife.

HISTORICAL   **ONTOLOGICAL**   **FIELD**

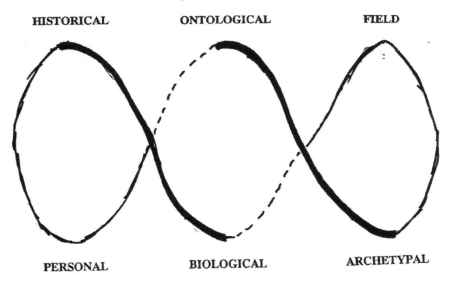

PERSONAL   **BIOLOGICAL**   **ARCHETYPAL**

This highly intuitive model is the result of twenty-two years of professional experience and reflection on human development around the world. In this model, there are six types of human energy: biological, historical, psychological, or personal, ontological, archetypal, and field energy. This entire pattern of connectivity is a non-radiating energy packet that constitutes the human journey. In it, there is one journey with four inter-related patterns of energy connectivity. First, there is the centering of oneness which is the super-conductivity of a human life. Next, there is a duality of contrasts between your biological me-ness and your ontological me-ness. Next, there are two sets of triangles of dynamism: one made up of biological, historical, and psychological energies. The other made up of ontological, archetypal, and field energies. Next, there is a quaternity of stability. This is made up of historical, psychological, archetypal, and field energy. Within this DNA of human energy patterning, the journey of the self begins with biological energy at birth. The self then is attracted to the historical energy pole as it enters conscious spacetime. Next, the self is attracted to the psychological energy pole as it matures and develops its ego structure. The movement from psychological energy to ontological energy is experienced as discontinuous because there is a cross-over of energy patterns. At the ontological energy pole, the self experiences its groundedness in Being as a unique aspect of being. Next, the self is pulled into archetypal energy as the psyche begins to dialogue with the great forms – the gods, and goddesses, the great images that appear to be universal (Jung). Next, the self is flung into field energy as it experiences that it is a field within fields, part of a holographic system of all that is. When the self next moves back toward reexperiencing its biological energy, it again experiences a discontinuity as the energy flow once again crosses over another energy flow pattern. This flow toward attractor after attractor, along with the experience of radical discontinuities is the human energy system.

Again, whether this is exactly the way it is is not our focus. What we are exploring is a complex, dynamic, flow and pulsation of different energy sources which constitute the human phenomenon. Having touched base with this larger story of human energy, we will now shift to a discussion of organizational energy and how it can be orchestrated.

Organizational Energy (ICA)

In 1987, the ICA developed a model of Organizational Energy: a Dynamic System of Energy-in-Motion. Since then, it has been useful in assisting organizations in their own development and transformation. This model was designed to act as a vision of a highly effective organization rather than as a description of dynamics within all organizations.

There are eight energy factors operative in an effective organization: Communication and Mindspace, Myth and Environment, Adaptation and Learning, and Commitment and Achievement. These are aspects of the culture of the organization.

There are four energy dynamics of effective management: Managing Diverse Participation, Inspiring Enterprising Action, Empowering Individual Performance, and Framing a Compelling Vision.

There are five energy flows that bring the organization into optimal energy patterns: Integrity as that which flows between Vision and Participation; Innovation which emerges from the tension of the two poles of participation and action; Creativity which springs out of the relationship between Performance and Action; Commitment which is cultivated when Vision and Performance are intensified; And Learning, which takes place when Participation and Performance are honored, reflected upon and deepened.

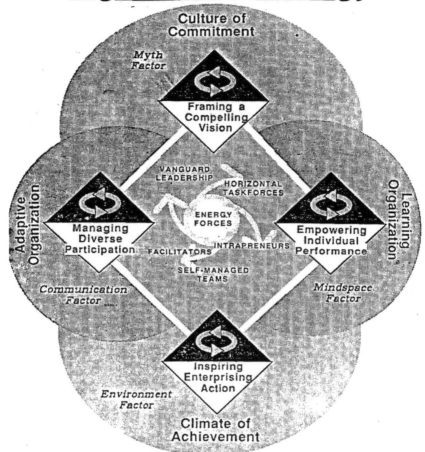

Organizational Energy

Dynamic System of Energy-in-Motion

Finally, there are four energy forces at the center of the highly effective organization. These are the sources of power for the organization, "power" defined as the basic energy to initiate and sustain action translating intention into reality". These energy forces are: Facilitators, Intrapreneurs, Self-Managed Teams, Horizontal Taskforces, and Vanguard Leadership.

Venezuelan Corporate Culture

Before your final thought-experiment, I want to shift from these energy models and share some concrete learnings which I had in Venezuela in 1988-1989 in conducting a Corporate Culture Research Project involving six Venezuelan organizations, including PDVSA, Corpalmar, Electricidad de Caracas, Centro Medico Docente La Trinidad, Fundacion de la Vivienda Popular, and Empresas Lansberg. We discovered that managers in Venezuela experienced that "the world as we have known it in our generation is radically changing". This change can be seen in four dramatic ways.

First, Venezuela is changing because of increased pressures from many sources. There is more corruption. This is particularly poignant because resources are more scarce, due to the economic situation (the collapsed price of oil). It is therefore impossible for the government to provide its usual vast number of jobs and to subsidize prices of food, transportation, and communication as it had become accustomed to do. All of this puts more attention and pressure on the private sector to provide jobs and services. However, with the the overall deterioration of the economy, consumer demand has dropped (in 1988) by an average of forty percent which linked with high interest rates and high inflation means less need for a large labor force and large inventories. Also, the uncertainty in the environment makes it difficult to visualize the future. One corporation which had pioneered in strategic planning has now decided that it must operate in a reactive mode daily due to the chaos of government policy and uncertain markets.

Secondly, Venezuela is changing because of new demands on its economic development. The quality of products and services has become essential. Also, it is imperative to improve production and expand markets. In a previous time of subsidies, price controls and a protected national market, the private sector did not have to focus on quality and marketing. Now that Venezuelan corporations are operating in an open, global market, these are becoming a matter of life and death. Also, companies are becoming more complex with mergers and new affiliates being created to respond to the demands of a more competitive marketplace.

Thirdly, Venezuela is changing due to the generational shifts taking place. There is the experience of the potential of youth. "Now is the hour for more participation in decisions". More people, especially young people, are demanding that their voice be part of the societal dialogue. The younger generation is seen to be different, but there are mixed reviews about what the difference is. Some people perceive a more motivated, well trained, young manager. Others see a lack of social concern and international orientation. Probably, both are true. There is also a movement "beyond patriarchy". In this generation, the founders of some of the major corporations are passing the leadership to a younger, professional management away from the roles of the family which owns the corporation. There is also an increasing interest in the role of the private sector in society as the patriarchal role of the state is further weakened.

Finally, Venezuela is changing as a new style of manager is emerging within the society. As the role of the unethical, *caudillo* (strong man/patriarch) is seen to be dysfunctional in motivating both public and private sector organizations, a young, dynamic, ethically sensitive manager is emerging. This new manager sees and experiences the necessity for more flexibility and capacity to react to and interact with the environment. These new managers are the "transition molders" who are responsible for societal, economic, and generational change. We see such managers in the Cabinet – the Minister of Education, the Minister of Industry, etc., as well as in private companies and in the movement of neighborhood associations, etc. In as much as the manager can embrace and process these changes, he or she will embrace and process the future of Venezuela, Latin America, and the planet.

In 1989, one could see that the entire system was adjusting to the new situation. Economically, this could be seen in the shift to unsubsidized food prices. Politically, there were the historic elections of governors and later were to be direct elections at the municipal level. Culturally, there was a greater self consciousness that attitudes, and behavior must adjust to a radically new situation. The President of Venezuela said in his inaugural speech that Venezuela was not only undergoing an economic and social transformation but a cultural transformation – a change of values, assumptions, and behavior commensurate with the new reality which Venezuela had been given.

How can these energies in organizations and in the society be orchestrated to achieve greater productivity and quality? What if the key were not in a book on management written by a Japanese, a West German, or a North American but was found in Venezuela? What is the music that will energize people to dance the dance of productivity and quality? Is it not the salsa, the joropo, the music of Barlovento, the music of the Andes, the music of the Yanomami? I do not think that it will be Korean music and energy that will create an economic miracle in Venezuela.

Your County and Culture
Now, returning to consider your own country and its culture, think about five aspects of management based in your country's culture, including the timing, the rhythms, and the energy of its music and dances. Look back at the positive and negative features you brainstormed. What are five elements of your vision of what needs to be done to honor, release, and orchestrate these energies toward greater productivity and quality? What are ten action-elements to realize your vision? What music do you hear? What would you call it? What would you name the dance of effectiveness in your country? How can you begin to share this? Implement this?

I hope that you have enjoyed this essay. What do you remember? What ideas, words? Feelings? What did you find most useful? What images? If someone asks you what you read, what would you tell them? What would you title this essay? How can you continue this kind of thinking and action in your own life and work? How are you different because of reading this essay?

Essay Bibliography

Bentov, Itzhak. 1977. *Stalking the Wild Pendulum: On the Mechanics of Consciousness.* Destiny Books.

Calder, Nigel. 1983. *Timescale: An Atlas of the Fourth Dimension.* Chatto & Windus.

Capra, Fritjof. 1976. *The Tao of Physics.* Bantam.

Darling, David. 1989. *Deep Time: The Journey of a Single Subatomic Particle from the Moment of Creation to the Death of the Universe and Beyond.* Delacorte Press.

Hall, Edward. 1983. *The Dance of Life: The Other Dimensions of Time.* Anchor Books.

Harman, Willis. 1988. *Global Mind Change: The Promise of the Last Years of the Twentieth Century.* Knowledge Systems.

Houston, Jean. 1982. *The Possible Human: A Course Enhancing Your Physical, Mental, and Creative Abilities.* Tarcher.

Institute of Cultural Affairs. 1987. "Organizational Energy." Unpublished (Chicago)

Maturana, Humberto, and Francisco Varela. 1988. *The Tree of Knowledge: The Biological Roots of Human Understanding.* New Science Library.

Wilber, Ken. 1983. *Eye to Eye: The Quest for the New Paradigm.* Anchor Books.

Toward a Whole Systems Analysis and Strategy of Sustainable Human Development (SHD)

(June 1994, New York)

I wrote this piece while I was in UNDP in order to clarify my thinking related to my work as a policy adviser. In it, I introduce the integrative concept of socio-ecological and the planning dynamics of vision, blocks, strategies, and actions.

What happens if we apply a few concepts of whole systems thinking to sustainable human development (SHD)? This approach allows SHD to be conceptualized both in a holistic and a holographic perspective. If this way of framing SHD is useful, it could be expanded in a more concrete presentation using program examples.

To provide a comprehensive theoretical framework for SHD, we need a whole systems analysis of socio-ecological reality. By socio ecological we mean the integration of social and natural systems. First, we acknowledge that the fundamental system is the planetary system of land, air, water, and a vast variety of species of plant and animal life. This we are referring to as the ecological or natural system. Within this system, we find the sub-system of the human species about which we are highly concerned as it is our own species. This we are calling the social system constituted by several dynamics which can be subsumed under economic, political, and cultural processes.

The natural system can exist without the social system, whereas the social system cannot exist without the natural system. This is the central, defining fact of our socio ecological reality. This was the wake-up call of the Earth Summit. This leads to the issue of sustainable development. On the other hand, being human, we are preoccupied with the survival and development of our own species. This in turn leads to the issue of human development.

Taken together, we arrive at the formulation of sustainable human development (SHD). SHD, therefore, is concerned with the development of the human species in its integral relationship to the natural environment. This configuration gives us a people-centered model within a planetary context. The objective of SHD, then, is social development in harmony with natural development. Harmony between the primary system and the sub-system is a fundamental aspect of our theory.

Also, within each type of development we find the objective of harmony. With social development we find the goal of social harmony within economic, political, and cultural dynamics. Our vision of social development is a harmoniously functioning system based on the principle of equity. Equity is the understanding that each human being by virtue of having been born should participate fully in its own development or unfolding. In the 1994 *Human Development Report* (Oxford/UNDP) this is called the "universalism of life claims."

In the same manner, natural or environmental development has the goal of ecological harmony. Our vision of ecological development is a harmoniously functioning system based on the principle of mutuality. Mutuality is the understanding that each aspect of the planetary system, be it air, water, land, plants, or animals, by virtue of being part of planet Earth should participate fully in its own development or unfolding.

In summary, our first-order principle is harmony, and our second-order principles are equity and mutuality. These three principles have enormous implications for human behavior in its economic, political, and cultural dynamics. What we know about systems is that they are guided by operating principles.

Given this scenario of optimal functioning of our socio-ecological system, we must acknowledge the current state of the system. The current operating principles of these systems are well known to all of us. The current first-order principle is not harmony but is hostility. The second-order principle of the social system is disparity. And the second-order principle for the natural system is conflict.

Through a process both analytical and intuitive, UNDP has arrived at four focus areas for promoting SHD. These are poverty alleviation, environmental regeneration, advancement of women, and productive employment. Each of these is a response to either a systemic dysfunction or a major societal gap. Each area moves toward SHD from a distinctive perspective and, in a holographic manner, includes each of the other areas.

Poverty is a systemic dysfunction of the social system – a system-wide condition of social inequity manifest in policies and programs and in attitudes and behaviors. Poverty results in a massive loss of human productivity within the social system. SHD, therefore, requires the alleviation of poverty. Poverty alleviation includes environmental regeneration, the advancement of women, and productive employment. This is in marked contrast to the dominant paradigm of individualism, wealth accumulation, social disintegration, and discrimination.

Environmental degradation is a systemic dysfunction of the natural system – a system wide condition of ecological imbalance manifest in policies and programs and in attitudes and behaviors. Environmental degradation results in a massive loss of human sustainability within the natural system. SHD, therefore, requires the regeneration and· protection of the environment. Environmental regeneration includes poverty alleviation, the advancement of women, and productive employment. This is in marked contrast to the dominant paradigm of the instrumentalism of nature, the linkage of economic productivity to environmental pollution, the linkage of unsustainable lifestyles to resource depletion, and the reduction of human awareness to a time frame of immediacy.

Inadequate participation of women is a major politico-cultural gap in the social system – a system-wide condition of gender discrimination manifests in policies and programs and in attitudes and behavior. Inadequate participation of women results in a massive loss of human creativity within the social system. SHD, therefore, requires the full participation and partnership of women within the social system. Women's advancement includes poverty alleviation, environmental regeneration, and productive employment. This is in marked contrast to the dominant paradigm of a culture and politics oriented to forty-nine percent of the human population.

Unemployment is a major economic gap in the social system – a system-wide condition of financial and market control manifest in policies and programs and in attitudes and behaviors. Unemployment results in a massive loss of human sustenance within the social system. SHD, therefore, requires the creation of sustainable livelihoods for individuals and families within the social system. Productive employment includes poverty alleviation, environmental regeneration, and women's advancement. This is in marked contrast to the dominant paradigm of efficiency, productivity, profitability, and open global markets.

The focus areas of SHD provide a holistic vision viewed from four perspectives. To operationalize this vision we cannot, however, simply take these four areas and implement them. There is a missing step which if left out will frustrate operationalization. This step is the identification of the constraints, gaps, impediments, and contradictions which block the realization of the SHD vision. These blocks are attitudinal, structural, and systemic. For example, if we attempt to "alleviate poverty" we will run into many blockages including attitudes of superiority of the social elites and inadequate structural access to credit, land, and basic services.

There is another level of contradiction which holds all these constraints in being. This might be, in this case, the belief that "the poor you will have with you always" or it may be the principles of wealth accumulation and profitability. Identifying these deep underlying contradictions is the key to building effective strategies. To realize the vision of poverty elimination moving toward social equity, we must develop strategies which deal with these blockages and the underlying contradictions. This might include strategies of changing the attitudes of the elite, creating new structural access to credit, and changing the myths or cultural assumptions of the inevitability of poverty. This process of strategy creation, to be effective, must take place at the country and local community levels as well the international.

A whole systems analysis and strategy of SHD provides a theoretical framework for UNDP's programming. Within this framework, specific entry points can be identified at the country level. UNDP's role is to act as a facilitator of dialogue and collaboration which together move a society towards its own vision of SHD.

Development Epistemology:

A Whole Systems View

(1994, New York)

In this piece, I introduce the use of Ken Wilber's integral quadrants model of mindsets, behaviors, cultures, and systems for analysis and planning.

"If all you have is a hammer, everything looks like a nail." The tools of analysis by and large determine or at least influence perception and judgment. This is not bad; it is natural and inevitable because the human being is a creature of perception and perspective.

In the business of development, one's training and experience go a long way in determining and influencing how one views development. Take for example a society of a million and a half people, for instance, Trinidad and Tobago. When analyzing this society, it is natural for an economist to see economic systems, a political scientist to see political systems, a cultural anthropologist to see value and ethnic systems and for an environmentalist to see ecological systems. If these experts share their analyses with each other, they will find that they have used different tools and frameworks with which to analyze the very same society, and they have come to some quite different conclusions. Or is it the same society? Is it not the case that perspective determines perception that determines reality? Do we not see what we are looking for, from a particular vantage point and through particular "lens"? Is it not the very nature of consciousness to do so?

How then do we go beyond an analytical perspective of development that divides reality into different categories to an appreciation of a *whole social system?* Or is this even a possibility?

Fortunately, there is a growing body of knowledge concerned with just this effort. It is called by different names and has different dimensions, but it leads in the same direction. These approaches are variously called a systemic approach, a multi-disciplinary approach, a cross-sectoral approach, an integrated approach, a holistic approach, or a whole system design approach.

The simple idea behind most of these approaches is that a society or any reality for that matter is assumed to be one fabric with every aspect related inextricably to every other aspect. It is also assumed that there are indeed many perspectives from which to view this one reality. In fact, this is the social enterprise of "bringing forth a world together", as the cognitive biologists would say (Humberto Maturana and Francisco Varela).

Why are these concerns important, even critical, to the United Nations and especially to UNDP? Even though the UN is a club of nation-states (and therefore tends toward a political perspective), it has throughout its history attempted to take the widest possible view of social reality. It has done so by spinning off specialized agencies that take a particular perspective: the welfare of children – UNICEF; the welfare of women – UNIFEM; the welfare of workers – ILO; the cultural perspective – UNESCO; the health perspective – WHO; and so forth. This was a grand effort to view society from its many perspectives. What has happened, however, is that each agency has become an institution which naturally wishes to protect and promote its own perspective and its own institutional interests.

Is it possible for this diverse family to come together to give the UN a holistic perspective on society and the problems of development? This is where the series of UN conferences in the 1990s and UNDP come into the picture.

The series of UN conferences in the 1990s did attempt to bring the whole UN family of agencies, the world community of nation-states, and the growing non-governmental community together to view common issues from multiple perspectives. Again, this was done, however, by dividing, for the sake of analysis, the whole of societal reality into pieces – gender (Beijing), poverty and social integration (Copenhagen), human rights (Vienna), population (Cairo), human settlements (Istanbul) and so forth. Some progress was made nevertheless in establishing a more holistic vision of development.

Now enter UNDP. UNDP is not a specialized agency. As coordinator of the UN development system at the country level (through the Resident Representative/Resident Coordinator [RR/RC]) and at the global level (through chairing the UN Development Group (UNDG), it has attempted to take a more holistic rather than analytical perspective of development. This attempt resulted in the human development or sustainable human development paradigm and approach, launched in 1990 with the Human Development Report (HDR) and later with the concept of Sustainable Human Development (SHD). But because UNDP is also a bureaucratic agency, this perspective has tended to become identified with the institution rather than as a common currency or language of the whole UN system. On the other hand, many groups, including the World Bank, now sound more and more like UNDP in their language and concerns.

Now, at a time when we development practitioners must acknowledge the many failings of the past fifty years as well as some of the notable gains in social and economic indicators, and as we find ourselves in a explosive moment and movement of multiple-izations (e.g., globalization, urbanization, democratization, marketization), we have the opportunity (and some would argue, necessity) to step back and take a genuinely holistic or whole system view of the development enterprise.

This is necessary because we have become aware that all the great development issues that confront us – from poverty, HIV/AIDs, environmental degradation, gender inequality, to lack of accountability and transparency in governance – cannot be solved from a sectoral approach alone but are multi-dimensional issues requiring multi-dimensional approaches.

Take poverty for example. It is widely acknowledged that poverty has dimensions of income disparity, poor access to healthcare, education and credit, weak political voice, gender inequality, negative environmental impacts, and so forth. Likewise, the eradication of poverty requires a multi-dimensional approach that includes all these sectors from the policy levels to programs and projects.

Or take HIV/AIDs. This is not only a health issue. It includes the dimensions of gender roles as well, legal frameworks, insurance systems, care of orphans, psychological trauma, social disintegration, and so on. Therefore, the epidemic must be approached in all its dimensions.

Sectoral analysis and sectoral policies and programs are still needed. But someone somewhere must have a bigger picture – seeing how all the pieces make a larger whole and how that larger whole is or is not being addressed. This is the enterprise of whole systems design.

A whole systems approach looks at the interconnections of all the dimensions of being human – the political, social, economic, cultural, psychological, spiritual, physiological, and environmental dimensions. The key word here is *interconnections*. These are not separate realities but different perspectives on a singular reality. We must return again and again from our analytical excursions to the reintegration of a holistic perspective of the whole system. Then we can have breakthrough insights into policy and program formulation. Then we can identify creative approaches to capacity development at the individual, organizational, institutional, and system-wide levels.

Again, it is not either/or. It is not either sectoral analysis or holistic integration. It is both/and and much, much more.

Mapping a society as a whole system is not only to map its exterior or surface reality but also its interior or depth reality, and not only its collective reality but also the reality of the individual person. These four categories can be combined to produce a highly inclusive map of four dimensions: exterior/collective; exterior/individual; interior/collective; and interior/individual. (Ken Wilber)

Before describing this map further in a theoretical manner, let us apply it to the mapping of an institution – the parliament of a developing country – to see the implications for development.

The usual manner of analyzing a parliament would be to view it as a political institution and therefore to analyze it from the perspective of political science and institutional development. This would map the exterior/collective dimension but not much more. In addition to this dimension, a parliament has an exterior/individual dimension. This is the dimension of the behavior of an individual parliamentarian. This would deal with issues such as corruption, representation, and accountability. The third dimension is that of the interior/collective. This deals with the corporate culture of the parliament – the hidden or manifest "rules of the game" that guide the behavior of the parliament as an institution and parliamentarians as individuals. Finally, there is the interior/individual dimension. This is the most hidden and subtle – the realm of psychology, consciousness, and spirituality. Who is each parliamentarian in his or her heart and soul? What are their intentions? Perceptions? Fears? Hopes and dreams? How "ethical" is the person?

How does this four-dimensional map help us as development practitioners strengthen a parliament? It gives us a multi-dimensional perspective of this institution that allows our analysis of constraints and our proposals to achieve improvements to be based on a thorough and in depth reading of the institution in four dimensions rather than only one or two.

As an example, let us take the four dimensions and look at possible problems and interventions:

PARLIAMENT

Dimension	Problem Analysis	Proposed Actions
Exterior/Collective (Social System)	Low salaries Poor information analysis Election fraud	Increase incentives Conduct public opinion polls Improve election processes
Exterior/Individual (Behavioral)	Rude interactions Absenteeism	Recognize good behavior Recognize good attendance
Interior/Collective (Cultural)	Corruption expected "Winner takes all" mentality	Hold public forums on corruption Utilize consensus building approaches
Interior/Individual (Mindset)	Low level of education Motivated by self interest only	Offer seminars Offer retreats Create citizen feedback mechanisms

In this way, the parliament not only needs a computer system, a serviceable building, and written procedures. It also needs to develop the capacities and attitudes of the individuals that comprise it, reward good behavior, strengthen the connections of accountability and responsiveness between parliamentarians and citizens and build a corporate culture of trust, transparency, and consensus. Also, in this comprehensive approach we will see the linkages of the parliament strengthening program with other development issues such as gender equality, HIV/AIDS, poverty, environment, the role of the media and civil society and so forth. We are viewing the parliament not so much as an impressive building and set of procedures but as a system-wide set of relationships reaching throughout the society and beyond, built as much of intentions, culture, and behavior as of brick, mortar, and political appearance.

Now, as UNDP focuses all its energies on the reduction of human poverty by 2015, the challenge is to help countries design an interlocking policy framework that addresses the multiple dimensions of human poverty both from a holistic and sectoral perspective. Thus, our policy advice may utilize any sectoral entry point (e.g., health, credit, local governance, water, energy, or gender) but will always link that entry point with the other dimensions of human poverty reduction.

As UNDP's Bureau of Development Policy (BDP) moves to provide its services to Country Offices both from headquarters and from regional or sub-regional technical clusters of policy specialists, one of the challenges that faces us is the methodology that will allow us to combine a sectoral entry point approach within a holistic policy framework. How do we combine depth expertise in each sectoral area (either our own or that of a partner institution or senior consultant), the interconnectivity with other policy sectors and institutions, and the four dimensions of the model mentioned above (exterior/collective, exterior/individual, interior/collective and interior/individual)?

The Capacity Building Facility: Facilitating Governance as a Process of Participatory Partnership

(25 August 1994, New York)

This note is based on UNDP's Local Initiative Facility for Urban Environment (LIFE) that I helped develop and coordinate.

CONTEXT: WHOLE SYSTEM TRANSITION

We live in a time of whole system transition. Virtually every aspect of human society is changing with the breakdown of old forms and the breakthrough of emerging, new forms. Some of the major trends driving this transition – democratization, decentralization, rapid population growth and urbanization, "marketization", ecological awareness and "planetization" – are changing the very nature of human society. Beyond any specific set of changes, however, there appears to be a fundamental shift taking place in the perception human beings have of themselves as a species and of their role on this planet. Therefore, this transition is not merely the change of a few specifics but is a transformation of the social system. The World Summit on Social Development, taking place March 1995 in

Copenhagen is a natural opportunity for global dialogue concerning this phenomenon.

CAPACITY BUILDING: FORMATION OF SOCIAL CAPTIAL

Most organizations of the public, private, voluntary, and community sectors, born of another era, are overwhelmed in the face of this whole system transition. In addition, each social actor harbors negative images of the other social actors which block cooperation and synergy. To meet these and other challenges, organizations and the individuals which constitute them require new skills, new attitudes, and new approaches to carry out the daunting task of facilitating the process of governance which must involve all the social actors including national and local governments, non-governmental organizations, community based organizations, and the private sector. To equip each sector to fulfill its societal function, organizational officials must learn the skills of "facilitating a process of participatory partnership."

The learning and application of these new skills will bear fruit in social development including reducing poverty, promoting sustainable livelihoods, integrating diverse groups, and regenerating the environment. These skills of "facilitating governance" are best acquired in a learning-by-doing mode rather than in an academic mode, although some formal training is needed. The exercise of these skills increases the formation of "social capital" – the strengthening of voluntary relationships within a society among social actors which energize social bonds and result in improved economic, political, and cultural transactions. This type of capacity building catalyzes systemic change – a transformation of the modalities of societal interaction.

A PROCESS OF PARTICIPATORY PARTNERSHIP

Involvement in the "process of participatory partnership" requires, among others, three skills: (a) systems thinking, (b) strategic design, and (c) the implementation of multi-actor modalities of action and reflection-in-action. This process gives rise to social experimentation, social innovation, and social learning.

Systems Thinking

Systems thinking skills are required so that the social actors can grasp the relationships inherent between specific sectoral issues and the entire system of economic, political, cultural, and environmental processes. A systems approach enables recognition, conceptualization and description of the complex and recurring patterns found in both social and natural systems. Operating out of this understanding of systemic relationships within a holistic framework, the social actors can move beyond debate to dialogue. This type of dialogue requires a suspension of certainties, awareness of multiple perspectives, and an openness to the emergence of creative breakthroughs. Learning about holism allows for a recognition of systemic wholes which are more than the sum of the constituent parts. This way of viewing social reality provides objectivity and rationality to otherwise highly emotional and confrontational relationships. Systems thinking builds the capacities necessary for analysis, synthesis, and creative innovation.

Strategic Design

Skills of strategic design are necessary for the social actors so that processes of change are directed toward intended future conditions rather than in reaction to present problems. This is a shift from a problem-solving, or reactive mode to a future-design approach or proactive mode. Strategic design includes facilitating: (1) the articulation of the latent vision of the future held by a society, community, or organization; (2) the discernment of both the inhibiting and enhancing factors related to the hoped-for vision; (3) the creation of a set of strategic directions which take advantage of the enhancing factors, deal with the inhibiting factors and move the society, organization, or community toward its vision; (4) the identification of tactical action arenas which will set the strategic directions in motion; (5) the preparation of a set of action steps within a specific time frame which provide implementation of the tactical arenas and clarify (a) what will be done, (b) when it will be done, (c) where it will take place, (d) how it will be carried out and (e) by whom; and (6) on-going reflection-in-action which provides feed-back of lessons, insights, questions, data, models, and methods into the above-mentioned cycle.

Strategic design most effectively takes place in workshops, seminars, consultations, conferences, colloquia, and fora with the active participation of representatives of all relevant social actors, the use of participatory methodologies, and with the assistance of trained, group facilitators to guide the process. Strategic design builds the capacity to orchestrate and facilitate multi-actor dialogue and collaboration focused on specific issues or cross-cutting themes. Strategic design includes combining creative inquiry and innovative leadership. Individual development as a learning component is an inherent and critical aspect of strategic design in that only in understanding oneself holistically and in pursuing personal growth can one be of genuine service in applying strategic design within an organizational or societal setting. Strategic design involves several phases including preparation, immersion, divergence, convergence, incubation, cognitive leap, creative stage development, innovation stage evaluation, and synthesis.

Multi-Actor Modalities of Implementation and Feedback

In addition to the skills of systems thinking and strategic design, the skills of forming multi-actor mechanisms for implementation and learning are essential. Such mechanisms of collaboration and partnership include, among others, the formation of preparatory committees, task forces, and legal entities at the national, provincial, municipal, and local community levels. The key to the effective operation of collaborative organizational structures is the sense of ownership of the process by each actor. This sense of ownership is most effectively instilled through open and transparent processes of dialogue, planning, and evaluation utilizing the skills of systems thinking and strategic design as outlined above. Multi-actor modalities of action and learning build the capacities for effective social change at any level.

PROGRAM DESIGN OF THE CBF

Local/National Activities
The dynamic framework for the Capacity Building Facility (CBF) at the country-level begins upstream, moves downstream, and then moves back upstream. This upstream-downstream-upstream (UDU) approach includes the following steps, probably, but not rigidly, in this sequence:

Upstream:
First, the identification of a national facilitator should take place. The Terms of Reference for this person or organization are to facilitate, i.e., enable and catalyze, not coordinate or control, the process of participatory partnership. The national facilitator begins a dialogue with representatives of relevant social actors to identify a strategic, entry-point issue. This can be any issue from credit provision, access to basic services to environmental protection. After the strategic, entry-point issue is determined, the identification of the actors which are the stakeholders related to this issue should take place. Next, a national Preparatory Committee (PreCom), made up of representatives of the relevant actors, should be formed. This group is an ad-hoc body with the Terms of Reference (TOR) to set up a national consultation on the entry-point issue. A national consultation workshop is then held to focus the entry-point issue and to identify priority sub-issues, strategies for dealing with the issue and criteria for successful initiatives related to dealing with this issue. Following the national consultation, a national taskforce is formed to provide guidance to this process.

During this phase, the national facilitator, the PrepCom and the national task force will participate in a series of training sessions on systems thinking and strategic design.

Downstream:
After the formation of a national task force, small-scale demonstrations of strategic responses to the entry-point issue are identified, supported and implemented. This provides a new generation of innovations for social learning. These small-scale initiatives are identified in the following manner. The national task force invites the submission of project proposals for small-scale initiatives drawn up by collaborative teams of social actors, e.g., NGOs, CBOs, and government. Utilizing a selection criteria developed in the national consultation workshop, the national task force selects the most promising proposals and provides funding, either as a loan, grant, or combination of the two. The national facilitator and the national task force then assist the small-scale initiatives through technical assistance, monitoring, networking, and training, including training in systems thinking and strategic design.

Upstream:
Following the completion of a small-scale activity, the national taskforce aids participatory documentation and evaluation of the project. Based on an analysis and synthesis of these studies, lessons-learned are compiled and disseminated through workshops, publications, videos, and the mass media. Following this dissemination process, policy dialogue conferences are conducted at the municipal, provincial, and national levels, which can result in new policies, programs, and projects.

Regional, Inter-regional and Global Activities
Regional, inter-regional, and global activities will include the documentation, dissemination, interchange, and transfer of lessons-learned at the local and country levels to other countries through the various levels. Specific activities include

conducting workshops and conferences, producing videos and publications, utilizing the mass media, conducting research projects, and transferring actual innovations between countries.

INSTITUTIONAL ARRANGEMENTS FOR THE FACILITY

Role of the National/Local Actors

As indicated above, the local and national actors play the major roles in the CBF country-level activities. At the regional and inter-regional levels, international NGO networks, intergovernmental bodies and research and training institutes can play a role. The reason for placing the CBF process entirely in the hands of the local and national actors is on-the-job capacity building experience including reflection-in-action.

Role of International Actors

International assistance of two types is needed. On the one hand, technical and operational assistance of the global program is needed. This provides the program with the necessary global perspective ensuring inter-country linkages, common guidelines, and capacity for analysis and synthesis of lessons-learned at a global level. On the other, major financial flows are required both in the form of grant funds and loan financing. This ensures the availability of capital for each phase of the UDU process.

Role of UNDP/UN

UNDP, through its 131 country offices, the five Regional Bureaus, the Governance and Development Management Division (GDMD) and the Office for Project Services (OPS), will provide the overall technical, operational, and administrative coordination. UNDP's Resident Representatives, who are also the Resident Coordinators of the UN system at the country level, will provide their assistance in introducing this process to Government. The Rgional Bureaus provide direct contact between Headquarters and the country offices. GDMD, with its considerable experience in backstopping global program such as the Management Development Program (MDP), the Urban Management Program (UMP), and the Local Initiative Facility for Urban Environment (LIFE), will provide the analytical and synthesis functions and help ensure the quality of the program. Likewise, OPS, with its vast experience in executing hundreds of projects worldwide, will provide the necessary administrative support. UNDP will involve the specialized agencies of the UN system in providing their expertise in the operations of the CBF.

Role of the Funds Providers
The funds providers, e.g., The World Bank, the regional banks, and bilateral donors, will be full partners in the operations of the CBF. Their representatives will participate in the CBF Global Advisory Committee for ongoing program review and planning. The banks will provide loan funds at concessionary rates and the bilateral donors will provide grant funds. The total initial allocation to the CBF is expected to be $10 billion. Various mechanisms will be utilized to make this fund available including, among others, debt reduction schemes and debt-for-development swaps. The funds providers will ensure financial monitoring of the CBF.

CONCLUSION
The Capacity Building Facility (CBF) will provide developing countries with access to state-of-the-art methodologies and processes and the catalytic financial resources to engage in their own capacity building exercises. Through a combination of learning-by-doing and formal training the CBF provides an opportunity for both structural and attitudinal change. By focusing on strategic, entry-point issues, the CBF offers an indirect approach to capacity building. This keeps the focus of the program on the "what" of social development and allows the "how" of capacity building to be an appropriate means to that end. As a global program the CBF provides an inter-country

network of learning, dissemination, and policy dialogue on social development.

It would be highly appropriate to launch the CBF at the World Summit on Social Development in March 1995 at Copenhagen. For this to happen, intensive consultations within the UN, the multi-lateral banks, the bilateral donors, national and local governments, NGO networks and research and training institutes must take place over the next six months. UNDP stands ready to facilitate this process.

NOTES

1. Ms. Jean Houston, Ph.D., Co-Director of the Foundation for Mind Research, Pomona, New York, has written extensively on the topic of whole system transition.
2. The concept of "social capital" is elaborated in the UNDP Discussion Paper, "Sustainable Human Development: From Concept to Operation: A Guide for the Practitioner", 1994.
3. The literature on systems theory and system thinking is quite large. The understanding of whole system design is articulated by the Whole System Design Program of Antioch University, in Seattle, Washington.
4. The definition of dialogue is from The Dialogue Project, which is part of the Organizational Learning Centre at MIT.
5. This process of strategic planning is found in the book *Winning Through Participation: The Technology of Participation (ToP)* by Laura Spencer.
6. This Upstream-Downstream-Upstream approach is currently being tested by UNDP's Local Initiative Facility for Urban Environment (LIFE).

Whole Systems Change and HIV/AIDS

(1994, New York)

This was written for the Inter-Country Consultation in Africa on Ethics, Law and HIV, 27 June - l July 1994, Dakar, Senegal. The purpose of the note was to share a reflection on the HIV/AIDS epidemic from the perspective of whole systems change. At the time, the author knew little about HIV/AIDS but was eager to learn. This inter-country consultation was a first step in this learning process. This paper attempts to share a few thoughts, as we confront the challenge which HIV/AIDS brings to our species at this moment in history. Now in 2021 during the COVID-19 pandemic, it is highly relevant.

A Metaphor for Our Times
We live in a time of breakdown and break through. The membranes which have heretofore separated cultures, races, nations, and religions are rapidly breaking down. It is as though the immune system of our species is becoming permeable. We wear each other's clothes, sing each other's songs, eat each other's foods, and live in each other's countries as we rush headlong into what some would call "planetization". The breakdown through HIV/AIDS of the physiological immune system is mirroring this larger, global, cultural breakdown.

HIV/AIDS is a holistic disease. It is not simply a medical phenomenon but is also psychological, cultural, familial, legal, educational, sociological, philosophical, governmental, and economic. Therefore, to respond to the phenomenon of HIV/AIDS requires a holistic response – a whole systems shift in the very nature of human sociality. HIV/AIDS exposes the systemic inequities in society and the operating principles at work in societal systems, e.g., fear, hostility, and inequality. In this way, the tragedy of HIV/AIDS is a doorway, an opportunity, a beckoning, to create a new kind of human society. This is the breakthrough that is happening.

Emerging Vision
What would this new society look like? What would be the operating principles of such a social system? This new social vehicle would be based on many of the principles which have been discussed in this inter-country consultation, e. g., shared responsibility, courage, compassion, equity of opportunity, and social harmony. Thus, our discussion of ethical principles is central to creating this new society. Social systems operate from the "software" of shared principles, values, images, and assumptions. These are the motivating impulses that drive our economies, our politics, and our very cultures. These principles are then expressed in various systems including legal systems, health systems, educational systems, financial systems, and governance systems. These principles arise from many sources such as the dialogue between the universal imperatives of the historic, world religions and the intuitions and wisdom of local people everywhere.

Let us take one of these principles, "shared responsibility", and relate it to HIV/AIDS and a new societal system. In shared responsibility, the individual is responsible not only for him/herself but for the community and society. Conversely, the community is not only responsible for the common good but for the well-being of each person. This is the inevitable mutuality and reciprocity of sociality. The person infected with the

HIV is not only responsible for caring for his/her life but is also responsible for the well being of other people. Likewise, the community is not only responsible for reducing and stopping further infections of HIV but is responsible for the care and nurture of the individual already infected. In shared responsibility there is no juxtaposition of public health and individual rights. In its essence, responsibility entails both freedom and obedience. Without the exercise of individual free will, responsibility would be a form of slavery. And without obedience to the needs of others, responsibility would be at-best selfishness and anarchy.

Underlying Contradictions -
Given this emerging vision of social equity and, we must add, environmental regeneration (which some have named, "sustainable human development") what then are those forces, attitudes and structures which are blocking this vision from being realized? We can, of course, think of many such factors, e.g., fear, discrimination, inadequate access to basic services, credit, land and shelter, unjust laws, submission of women, environmental pollution, and disease, including HIV/AIDS. And underneath these many and seemingly unrelated challenges are deep, concentrations of blockages or contradictions. These underlying contradictions are like the powerful roots of a huge plant anchoring it firmly in the soil. These must identified and named so that they can be dealt with creatively. Otherwise, our attempts to move toward our vision of a new society will be frustrated and stopped entirely. These underlying contradictions include, among others, poverty, environmental degradation, the submission of women, and unemployment.

In the case of HIV/AIDS, what are the underlying contradictions which are blocking the eradication of the epidemic? At first glance, it appears that these include unprotected sex, the sharing of needles, and contaminated blood. This is so, but what is maintaining these conditions? Is it not such phenomena as multiple sexual partners, inadequate access to condoms, drug addiction, inadequate access to clean needles, and unchecked blood. This too is so, but, looking deeper, what is allowing these conditions to exist and persist? Do not these deep underlying attitudes and structures include discrimination, fear, misinformation, poverty, the submission of women, inadequate education, unjust legislation, and inadequate health care? To devise meaningful strategies, we must first identify these deep, underlying contradictions. These negative attitudes and debilitating structures then become our challenges, providing a doorway into the future. Strange as it may sound, these are not our enemies but our odd friends.

Strategic Proposals
If these are some of the underlying contradictions which are keeping us from realizing a new society of equity and health for all, what are the strategic proposals which will deal with these contradictions and move us toward our emerging vision. Here we must ask what are the broad strategic directions which will deal with this matrix of contradictions. We will need strategies to stop further infections, to care for the already infected, and to deal with the consequences of the epidemic, e.g., the orphans, single parents, societal depression and despair, and rapid population decrease in the public and private sectors. We will need strategies of poverty alleviation, productive employment, advancement of women, and environmental regeneration.

We will need to create strategies which bring into being new systems of health care, legislation and policy, education, finance, insurance, and employment. We will need strategies at various levels, e.g., the individual/familial, the community/city, the provincial, the national, the regional, and the global. We will need to catalyze and maintain national movements and an international movement. Some of our strategies will be focused on changing attitudes, images, and values, which consequently will change individual behavior. And other of our strategies will be focused on changing societal structures, which will result in changed community behavior. In this way our strategies will not only be problem-solving, or past oriented in nature, but will be designing a new system of equity of opportunity that is future-oriented in nature.

Tactical Systems
After designing our strategic proposals, we will need to build our tactical systems. These are the policies, programs, and projects, the modalities, mechanisms, and processes which will achieve our strategic proposals. These will include, among many others, policies of just legal frameworks, programs of universal health care, projects of home care for the infected, modalities of public-private-community partnerships, mechanisms of credit availability, and processes of participatory decision-making at all levels.

Action Steps/Time Frame
Once our tactical systems have been designed, we are ready to decide the specific action-steps to be taken, and to decide when they should be taken, how they should be taken, where they should happen, and taken by whom. These action-steps are then placed on a time frame for the next several months to guide us daily and weekly. Of course, this plan will need to be revised and adapted to new circumstances, insights, and opportunities, but it will act as a map and compass for our actions. Then on a quarterly and yearly basis, we will want to go through this exercise again, if possible, with trained facilitators guiding us through the process.

Conclusion
Precisely because HIV/AIDS is so frightening and threatening, it is demanding that our species grow up and re-invent more equitable and sustainable societies. We will either grasp this opportunity or it will slip away from us. In our discussion of Rwanda, we could see that it was no accident that this society disintegrated into genocide, suffering, and chaos. In fact, we

are beginning to identify the conditions and factors which lead to massive social disintegration. These factors include poverty, disease, famine, inequity, unemployment, discrimination, and environmental degradation. If our species experiences these conditions anywhere on our planet, we are all at risk. For poverty, disease, and pollution carry no passports. Either we have a common future, or we have no future at all. One of the clear messages of this inter-country consultation is that in HIV/AIDS a door has been opened for us, and we see a ray of hope shining through. Let us go through this door together with open eyes and a vision of sustainable human development.

The Journey of a Reflective Practitioner

of Whole System Change

(1995, New York)

In April 1995, at the invitation of professor Harold Nelson, PhD, the program's designer, and director, I made a presentation to the "Systems Theory Revisited" module of the Whole System Design Graduate Program of Antioch University, in Seattle, Washington, USA. At the time, I was a policy adviser with UNDP on my way from New York to Tokyo and stopped in Seattle to speak to this class and later a group of colleagues of the Institute of Cultural Affairs. The purpose of my session was to help the students clarify how an individual can apply systems theory in a variety of settings and challenge them to be reflective practitioners of whole systems change. The paper that I presented shared my journey as a reflective practitioner of whole systems change designing a life of whole system design. This was an experiment in using vignettes from my life story as a pedagogical tool, and thus could also appear in the Self Transformations Collection.

Here and now. Together. We bring forth a world. What is the world we are bringing forth? How does this bringing forth happen? How are we "together?" Are we truly here? Are we fully now? As you know, these statements and questions

are based on the words of Humberto Maturana and Francisco
Varela. What do you think of these questions? Let us begin
by scanning this particular here, this particular now, this particular we, the particular world which is coming forth. Look
around. Look within yourself. Look within someone else. Look
from outside this situation. What is being called forth?

I must first tell you that my interest in these questions is not
incidental, not academic, not an abstract musing. Everyday, I
am driven by a related question: If the socio-economic world is
a human construct, a human invention, why cannot we invent
another world – more equitable, more just, more sustainable?
Why must billions of our fellow human beings live in grinding
poverty, without adequate housing, without healthcare, without education, without jobs, without dignity, without meaning?
Why must the natural environment systematically be destroyed?
What is holding this present construct in being? What is blocking the creation of a new human social invention of greater
equity, sustainability, and meaning? What would enable this
creation to come to be? What is my role in this enablement, this
catalysis? These are the questions of a reflective practitioner
of sustainable human development. How do these questions
come to you? What do they evoke? How have these questions
come to be a driving force in life, in my life, the lives of many
others, perhaps in your life? This begs a story – the story of a
particular life. As I tell this story, please think along with me
about your own life.

I must begin by asking: what is the significance of one
human life within the unimaginable vastness of the space-time
universe, within the immensity of a 13-billion-year universe
story? This is one of the greatest of mysteries. I believe that
every human life is a once and for all, never again, opportunity
for the universe to become conscious, to become expressive, to
celebrate its existence. I am such an opportunity. You are such
an opportunity. Each person is such an exquisitely precious
opportunity. Someone else has said it beautifully – you are a
star's way of looking at a star.

I would like to share with you one such life story as reflected in 17 images on the arrow of time. How does one become aware of systems, aware of design, aware of creativity? This is the story of an evolving whole system designer who is becoming a global practitioner. I have taken note that in your program you place great emphasis on the individual journey. With the KC4 curriculum component in your course, you have looked at global transformation with Willis Harman. Next with KC6, you will look at individual transformation. As part of your current KC5 mandate, this story will deal with the connection between planet and person. This story will be told as biography rather than autobiography, as a journey of consciousness rather than of an ego, from a transpersonal rather than a personal perspective.

1. It is 1949 in a small town in southeastern Oklahoma. A little boy of five sits in a barber chair. He is fascinated with the reflection he sees in the barbershop mirrors in front and behind him. He sees his own image, the barber, the barbershop. He sees this image not just once, but repeated again and again, becoming smaller and smaller, further, and further, refracted and reflected in the mirrors. This early experience becomes a fractal wave that repeats itself throughout his life – the awareness of images of reality reflected again and again, receding into an infinite distance. A reflective practitioner is unfolding. What is your earliest memory of your awareness that reality can be reflected upon again and again? What is a pattern in your life that repeats itself over and over?

2. November 1965, the boy is now a junior in college. After studying existentialism and poetry and marching for the civil rights of African Americans and women, the young man is suddenly struck by a transformational happening. In a weekend seminar in Chicago's westside

Afro-American ghetto, strewn with broken glass and broken lives, he experiences radical affirmation, a radical
possibility, a radical call, an intentionality, an opening.
This brief experience becomes the defining moment of
his life. What for you was an early defining moment?

3. The following year, fresh out of undergraduate school,
he is back in that same ghetto sitting in a lecture hall –
a model is being presented called the "Life Triangles".
One corner of the triangle deals with theoretical reality,
another with practical reality and the third with "un-
synonymous" (mysterious) reality. Suddenly all human
experience is reflected in this comprehensive model.
Other mental models are presented which awaken a deep
yearning in the young man – the desire to see what is really
there, a desire for Truth. One model deals with dimensions of human experience – with knowing, doing, and
being. One model deals with social reality – economic,
political, and cultural commonality – allowing society
to be viewed as an integrated system of dynamics and
relations. One model shows the geographic and social
relationships of the world in three spheres – West, East,
and South. Yet another model shows the relations of six
Ur images underlying human culture. These and other
models convince the young man that it is possible to
reflect reality in dynamic visual constructs, all the while
knowing that they are changeable and, as such, temporal approximations of what is otherwise mysterious,
unknowable reality. When and how did you become
aware of the power of mental models?

4. Accompanying these models are principles. Models
should be comprehensive – inclusive of all dimensions
of a reality; future-oriented – in response to the life
questions emerging from the distant future; archaic –
considering the wealth of human experience throughout history and evolution; and intentional – embody-
ing the principle of responsibility, willfulness, being a

self in the world. He begins to grasp. the implications of Kierkegaard's definition of the self: "The self is a relationship that relates itself to itself and in willing to be that relationship grounds itself transparently in the power that posits it." From these principles arises a stance – of being responsible to the Mystery for the world. To this stance are added methods – intellectual methods of study and pedagogy; social methods of community and organizational development; and spirit methods of personal transformation of consciousness. The young man, now twenty-four years old, is equipped with a few basic tools with which to change the world and to continually transform himself. What are some of the methods and principles which have been most formative for you?

5. It is amid the despair of this urban slum that hope is born in his heart. It is here amid social and economic decay that a model for the future of human community is being given living form. The young man is awakening to the possibility of catalyzing transformation within individual lives and within a community of sidewalks, buildings, children, and gangs. The vision of 5th City has emerged in his consciousness. When in your life have you been grasped by a motivating vision or hope in the possible?

6. From this local fragment of geography, the young man, recently married, takes a spin around planet Earth, and falls madly in love with her mountains, her seas, her peoples, her cultures. This journey, called a "Global Odyssey", takes only thirty days, travelling to Mexico City, Tokyo, Bangkok, Kathmandu, Calcutta, Varanasi, Addis Ababa, Cairo, Athens, Rome, Dubrovnik, London, and Reykjavik. Ten of the world's great cultures are encountered experientially. This experience itself is experienced through depth dialogue, journal writing, and reflection. A gestalt of the whole Earth as a single living system forms in his mind's eye. This vision never

leaves him throughout his life journey. He has been infected with the virus of globality and has become a loyal citizen of planet Earth. When did you become aware of the planet as a living system?

7. The time is now 1970; the place is Kuala Lumpur, the beautiful capital of tropical Malaysia. Leaving graduate school far behind, the young man and his beloved, enter a two-year journey with another culture – a luxuriant mixture of Malay, Chinese, Indian, and British cultures. The young man becomes conscious of his own culture as it bumps up against other cultures, and of his own assumptions as they collide with quite different assumptions. He is beginning to become aware of the systemic nature of culture itself. He asks a Chinese doctor if his Western body can be sustained on Chinese noodles, rice, vegetables, and fragments of chicken. The doctor replies yes, he will most probably be healthier with this diet. The young man conducts courses on leadership throughout Malaysia, Singapore, Thailand, and Indonesia and begins to awaken to a new dimension of his calling – being of service to people by transferring life methods which enable social and personal transformation. When have you become aware of another culture? of your own culture? Of the systemic nature of culture? Of your calling or vocation?

8. Korea – Land of Morning Calm – 5,000 years of history. It is here that our subject expands his family and helps transform a province and a rural village. After six years of trying to make a baby, the couple decide to adopt a little Korean boy. Immediately following this decision his wife becomes pregnant. Suddenly a family of two adults is transformed into a family system of four people including two little boys. What a shock! Soon after, the young man begins to help create a human development project, as a demonstration of systemic transformation of a local community. First, a week-long consultation is

held with representatives of an entire Island province. Then, a pilot village is selected. The village is situated on the slopes of the Island's central volcanic mountain affording a breathtaking view sweeping out and down to white foaming waves crashing on black jagged rocks. He moves his little family into this 15th century village of rock houses and mud floors, complete with ecologically sound, but quite surprising, pig toilets. It is here that the young man learns of the dramatic differences between urban and rural life. Suddenly there are no streetlights. No restaurants. No movie theatres. No drug stores. No paved roads or side walks. No hot water. No refrigeration. His consciousness is raw with discomfort and disorientation. The village begins its transformational journey toward modernity and development. At the end of six years in Korea, he helps host a "World's Fair of Human Development" with people coming from projects in the 24 time zones of planet Earth to the tiny village of Kwang Yung II Ri to celebrate their diverse journeys of human development. When did you become aware that a family is a system? When did you become concerned to change the world?

9. It is 1978 in Indiahoma, Oklahoma, USA. Our protagonist, now thirty-four years old, returns from eight years in Asia to his home state of Oklahoma to conduct a human development project in a small town populated by poor whites and Comanche Indians. A new water tower is built; a HUD grant is received; he directs a Vista project to renew the town; a "Festival of Hometowns" is held to celebrate every hometown. After six years in Korea, he cannot stop bowing to people. Even so, he is falling in love perhaps for the first time with the people of his native land. When did you return to your home with new eyes? What did you experience?

10. It is now 1981. Our reflective practitioner and his little family are living in a small village, named Woburn

Lawn, situated high in the Blue Mountains of Jamaica. In Kingston, he is working with a National Committee of government officials, volunteer organizations, private companies, and community groups to conduct a national consultation on human development for the 1980s called "The Jamaican Potential". He also directs a comprehensive development project in a cluster of villages in the Blue Mountains. In addition, he is conducting strategic planning consultations with organizations including the National Commercial Bank, the Anglican Diocese of Jamaica, the Girl Guides, and UNICEF's Inter-ministerial Basic Services for Children Project. He sees himself engaged in the system-wide transformation of a nation from the micro to the macro level. When did you first see the need for national transformation?

11. In 1984, our systems designer takes a delegation of fifteen Jamaicans, including the Minister of Community Development, to New Delhi to participate in the International Exposition of Rural Development (IERD). The theme of the exposition is "Sharing Approaches That Work." The delegation takes with them a professional exhibition, including videos, of Jamaican projects. Leading up to this international event, he has assisted in documenting rural development projects throughout the country and in holding a national rural development symposium. When did you become aware of the need to "share approaches that work?"

12. In that same year, our subject begins to awaken to a "new paradigm of reality." He reads *The Tao of Physics* and the *Dancing Woo Li Masters*. He reads *Lives of a Cell, Cosmos, The Aquarian Conspiracy, No Boundaries, Eye to Eye, The Possible Human*, and many other works. His mind begins to open to a universe of quantum mechanics, a holistic universe, the perennial philosophy, a universe animated by consciousness. This paradigm is quite ancient and is in sync with his earlier models and principles. What is

new is the articulation of this paradigm within a scientific, historic, and mythic framework. He is fascinated with the vision that is emerging but also asks himself the question: What does this vision have to do with my daily life and work? He becomes aware that the consciousness which he has been developing for forty years is corroborated by a wide body of literature and experience both scientific and religious. He is introduced to insight meditation. He sits in the lotus position for the first time. He becomes fascinated with the way of the Buddha. When did you first encounter the "New Paradigm", the "Perennial Philosophy?" What difference did it make in your life?

13. And in that same year, he and his family move south to Venezuela, to Caracas the Capital, to a small barrio called Las Minas de Baruta - the Baruta mines. His task is to build a national organization – a non-governmental organization – with a strong Board of Directors, a portfolio of projects in community and organizational development. He studies and learns Spanish. He secures contracts and grants for the organization. He develops local staff and receives a downtown office for the organization. He conducts strategic planning workshops with Colgate Palmolive, Citibank, and Household Finance. He conducts community development consultations for the oil companies in the prairies of Venezuela and in the tropical rainforests east of Caracas. The organization purchases an old mansion in need of renovation to provide residences for the staff. Then suddenly, everything begins to change, to be change. When have you created something which seemed solid but later changed radically?

14. In 1986, he encounters Dr. Jean Houston. In her seminar on Sacred Psychology, he rediscovers his own tears, his own pain. He discovers that he is a dancer. He discovers that he is a whole being of body, mind, and spirit.

He begins a journey with Ms. Houston that encompasses four levels of consciousness – the sensory/physical, the psychological/historic, the mythic/symbolic, and the unitive/integral. Later he participates in her think tank on whole systems transition and in her Mystery School. All the while his sense of individuation and wholeness is deepening. When did you discover or rediscover the wholeness of your own being?

15. In 1988, he and his colleagues decide to participate in an experiment called "whole system transformation." This experiment begins to alter the controlling images of the organization and community of which he has been part for the past twenty years. A transformation takes place from being a family, religious order to a profit-making service organization. From being a prior, he becomes a CEO. From having a volunteer staff, he hires a professional staff. From living in community, he moves his family into their own apartment in downtown Caracas – complete with swimming pool. From focusing on rural development, he invites Willis Harman and Jean Houston to Caracas to conduct seminars on the metaphysics of consciousness and the possible human. When did you experience a transformation in an organization or community of which you were part? What provoked this transformation?

16. In March 1990, he takes yet another journey – this time returning once again to his native country, stopping in New York City. He returns with $900 in the bank, with no job, no home, and no insurance, and with a family, one son entering college, and another entering high school. After working with the Mega Cities Project at New York University, he is invited to work with the United Nations Development Program (UNDP) in urban development and management. He is attracted to UNDP by its annual Human Development Report and his lifelong admiration for the United Nations symbolized for him

by Dag Hammarskjold, the Secretary-General whose journal of spiritual reflections, *Markings*, was published after he was killed in a plane crash on a peace mission in Africa. First as a consultant and later as a staff member, our own reflective practitioner travels for the UN to Nairobi, Paris, Kuala Lumpur, Bangkok, Islamabad, Bombay, New Delhi, Madras, Rio, Kingston, Dakar, Dar es Salaam, Mwanza, Cairo, Rabat, Fes, Geneva, Vancouver, Honolulu, San Francisco, Washington, D.C., Mexico City, Bogota, and Cartagena. As coordinator of a global program on urban environmental improvement in the slums and squatter settlements, he begins to perturb the system of international development cooperation with images and methods of participation, partnership, and process, of systems thinking and strategic design, of consciousness and culture. He creates a visual model of UNDP's vision of sustainable human development. The LIFE Program (the Local Initiative Facility for Urban Environment) takes root in twenty countries with fifty small-scale projects in waste management, water supply and quality, canal rehabilitation, reforestation, sanitation and drainage, income generation, environmental education, and environmental health. When did life give you exactly what you had always wanted?

17. It is now December 1993. At the International Healthy Cities Conference in San Francisco, our protagonist meets your esteemed director, Dr. Harold Nelson. They have lunch together and talk for hours about whole system design. Our reflective practitioner is fascinated with what he hears. When have you met someone with whom you knew you wanted to talk and learn?

And now, here, we are together, bringing forth a world. What is that world which we are bringing forth? The challenge facing us as a species and as individuals is posed by Pierre Teilhard de Chardin: The task before us now, if we would not perish, is to shake off our ancient prejudices and to build the Earth. How are we to do this, all of us together?

Questions:

1. How did your childhood prepare you to practice Whole System Design (WSD)?
2. What early principles, methods, and stance prepared you for the WSD journey you are on?
3. When did you first become aware of systems?
4. When did you first try to help design a whole system?
5. What have you learned about designing systems?
6. How has systems theory helped you in designing systems? Which concepts? Which theorists? How?
7. What do you see is the greatest challenge of WSD?
8. Where are you called to practice WSD?
9. How does reflection on your practice help your practice?

THEME

Sustainable Human Development

This theme contains essays related to my views on UNDP concepts, strategies, and programs. Some of the topics dealt with include urbanization, urban development, governance, and people and planet centered development. Authors referenced include Joseph van Arendonk, PhD, William Draper, Jean Houston, PhD, and Joseph W. Mathews.

Human Development and Urbanization:
A Planetary Perspective

(December 1990, New York City)

This was written for an international think tank on whole systems transition meeting in Bocono, Venezuela, 10 – 16 December 1990. I helped arrange for the meeting but did not attend due to my new position at UNDP in New York City. Jean Houston, PhD, led the discussion. From the 1990 introduction: "The paper attempts to review a sociological context for human development and urbanization and to expand this view to the multiple perspectives of whole systems transition. It was written because of the author's many years of life and work with the Institute of Cultural Affairs (ICA) in human development in villages, cities, and organizations, and because of his current work in urban development. It is concerned with touching base with some of the factual data and with some of our feelings and thoughts about where we are headed. It is an attempt to weave the outer and the inner together into one fabric that is urbanization." The reader will note that the statistics in the paper are from 1990. The context, conclusions, and recommendations, however, are relevant in 2021. In the last few pages, I share my own reflections and make use of Jean Houston's four level framework.

In 1986, Joseph van Arendonk, PhD, Deputy Executive Director of the United Nations Fund for Population Activities (UNFPA), posed two profound questions to an international conference of the Institute of Cultural Affairs which I was attending. He said that we must ask the questions of "What is Man (or humanness)?" and "What is development?" To this day, these two questions ring in my ears. Van Arendonk said that these are not only philosophical questions; they are urgent, practical questions. He said that the reason that we must stand before these two questions as questions is that we already have our own assumptions about the answers to them. Our assumptions and answers block us from thinking afresh about these fundamental concepts, thus disrupting the social dialogue and creation of participatory answers. It is most certainly not bad to have answers; in fact, it is inevitable and necessary. The issue comes when my answer keeps me from hearing other people's answers and from acknowledging the validity of other answers as representing the integrity of a human life. This kind of awareness does not lead to a relativism that concludes that, therefore, all answers are legitimate, and it makes no difference what one's answer is. Rather, this openness to participating in a lively dialogue with other people is the very essence of a learning society, a concept we will elaborate elsewhere.

Our answer to the first question springs forward from our acculturation and socialization as provided by our nation, region, culture, religion, political ideology, class, race, age, and sex, as well as our own individual history. Some say that human beings are basically evil and therefore must be kept in check by the structures of society. Others believe that human beings are a resource, a human resource, like a natural resource, for economic productivity. Others know that human beings are spirit or consciousness and are on a journey of self-realization or self-transcendence. Others are convinced that human beings are made in the image of God. Others think that the human being is merely an intelligent animal. Some are certain that only their group is truly human and that all others are barbarians or infidels or the "poor" and, therefore, less than human. And the answers go on and on. Again, the point is not that it makes no difference what one's answer is. The issue is that implicit in one's answer about the meaning and ultimate valuation of the human phenomenon is a theory of development.

Our answer to the second question is all too universal: "Development has to do with progress, with industrialization, with modernization. It has to do with increased production and consumption of a society. It has to do with Gross National Product (GNP) and GNP per capita." This is the definition of development which the West has successfully sold to almost the entire world. Here we can clearly see that implicit in this definition of development is a definition of humanness.

These two questions, as authentic questions, questions which must be faced by each person and each community in each era, are the backdrop for this paper. In the final analysis, the only answers in which we are interested are the composite answers which 5.2 billion human beings on this planet are "bringing forth together", as Maturana and Varela would put it, through social interaction and discourse and with their very lives.

A further condensation of these two questions might be the one question of "What is Human Development?" This is the form of the question which we will use in this paper. We will first review the debate which the United Nations Development Program (UNDP) has opened concerning this question. We will then place urbanization, one of the most pervasive phenomena of the past two hundred years of human history, within this context, focusing particularly on the so-called developing world or the South.

The Human Development Debate

Earlier this year, the UNDP published its first annual *Human Development Report*. In this 189-page document, the dialogue about human development is reopened. In the foreword of the report, the Administrator of UNDP, William H. Draper III, states that during the many stirring and surprising events of our moment in history, "we are rediscovering the essential truth that people must be at the center of all development. The purpose of development is to offer people more options. One of their options is access to income – not as an end, but to acquiring human wellbeing. But there are other options as well, including long life, knowledge, political freedom, personal security, community participation, and guaranteed human rights. People cannot be reduced to a single dimension as economic creatures. What makes them and the study of the development process fascinating is the entire spectrum through which human capabilities are expanded and utilized." (page iii)

This statement, coming from the representative of the senior agency of the UN family, is laudable. In Mr. Draper's words, the report "opens the debate." We are now looking at nothing less than the whole human person within the context of the whole planetary society. There is now room for the philosophers and anthropologists to enter the dialogue with the economists and statisticians. And, more importantly, with "people at the center of development", there can be no debate that excludes the village woman, the urban bus driver, the suburban school children, and the elderly. We are acknowledging the "multilogue" which has always been the way society and history are created and recreated. What are the indicators of human development? How can they be identified and measured? How can peoples' voices be heard and considered? These are some of the questions which we will address later.

Mr. Draper goes on to say that "the central message of [this report] is that while growth in national production (GDP) is absolutely necessary to meet all essential human objectives, what is important is to study how this growth translates – or fails to translate – into human development in various societies. Some societies have achieved high levels of human development at modest levels of per capita income. Other societies have failed to translate their comparatively high-income levels and rapid economic growth into commensurate levels of human development."

Economic development is a means to human development. People can no longer be seen as simply a resource and a means for economic development. Societies can be held accountable for their strategies and results of human development. The overview of the report states that "human development is measured . . . not by the yardstick of income alone but by a more comprehensive index – called the human development index – reflecting life expectancy, literacy, and command over the resources to enjoy a decent standard of living." The overview goes on to summarize the central conclusions and policy messages of the report: 1) The developing countries have made significant progress towards human development in the last three decades. 2) North-South gaps in basic human development have narrowed considerably in the last three decades, even while income gaps have widened. 3) Averages of progress in human development conceal large disparities within developing countries – between urban and rural areas, between men and women, and between rich and poor. 4) Fairly respectable levels of human development are possible even at modest levels of income. [Here it is mentioned that Venezuela is one of the top fifteen countries that have achieved relatively high levels of human development within a reasonably democratic political and social framework.] 5) The link between economic growth and human progress is not automatic. 6) Social subsidies are necessary for poorer income groups. 7) Developing countries are not too poor to pay for human development and take care of economic growth. 8) The human costs of adjustment are often a matter of choice, not of compulsion. 9) A favorable external environment is vital to support human development strategies in the 1990s. 10) Some developing countries, especially m Africa, need external assistance a lot more than others. 11) Technical cooperation must be restructured if it is to help build human capabilities and national capacities in the developing countries. [Here it is said that emphasis must be made on improving the availability of relevant social indicators (something which Hazel Henderson and the South

Commission have been working on for years) and on assisting developing countries in formulating their own human development plans.] 12) A participatory approach – including the involvement of NGOs – is crucial to any strategy for successful human development. [The ICA, among others, has been utilizing a participatory methodology for over thirty years.] 13) A significant reduction in population growth rates is essential for visible improvements in human development levels. (Here the point is made that by the year 2025, 84% of the world's human population will be in the developing countries.) 14) The very rapid population growth in the developing world is becoming concentrated in cities. 15) Sustainable development strategies should meet the needs of the present generation without compromising the ability of future generations to meet their needs.

From these fifteen points, we can sense that something unprecedented has happened in the past thirty years and that something even more extraordinary is prefigured and called for over the next thirty years. The invention of societies is as natural to the human being as the creation of ant hills is for ants. However, whereas with the ant the model for the ant hill appears to be encoded in and easily accessed from the nature of the ant as a collective entity, with the human being, the model for a society seems to be the composite emergent form manifested from the individuals that make up that society as conditioned by historical and evolutionary forces. (Maybe this is not so different from the ant phenomenon, after all.) If this is somewhat descriptive of our reality, then we can assume that by changing our conditioning – our beliefs and images – we will alter our perceptions, resulting in new behavior and new societal forms. For example, if poverty has heretofore been an assumed component of any society, by changing this assumption to "poverty is an aberration not an inevitability", we can invent societies that do not manifest this systemic malfunction. Other examples can be made concerning unemployment, crime, wealth, racism, drug abuse, imperialism, environmental degradation, war, etc. The point is that societies can be restructured through a process of re-imaging, re-assuming, and re-conceptualizing by individuals, until a critical mass is reached, resulting in a new common sense, which in turn is manifested in new societal forms and behavior.

What we must face, however, is our residual resistance to these "changes of mind and heart." Our very identities, our very lives, as individuals and communities are tied up with our definitions of humanness and our assumptions about ourselves, our world, and the conscious or unconscious valuation we give to the universe itself. To repeat, our assumptions about concepts such as "urban and rural", "male and female", "rich and poor", and "North and South," govern our behavior and our societal structures. Changing these will not be easy but it is possible and desirable, if not critical, to change them now. In our section on proposals for whole systems transition, we will be exploring various scenarios.

What we need to do at this point is to celebrate the articulation of these fifteen points, as a voice related to the 159 member nation-states of the United Nations. The dialogue is open; trends and options are being clarified; and directions and mandates are coming into focus.

Each of the above fifteen conclusions is elaborated in the Overview, which ends by saying: "Far from answering all questions in this first effort, the findings and conclusions often point to issues requiring deeper analysis and research: What are the essential elements of strategies for planning, managing, and financing human development? What are the requirements of a practical framework for participatory development? What is a conducive external environment for human development?"

We will now summarize and highlight the report itself before we focus on urbanization and proposals for whole systems transition.

The Report has five chapters: Defining and measuring human development; Human development since 1960; Economic growth and human development; Human development strategies for the 1990s; and A Special Focus – Urbanization and human development. Throughout, there are numerous boxes, tables, and figures that give graphic and detailed explanations of major concepts.

The first chapter begins with quotations from Aristotle and Kant in a discussion of "What is human development?" A working definition is suggested, (in summary): Human development is a process of enlarging people's choices and has two sides: the formation of human capabilities and the use people make of their acquired capabilities. In measuring human development, the Report suggests a focus "for the time being" on three essential elements of human life – longevity, knowledge, and decent living standards. The human development index (HDI) is based on a composite of these three indicators. The HDI ranks countries very differently from the way GNP per capita ranks them. For example, to quote: "Sri Lanka, Chile, Costa Rica, Jamaica, Tanzania and Thailand, among others, do far better on their human development ranking than on their income ranking, showing that they have directed their economic resources more towards some aspects of human progress." The two curves of human development and GNP reveal that the disparity among countries is much greater in income than in human development. The chapter ends with a promise that future editions of the Report may consider other choices that people value such as: economic, social, and political freedom, and protection against violence, insecurity, and discrimination.

Chapter 2 gives an overview of the significant progress towards human development in developing countries since 1960. For example, life expectancy at birth increased from 46 years in 1960 to 62 years in 1987. Adult literacy rates rose from 43% in 1970 to 60% in 1985. However, the North-South income gap has continued to widen over this period. The South's average per capita income in 1987 was still only 6% of the North's. The most extreme contrast that we find on our planet today is between the African nation of Guinea Bissau, with a life expectancy of 39 and a GNP per capita of $160 (both the lowest in the world), and the nation of Japan, with a life expectancy of 78 (the highest in the world) and a GNP per capita of $15,760 or Switzerland with a life expectancy of 77 and a GNP per capita of $21,330 (the highest in the world). There is still tremendous human deprivation in the developing world: nearly 900 million adults cannot read or write; 1.5 billion people are without access to primary health care; 1.75 billion people are without safe water; around 100 million are completely homeless; some 800 million people still go hungry every day; and more than a billion survive in absolute poverty. Of these, women and children suffer the most.

The chapter then goes on to illustrate developments in expanding human capabilities in relation to life expectancy, literacy, income, access to basic goods and services (including food, health services, water and sanitation, and education). Significant improvements have been made in all areas. But at the same time, it is mentioned that "poverty is by no means a problem of the developing countries alone. In the United States, after 200 years of economic progress, nearly 32 million people, about 13% of the population, are still below the official poverty line."

The section on "using human capabilities" focuses on employment, migration, popular participation, and the NGO movement. Still, even with the many advances in the developing world, "for more than half a billion poor rural women, there has been little progress over the past 30 years." Next there is a discussion of the "deformation of human development", especially in terms of crime, the drug trade, environmental degradation, refugees, and displaced persons, changing household patterns, and tropical diseases, and the AIDS epidemic.

The third chapter covers economic growth and human development and elaborates on a typology of three types of country experience in development: sustained human development, as in Botswana, Costa Rica, the Republic of Korea, Malaysia, and Sri Lanka; disrupted human development, as in Chile, China, Colombia, Jamaica, Kenya, and Zimbabwe; and missed opportunities for human development, as in Brazil, Nigeria, and Pakistan. The main policy conclusion is that economic growth, if it is to enrich human development, requires effective policy management.

In chapter 4, human development strategies for the 1990s are explored. We read: "The 1990s are shaping up as the decade for human development, for rarely has there been such a consensus on the real objectives of development strategies. The UN Committee for Development Planning summarizes this emerging consensus best: 'In the 1990s people should be placed firmly in the center of development. The most compelling reason for doing so is that the process of economic development is coming increasingly to be understood as a process of expanding the capabilities of people.' Any development strategy for the 1990s will combine several objectives: among them, accelerating economic growth, reducing absolute poverty, and preventing further deterioration in the physical environment."

This chapter deals with the policy measures that could accelerate progress in human development in the 1990s, including: growth with equity; meeting the needs of all; tackling disparities; and promoting private initiative. It also lays out global targets for the year 2000: Complete immunization of all children. Reduction of the under-five child mortality rate by half or to 70 per 1,000 live births. Elimination of severe malnutrition, and a 50% reduction in moderate malnutrition. Universal primary enrolment of all children of primary school age. Reduction of the adult illiteracy rate in 1990 by half, with the female illiteracy rate to be no higher than the male illiteracy rate. And, universal access to safe water.

The operational feasibility and overall credibility of global targets in human development will increase considerably if four criteria are met: 1. The number of global targets should be kept small; 2. The implications for human and financial resources must be worked out in detail; 3. Different targets should be fixed for different groups of countries; and 4. National strategies for human development should bridge national planning and global target-setting. This chapter ends with the words, "If human development is the outer shell, freedom is its priceless pearl."

Urbanization and Urban Development
The fifth and final chapter deals with a special focus on urbanization and human development. We will now not only summarize this chapter but bring in other data and reflections pertaining to urbanization.

In the past seven months, I have become aware of a startling fact and a surprising awareness. The fact is that the human population on our planet is fast becoming an urban phenomenon; and the awareness is that cities are not evil but are a natural, evolutionary form which is filled with possibility, creativity, and challenge.

After millions of years of rural existence with few concentrations of human population, our species is racing toward intensely dense and expansive agglomerations, now known as Mega-Cities. Governments have tried for decades to stem the tide of migration from the countryside to the city with little or no success. People want to improve their lives. The city acts as a great magnet that pulls men, women, and children out of dusty, muddy, dim villages to the concrete streets, and bright lights, of opportunity.

Urbanization is taking place as a subset of the larger phenomenon of the rapidly accelerating increase of the human population. Humans who numbered 1 billion only 170 years ago and 1.8 billion 70 years ago, now number over 5 billion and in 60 years will be at around 10 billion. This skyrocketing growth curve is the result of several factors, all under the heading of development – improved nutrition, improved health care, improved sanitation, an increase of the birth rate, longer life expectancy, and so on. Our race is growing rapidly toward a complexity which Peter Russell calls the "Global Brain" – around the magnitude of 10 billion. We will discuss this hypothesis later.

In chapter 5 in the *Human Development Report 1990* we read: "This is the century of the great urban explosion. In the 35 years after 1950, the number of people living in cities almost tripled, increasing by 1.25 billion. In the developed regions, it nearly doubled, from 450 million to 840 million, and in the developing world, it quadrupled, from 285 million to 1.15 billion." The world population is becoming increasingly urban and is increasingly found in the developing countries. In 1980, 75% of the world population was in the South; and in 2025 it is projected to be 84%. At the same time, the growth of cities is predominately a reality of the South. Continuing from chapter 5: "In 1960 just three of the world's 10 largest [cities] were in the developing world... By 2000 there will be 18 cities with more than 10 million people in the developing world, and eight of them will be among the 10 largest cities in the world. By 1960 there were 19 cities in the world with more than 4 million inhabitants, nine in the developing world. In 1980 there were 22 in developing countries. By 2000 there will be 50 – and by 2025, 114 of a total of 135 in that year."

I suppose that throughout my life, I have assumed that urbanization was a necessary evil and more evil than necessary. My image of the city was that it was dirty, noisy, impersonal, dangerous, filled with evil characters and dark alleys, rather nasty and brutish at best. Of course, there were also a few attractive features about cities. There were more entertainment possibilities, museums, famous institutions, international conferences, and so on. But the bad far outweighed the good in my mind.

How surprised I was when I learned that cities in the developing world, with one third of a nation's population, produce two thirds of the GNP; that cities are the locus of creativity and innovations in all fields of endeavor; that birth rates go down and literacy rates go up in cities; that people's standards of living go up in cities; that cities are more alive, interesting, and fun. Cities are not evil. Cities are good. They are the locus of possibility for millions of people to live a healthier, longer, happier life.

But of course, there are also the problems, the challenges, and the tragedies in the cities. Poverty has also found a home in cities. Urban poverty is growing as fast as cities are growing. There is inadequate revenue to maintain infrastructure; people do not have access to land and housing to purchase; municipal governments are unclear about how to manage this vast sea of humanity; and the urban environment suffers from pollution of every kind. The city is the home of violence, drugs, homelessness, and AIDS.

But still, cities are good. Why? Because cities are the result of the human desire and drive to associate, to interact, to create together, in short, to be social. Cities are sheer potentiality, a challenge to human ingenuity to solve vastly complex, mega-problems, utilizing the human resource of problem-solving and cooperation.

Instead of pitting the urban against the rural in some false dichotomy and antagonism, let us look at a model of a "whole system of human settlement" — the urban-rural spectrum. The urban-rural spectrum is a macro-ecology of density and sparsity, of vegetation and concrete – a natural flow of goods, services, information, and people back and forth over space and through time, each needing the other, each serving the other, each needing to be careful of the special reality of the other. Rather than an either/or or "us and them" modelling of reality, we see a natural, sea and shore, rock and sand imaging of the city-countryside.

Of course, this macro-ecology faces many challenges: how does the countryside feed the city; how does the city provide seasonal jobs for the countryside; how does the rural area provide recreation and natural beauty for the city dwellers; and how does the city offer opportunities for cultural activities, international interchange, excellent medical and educational facilities to the country folk?

What we see in many instances is in fact a blending and overlapping of who is who. In Venezuela, some villagers in Barlovento also have a small home in Caracas in the barrio. In the city they find work when there is no cacao to tend; they earn additional income which they take back to their village. They love their villages because of the slow, quiet, natural way of life. They also like the city for its opportunities of income genera-tion and self improvement. Likewise, the city dweller is also a naturalist at heart – leaving the city on week ends and holidays to hike, fish, farm, and so forth. The relationship between the urban and rural can be seen to be mutual, symbiotic, dialogic, a reciprocity – a dance back and forth, to and fro, a yin and yang, night and day, male and female.

How can this view change the way we live? How can it change the way we manage our cities and our rural areas? Two of our presuppositions are: that the people with the problem can solve the problem better than outside experts; and that the solution already exists in someone's mind or in some groups ability to act. What is an example of this?

Take the problem of air pollution. People invented the automobile to save time and effort in getting about. People also decided to create cars that burn fossil fuels that emit noxious gases into the atmosphere endangering animal and human life and damaging the ozone layer of the atmosphere. We invented something to save time and effort and inadvertently placed ourselves in danger. What to do? Invent something else! Either use a fuel in your car that does not have toxic byproducts or use a different means of transportation which does not use such a fuel. Of course, the issue then becomes one of invention, regu-lation, and management of the new system. With the political will we can solve our problems.

Chapter 5 mentions four issues for managing cities in the developing countries for the 1990s: decentralization – from national to local management; generating municipal revenues; enabling strategies for shelter and infrastructure; and improv-ing the urban environment. The chapter ends with these words:

"Rapid urbanization is transforming the developing countries, creating ever new problems but also offering ever new opportunities. To solve the growing problems of cities – and to unleash the many possibilities for human development – is going to depend heavily on better urban management, considerably better."

Proposals for Whole Systems Transition within Cities

What if in addition to this sociological analysis we take a more holistic view of human development and urbanization? What if we utilize the multiple perspectives of anthropology, cosmology, philosophy, theology, physics, biology, history, and psychology? What do we then see?

In other words, what if we perceive human development and urbanization at different levels of reality: the Sensory/Physical; the Psychological/Historic; the Mythic/Symbolic; and the Unitive/Integral, a typology developed by Dr. Jean Houston? What do we see, and what would we do?

SENSORY/PHYSICAL: At the sensory level, the city is concrete, glass and steel. It is cars, and buses, and subways; apartment buildings, shops, skyscrapers, houses; air pollution, garbage disposal, water, electricity, gas, telephones; TVs, radios, computers; schools, museums, streets, lamp posts, children playing, rats, taxis, helicopters, and so on. It is also our sensing of and our feelings about all of this – our seeing, our tasting, our hearing, our touching, and our smelling of the city: beautiful art and squalid slums, bland and spicy foods, baroque music at a concert and people cursing each other in an argument, the soft skin of a baby, and being pushed and shoved on a bus, the smell of perfume and car exhaust.

PSYCHOLOGICAL/HISTORICAL: Michael Ventura writes about the City as Psyche – the externalization or projection of our unconscious realm. The city is also the new forest, the new jungle, the new swamp – a place where we must confront the challenge of survival against the wild forces of nature. We fear the city. We dread what lurks in its shadows. We hurry from place to place hoping to escape being hurt. We become callous. We stop looking. We assume the worst of people. We also find companionship, our very own sub-group, and even love. In the city, the planetary ecology of cultures is bubbling in a pressure cooker. We turn a corner, and we are in China; we turn another comer, and we are in Italy, another and we are in Puerto Rico, another and we are in Kenya. The swirl of races, languages, foods, values, and lifestyles is awesome, intoxicating, enlivening.

MYTHIC/SYMBOLIC: Augustine writes about the City of God. Urbanization may be the trend toward that ideal. Peter Russell sees the emergence of the Global Brain. Cities may be the nodal concentrations of that nervous system and intelligence. Pierre Teilhard de Chardin has written about the noosphere. Urbanization seems to be accelerating that phenomenon. Maturana and Varela have outlined a cognitive biology of "bringing forth a world together". The city may be the most intense locus of that process of knowing what we know. From an evolutionary perspective, we see urbanization as the natural agglomeration of human cells into community into mega-communities and networks of mega-communities. The New Story is emerging within cities – how do we Earthlings live together? We work for each other; we serve each other; we eat each other's food; we dance to each other's music; we honor each other as the Other and yet as neighbor. The global village has become a global city.

UNITIVE/INTEGRAL: The Gaia Hypothesis presents the view that the Earth is a living organism. Cities may be Earth's mechanism for regulating human activity to care for the whole organism. The Form of Centeredness expresses itself in galaxies, solar systems, planets, cells, atoms, and human settlements, with the City as Center. The city is at-homeness, at oneness with our being, with our essence, which is radical sociality and radical individuation. In the city, unity consciousness is promoted by proximity and pathos. You are me, and I am you. We are one. I am the homeless man sleeping on the street. I am the lady bus driver who is yelling at her passengers "move it on back". I am the mayor delivering a difficult speech about the lack of municipal funds and necessary city employee cutbacks. I am the Korean grocery store owner proud of the beautiful rows of fresh vegetables and fruit. We are One – the one without a second – the unity that is Self, that is Being, that is Spirit.

From this perspective of perspectives, what if the solutions to urban problems and challenges were found in the new relationship we take to those problems as the very source of the solutions? What if the "solutions" to crime, drugs, AIDS, violence, environmental degradation, and poverty, were found within each of these realities and within the whole system itself? What is the common source of all these realities? Is it not human beings – human consciousness, human perception, human behavior? The "problem" is not that human beings are evil or that the city is evil. The possibility is to realize the true essence of humanness – to allow it to develop – to evolve – to transform. And what is this essence, which if realized will result in the solution to our problems? Is it not a fundamental goodness, universality, and oneness, that is each human being? How can we nurture the development of each human person within each community within each city within each nation within each continent within the planet as a whole? Must it not start with me, here, and now? Must it not start with us and our relationship? Does it not entail a change of heart and mind, that results in a change of behavior, that results in new social structures, new nations, and new planetary society? Is it not possible even at this moment?

In closing, I will make a proposal like one which I first heard made by van Arendonk three years ago in Bilbao, Spain: We must allow everyone to participate in the great dialogue concerning human development. Let us hold symposia at every

level – local, city, state, national, continental, regional, global –
at which two questions are posed for brainstorming and discussion: What is humanness – for us here and now? and What
is development – for us, now and here? We must combine philosophy and engineering, the spiritual and the material, to
transform our ever so human structures. And everyone must
participate, for everyone has an answer, and because no one has
the answer, and because "together we bring forth the world".
Together we can bring forth a world of human development.

Planetary sociality and planetary spirituality are two aspects
of one reality. In the 1960s and 70s, Joseph W. Mathews, the
dean of the Institute of Cultural Affairs, spoke about these two
aspects as the New Social Vehicle and the New Religious Mode –
"two sides of the same coin". Throughout history, human
beings have spoken about This World and The Other World.
We now speak of the outer and the inner. All these point to the
dual nature of our human condition – of being in but not of.
We are here and now and yet we participate in all space and all
time. Our condition is radically existential, and yet at the same
instance we participate in true essence. We must concern ourselves with food and clothing, with air and water, with money
and work. And yet, amid this world is another – there is a Land
of Mystery, a River of Consciousness, a Mountain of Care, and
a Sea of Tranquility. Human development has to do with learning to live in both worlds and to move back and forth with
facility. We are at home in both worlds as children of Earth and
children of Eternity. We live in the City of Men and Women
and in the City of God and Goddess.

Values and Principles

(1994, New York)

In this brief note, I clarify core values of human development. In 2013, I added justice, tolerance, and nonviolence, and changed equity to equality. Today, some would say that regenerative is more appropriate than sustainability.

What are the values and principles that should guide and motivate UNDP's actions to realize its corporate goals and strategies of poverty eradication and human development? These values and principles have emerged from the UN charter itself, the series of global conferences held in the 1990s and UNDP's own work in human development. The most fundamental values are *equity, sustainability,* and *participation.*

Equity is concerned with providing opportunities for all people regardless of their station in life. Equity assumes that every person is of infinite worth and potential, and it is concerned with the full realization of each person. All men and women should have opportunities to improve or maintain their well-being; and the vulnerable and excluded are targeted to provide security of well-being to all. Equity does not ignore the weak but gives special consideration to the poor, women, youth, the elderly, the disabled, minorities and any people who are marginalized. Without equity a society suffers the loss of the full energy and creativity of many of its members.

Sustainability is concerned with the wellbeing of future generations. Development must not only be concerned with improving conditions in the present but with the long-term viability of humans on this planet. Resources are protected and used with a view to optimize the well-being of people over several generations, ideally in perpetuity, without mortgaging the future. Therefore, sustainability has many dimensions – environmental, social, cultural, political, and economic. Without sustainability, the resources of nature and society would be lost for our children's children.

Participation is concerned with honoring the need that people must help determine their own future. It is based on the dignity of the human person and the creativity of people in shaping their own lives. All men and women should have a voice in decision-making, either directly or through legitimate intermediate institutions that represent their interests. Such broad participation is built on freedom of association and speech, as well as capacities to participate constructively. Participation has to do with governance systems that allow for a variety of approaches to self-organization. Without participation, societies would not benefit fully from the intelligence and care of all their members.

In addition to equity, sustainability and participation, several other values and principles are emerging as universal and should guide UNDP in its policy advice and program support. These include *transparency, accountability, responsiveness, empowerment, the rule of law, consensus-building, pluralism, subsidiarity, effectiveness, partnership, and strategic vision.*

Governance, Urbanization, and HIV/AIDS

(1994, New York)

This is another note that was written for the Inter-Country Consultation of the African Network on Ethics, Law and HIV, held in Dakar, Senegal, 27 June - 1 July 1994. The purpose of this essay is to reflect on the relationship between governance and HIV – both the impact of governance on the HIV/AIDS epidemic and the impact of the epidemic on governance. It also provides a brief reflection on the importance of both urban and rural strategies to deal with the epidemic. It is especially relevant in our time of the global COVID-19 pandemic in 2021.

Governance and HIV

The purpose of governance is to facilitate sustainable human development (SHD) including both social equity in the economic, political, and cultural spheres and environmental protection and regeneration. SHD is people-centered development which is pro-nature, pro-poor, pro-women, and pro-jobs.

The key to governance is social integration. This integration involves the healthy interaction of the public sector, the institutions of the civil society and the productive sector. The optimal functioning of governance systems includes a great variety of partnerships of the relevant actors concerned with any given issue. These partnerships provide a modality for the continuous increase of social capital – human relationships – of a society, alongside the formation of productive capital, human capital, and ecological capital. Partnerships include activities of problem identification, strategy building, implementation, evaluation, and feedback. Facilitation, not control, is needed in partnership modes.

The HIV/AIDS epidemic provides a serious challenge to and a critical opportunity for the further evolution of governance systems around the world. This is true especially for the African continent where the epidemic is growing at an alarming rate. Governance systems must undertake rapid changes to respond to the threat of the epidemic. Governance systems – legal frameworks, health services, insurance, social security – must be able to provide protection for those already infected with HIV, care for those ill with AIDS, protection of the families involved, prevention of the further spread of HIV, and care for the results of the epidemic, e.g., swelling numbers of orphans and elderly without adequate care, and reductions in the labor force and in public and private sectors. Through partnerships of organizations of the civil society, government, and business, new structures must be created to provide this protection, prevention, and care. For these new structures to come into being, new attitudes and behaviors of understanding, tolerance, compassion, and cooperation will be required.

These are not ordinary times. Our species is imperiled. Our response must be bold, rapid, and dramatic to meet this awesome challenge. Everyone will be affected if we are to turn back this devastating epidemic. Individuals and families, as well as new institutions, will be called to care for orphaned children and the isolated elderly. Legal authorities will need to exercise mature judgement in protecting both individual rights and community wellbeing. New forms of health care will need to be put into place to deal with the scope of the epidemic. New forms of insurance and social security will need to be invented. Mechanisms to ensure that the voices of those most affected by the epidemic are heard in the halls of power and deliberation will need to be created.

New NGOs are springing up and need to be supported to deal with the crisis. The private sector will need to do its part in the effort. Religious leaders will need to preach tolerance and compassion. Government leaders will need to maintain a climate of social integration and challenge the voices of intolerance, hostility, and panic. The media will need to provide objective information and avoid sensationalism. Government bureaucracies will need to become more efficient and effective in their service delivery. And most importantly, everyone will need to become more responsible – both for his/her actions and for other people.

Urbanization and HIV
It is well known that Africa is composed primarily of rural communities. What is not so well known is that Africa has the highest rates of urbanization in the world. Cities and towns are growing at an accelerating rate. This urbanization is being driven by several factors. These include "push" factors which drive people away from the villages such as famine, desertification, poor services, unproductive agriculture, and limited employment opportunities. In addition, there are the "pull" factors which attract the rural populations to the urban areas, e.g., greater opportunities for employment and the hope of improved basic services of health, education, water, and sanitation. For the above reasons, efforts to stem rural-urban migration have, by and large, been unsuccessful everywhere. We must now turn some of our attention to the swelling urban areas and respond to the challenges which face us.

Cities and towns have two faces. On the one hand they are places of wealth and opportunity and on the other hand they are the locus of growing poverty and environmental degradation. In Dar es Salaam, as only one example, 70 per cent of the population lives in informal, squatter settlements without adequate water and sanitation, and 75% of the residents work in the informal sector. These conditions are the breeding ground for disease and drug addiction. For these reasons, efforts to respond to the HIV/AIDS epidemic must include urban as well as rural strategies. Because the transmission of HIV/AIDS involves human contact and social relations and the consequences of the epidemic result in social disintegration, our current social systems including both prevailing attitudes and structures are being called into question. Governance, as the process of facilitating social integration towards sustainable human development, must be transformed to meet the challenges of this epidemic.

In addition, due to the rapid growth in Africa of cities and towns and the increasing numbers of urban poor, our strategies must deal with both the rural majority and the growing urban masses.

The clearer we become concerning the intricate, systemic ways in which HIV/AIDS interacts with every other part of our social systems and with processes of governance, both rural and urban, the more rapidly we can get about the business of transforming our individual attitudes and our community structures.

Achieving Sustainable Human Development (SHD) Through Urban Development Cooperation

(18 July 1994, New York)

When I was UNDP's urban development policy adviser, I wrote the following piece to highlight aspects of our urban development programs around the world.

SHD is a holistic vision. Urban development cooperation is one way in which this vision can be achieved. The success of UNDP's efforts to promote SHD in the urban setting depends upon team-oriented, multidisciplinary initiatives such as the Local Initiatives Facility for Urban Environment (LIFE) and the Urban Management Program and partnerships with other agencies in the UN system and institutions of civil society.

SHD in an Urbanizing World

Sustainable human development (SHD) is concerned both with social equity and ecological harmony. Social equity is people-centered development which ensures that the "universalism of life claims" (*Human Development Report* 1994) is

135

honored throughout the economic, political, and cultural structures of a society. Ecological harmony is planet-centered development which ensures that the eco-systems of land, water, air, and other species are maintained through a healthy relationship with the human species.

Our species lives in human settlements on a continuum of size and density from mega cities to tiny rural villages. Virtually all human settlements suffer from social inequity, manifest in poverty, unemployment and discrimination, and ecological dis-harmony, found in environmental degradation and natural resource depletion. SHD is needed in human settlements, both rural and urban.

Within this century an unprecedented shift in human settlements has taken place. After millennia of living predominately in rural settlements, our species is racing rapidly toward an urban destiny. By 2000, for the first time in history, over half of the human population will live in cities and towns. This shift is taking place with the greatest speed in developing countries. By the year 2025, eight of the ten largest cities in the world will be in developing countries.

The shift to the urban poses both positive and negative challenges to human ingenuity. On the one hand cities are the locus of increasing poverty and environmental degradation. For example, ninety percent of the poor in Latin America live in cities and towns. On the other hand, urban areas are the engines of social and economic growth and productivity, with sixty percent of the GDP of developing countries being generated in cities and towns. Because the world is rapidly becoming urban, it is necessary to promote an SHD strategy focused on urban settlements. As the Secretary-General, in his address to the Preparatory Committee of HABITAT II, pointed out: "The world's cities must become sustainable, safe, healthy, humane, and affordable."

Urban settlements provide an ideal laboratory for systemic, multi-sectoral strategies of SHD. Urban development includes the four program focus areas of SHD, e.g., poverty alleviation, productive employment, women in development, and environmental improvement. Furthermore, it provides an opportunity for integration of these focus areas within urban policies and programs. Cities serve as centers of employment, growth, and innovation. The urban informal sector provides an illustration of how a conducive policy environment could contribute to the promotion of employment opportunities, especially for the poor. In Mexico City, for example, a survey showed that over thirty-six percent of the city's population was employed in the informal sector. In Dar es Salaam, it is estimated that eighty percent of the residents work in the informal sector.

The urban environmental issues – waste management, environmental education, water supply and sanitation – affect the urban residents directly. Many of the problems and potential solutions affecting the global environment have their source in the urban areas, e.g., natural resource depletion and environmental pollution and damage.

Urban poverty is being recognized as one of critical issues in SHD. The estimates of the poor living in slums and squatter settlements in developing countries range from fifteen to seventy-five percent of the urban population. Residents in the low-income settlements lack access to basic services and means of livelihood.

Cities, with lower birth rates, provide greater opportunities for women's advancement through education, health services, and employment. The empowerment of women should increasingly be included in such urban policies and programs as shelter finance, access to land, and means of livelihood.

Criteria for Achieving SHD through Urban Development
The criteria for achieving SHD in urban settlements can be arranged in five components – alleviating poverty, promoting productive employment, improving the urban environment, advancing the participation of women, and building capacity for urban governance and management for SHD. The

program focus areas of SHD are causally related to these criteria as follows:

Alleviating Poverty
Providing and maintaining urban infrastructure in the low-income settlements; increasing shelter for the urban poor by improving their access to land, housing finance and construction materials; and providing basic urban services in squatter settlements such as education, primary health care and water supply and sanitation.

Promoting Productive Employment
Promoting income-generating activities for disadvantaged groups; improving the productivity and income of the urban poor by supporting informal enterprises and investing in human resource development; enacting appropriate economic policies to promote the role of the urban informal sector; and expanding job opportunities through economic growth of small and medium-sized cities.

Improving the Urban Environment
Upgrading waste management, energy use, and alternative transport systems; reducing air pollution; improving the living environment of disadvantaged groups, including women, squatters, and slum dwellers; enacting legislation for urban environmental management; and incorporating environmental considerations in urban planning.

Advancing the Participation of Women
Promoting the participation of women in shelter finance, vocational training, income-generating activities, and urban management; improving women's access to shelter, basic urban services, and government facilities; undertaking gender analysis of urban policies and programs; and promoting the organization of women.

Building Capacity of Urban Governance and Management
Decentralizing power and resources from the central government to municipalities, regional cities, and market towns, as well as strengthening the capacity of local authorities to plan and manage urban development programs; improving municipal finance, revenue generation, land management, and information systems; promoting participatory urban management through increased involvement of community organizations; encouraging private initiatives in the provision of urban housing and in the maintenance of urban infrastructure and services; and helping to involve NGOs and CBOs in the identification and implementation of local projects to alleviate poverty and improve the environment.

UNDP Strategy for Urban Development within an SHD Framework
UNDP's urban development cooperation is described in the book *Cities, People and Poverty*. UNDP is currently promoting SHD in urban development programs at the country, regional, and interregional levels. At the national level, UNDP helps with country-specific, directly targeted urban projects. As urban development involves multi-sectoral activities, assistance to a government is comprehensive and is coordinated with NGOs and agencies of the UN system to achieve a lasting impact. At the regional and global levels, urban development cooperation projects include creating forums for examining innovative policies and tools for urban development; strengthening regional institutions for operational research and technical cooperation; and contributing to the building of regional, national, and municipal capacity through exchange of innovative policies and practices for urban management and human settlements.

UNDP-assisted programs are executed by specialized agencies of the UN system and increasingly by developing country governments and NGOs. UNDP's main partner agency in urban development is UNCHS (Habitat). UNDP also works in close collaboration with UNICEF, ILO, WHO, UNFPA, DDSMS, the Regional Commissions, and the World Bank.

UNDP, including UNCDF, is assisting around 280 ongoing urban development and human settlements programs at a total cost of over $470 million. Urban programs and projects by category include poverty alleviation - 14%; environmental improvement - 17%; strengthening local government, planning and administration - 32%; and provision of infrastructure, shelter, and services - 37%. Two of the major, inter-regional programs promoting SHD are the ten-year Urban Management Program (UMP) and the innovative Local Initiative Facility for Urban Environment (LIFE).

The UMP strengthens capacities of urban management in five components – poverty alleviation, environment, land management, infrastructure and local administration and finances. Through country consultations the UMP brings the relevant actors together to formulate improved policies in the five program areas. The UMP is executed by UNCHS, in association with the World Bank, WHO and several bilateral agencies and with core funding and overall monitoring by UNDP. Regional offices in Kuala Lumpur, Accra, Cairo, and Quito provide panels of experts and responsiveness to country-driven requests.

LIFE, launched at the Earth Summit in Rio, promotes "local-local" dialogue and collaboration among NGOs, CBOs, and local authorities to improve the urban environment and alleviate urban poverty. LIFE conducts activities at the country, regional, and interregional levels. At the country level, LIFE supports small-scale projects in eight pilot countries, two per region: Pakistan, Thailand, Tanzania, Senegal, Jamaica, Brazil, Egypt, and Morocco. At the regional and interregional levels, LIFE supports documentation and interchange of successful initiatives by NGO networks and cities' associations including ICLEI, HIC, Mega Cities, ENDA and IULA.

In addition, the UNDP/ILO program entitled "Employment Promotion in Urban Works Program Through the Efficient Use of Local Resources" has examined the relevance of labor-intensive participatory methods in the construction industry, especially for various public works projects. It led to the preparation of guidelines, "From Want to Work: Job Creation for the Urban Poor."

UNDP is mainstreaming SHD with our UN partners, especially UNCHS (Habitat) and bilateral donors. This is being done in several ways: the use of special funds to promote multi-sectoral urban programs at the country level; providing the SHD methodology for UNCHS programs including Human Settlements Sector reviews; supporting HABITAT II through substantive inputs and holding the International Colloquium of Mayors on Social Development; and presentation of UNDP strategy to bilateral donors and other stakeholders to improve the visibility of UNDP as a substantive organization.

UNDP-assisted urban development programs are designed and implemented by governments and NGOs in developing countries. Assistance is channeled through our network of Country Offices with the support of the Regional Bureaus. To aid the Country Offices and the Regional bureaus, there is an Urban Development Unit (UDU) within the Management Development and Governance Division of BPPS. The Unit works in close cooperation with the urban development focal points in the Regional Bureaus and other operational units. This Unit is responsible for maintaining technical, advisory support to the Country Offices and operational units, providing technical coordination of innovative, interregional urban programs, such as LIFE, and monitoring UNDP-funded and agency executed programs, including the UMP. The Unit works in close collaboration with UNCHS (Habitat) and other specialized agencies of the UN system.

SHD Script

(12 December 1994, New York)

I wrote this script accompanied by a set of transparencies to introduce sustainable human development to people not familiar with it. It was very well received.

Introduction

Let us think together about an emerging paradigm of international development cooperation which we call sustainable human development **(SHD).** We will use a model for our discussion. As we know, no model perfectly reflects all dimensions of reality but gives us an approximate sense of a limited number of relationships.

People-Centered Development

Sustainable human development (SHD) is people-centered development. This is development that focuses on the actual wellbeing of people not simply on macro economic indicators. This concern is for all the people of a society including those most often forgotten – women, children, the poor, minorities, and the disabled. This is development by, of, and for the people.

Planet-Centered Development

Sustainable human development (SHD) is planet-centered development. In the Earth Summit, we woke up to the fact that if we do not care for the air, the water, the soil, and our fellow species of animals and plants, then the existence of our own species cannot be sustained. This fact compels us to employ a mode of development that is in harmony with the ecological systems of which we are part.

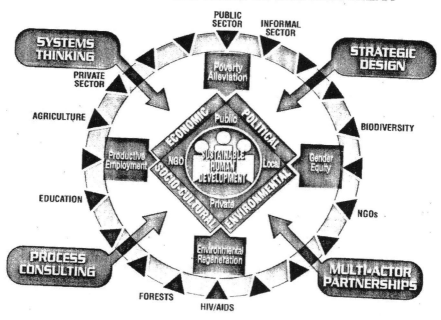

Multi-Actor Governance

Sustainable human development (SHD) involves governance by, of, and for all the social actors – in the public sector, the private sector, non-governmental sector, and the local/community-based sector. Governance is the facilitation of the healthy interaction of all the social actors moving the society towards sustainable human development

(SHD). Capacity building is needed to equip each of the social actors to play its role in this complex and complementary interaction.

Comprehensive Societal Dynamics
Sustainable human development (SHD) is development which is sustainable economically, politically, socio-culturally, and environmentally. SHD is economically viable, politically participatory, socio-culturally vibrant, and environmentally balanced.

Four Focus Areas
Because UNDP is a multi-sectoral organization, it has identified four focus areas of sustainable human development **(SHD),** in addition to governance which undergirds these four, for its program and policy work in 174 developing countries. These are poverty eradication and prevention, gender equity, productive employment and livelihood, and environmental regeneration. Poverty eradication and prevention is based in the assumption of social equity of opportunity. Gender equity is concerned with the full participation of half of the human population. Productive employment and livelihood are necessary for the self-sustenance of individuals and families. Environmental regeneration is the concern for the renewable use of natural resources and energy and the proper management of human waste.

   As UNDP's Administrator has said: "Sustainable human development is development that doesn't merely generate growth but distributes its benefits equitably; it regenerates the environment rather than destroying it; it empowers people rather than marginalizing them; it enlarges their choices and opportunities and provides for people's participation in decisions affecting their lives. Sustainable human development is development that is pro-poor, pro-nature, pro-jobs, and pro-women. It stresses growth, but growth with employment, growth with environment, growth with empowerment, growth with equity. Sustainable human development is not just a UNDP slogan, it is a unifying concept for all of us engaged in the business of development cooperation." This is a global task to ensure "our common future". Poverty, disease, violence, and pollution carry no passports. Every country and institution must play its role in this great venture.

Multiple Entry Points
Development organizations – UN specialized agencies, the Bretton Woods institutions, and NGOs – enter this comprehensive, holistic framework of SHD through a variety of entry points based on their mandates. For example, FAO enters through the entry point of agriculture. ILO enters through labor, WHO through health, UNICEF through children, and the World Bank through macro economic indicators. It is critical that conceptual and operational linkages are made between any given entry point and the other dynamics within the framework of **SHD.** For example, if one enters through the entry point of agriculture, the linkages between agriculture and poverty alleviation, agriculture and gender equity, agriculture and livelihoods, agriculture and environmental regeneration, and agriculture and good governance should be acknowledged. Agricultural development must be carried out in such a way as to be economically viable, politically participatory, socio-culturally vibrant, and environmentally balanced. In fact, agricultural development can be linked to virtually every other entry point as well. Agricultural development must be both people-centered and planet-centered. In this way, development can be both sectoral and holistic.

Within each country, strategic entry points need to be identified by the government and civil society. These can be, for example, HIV/AIDS, basic education, the urban environment, the role of the private sector, gender, public sector management, and so forth. From a given entry point, dialogue is stimulated among the relevant social actors concerning new policies, programs, and projects that link the five focus areas and move the society towards social equity and ecological balance. Harmonization of the social system and the natural system is what is needed.

Development Modalities
To catalyze sustainable human development (SHD), several effective modalities of technical cooperation have been identified. Among these are the formation of multi-actor partnerships, the use of systems thinking, the utilization of methods of strategic design, and the use of a process consulting approach to development. Multiactor partnerships of central government, local government, the private sector, NGOs, academic institutions, the media, and community-based organizations are necessary for dialogue and collaboration to move a society toward **SHD.** Systems thinking allows people and organizations to see beyond their narrow perspectives to a view of the whole system of a society and the inter-relations and multiple perspectives within the system.

Strategic design allows groups to move beyond reactive, problem-solving modes to proactive, future design modes. Process consulting moves beyond the expert-recipient mode to creating partnerships among the local/national actors and the external development agents so that situation analysis and program and policy planning, implementation, and evaluation are carried out by the relevant social actors.

Summary
In summary, SHD is not a fixed program but an ever-changing challenge. It is not one path but many. SHD is not a single formula for development but is the unique search of each country and community toward its own vision of people-centered, planet-centered development.

But this vision is not just a UNDP vision. Because of the positive response of the other agencies of the UN system to this vision, the Secretary-General has asked the Administrator of UNDP to coordinate all UN development activities within an SHD framework.

Once the concept of SHD is somewhat clear, the question becomes, how can it be operationalized? SHD is a holistic vision, but a nation cannot simply operationalize a vision. Each country and community must first analyze its enhancing and inhibiting factors and create strategies and action plans for implementation in policies, programs, and projects. This process requires activities both upstream at the level of policy and systems' design as well as downstream at the project, problem-solving end. The role of international development cooperation is to "facilitate a process of participation and partnership for sustainable human development (SHD)".

Discussion
Note: Following the presentation, another person should engage the participants in an interactive conversation. The following questions can be used to provoke and guide the discussion. The questions are divided into four types using the Institute of Cultural Affairs' ORID method.

Objective:
1. What do you remember from the presentation? What words? Images? What were the stages of the presentation?

Reflective:
2. What feelings did you have during the presentation? Where did your mind wander? What other images, words, stories, experiences did you think of during the presentation?

Interpretive:
3. What is the significance of this paradigm of development? At this moment in history? How does it make sense considering the past five centuries of development and the next five?

Decisional:

4. What are the implications of this paradigm for **UNDP?**
    For international development cooperation? What
    needs to be done to operationalize **SHD?** What are
    your personal resolves vis-a-vis operationalizing **SHD?**
    What further work needs to be done on the paradigm of
    SHD? How can this presentation be improved?

THEME

Visionary Social Activism

The essays in this theme are reflections on some of the major social and environmental challenges faced in 2017 – 2020 in the US and around the world, and on some of the actions that citizens can take to make a difference. Because my career was in international development, it was not until around 2013 that I became an activist in my own country, the USA. These essays are full of passion and resolve concerning what is needed to be done in our time. Because the essays are brief and direct, they have no introductions.

Is It Not Now or Never?

(26 October 2017, Swannanoa, North Carolina)

I am so sad. It appears that the other major political party is driving through their bill to cut taxes on the rich and harm the middle class and the poor. Perhaps it can still be stopped or made less toxic, but it does not look good at this point.

Why are many rich people so greedy? It is immoral and should be illegal. There should be a maximum allowed on income and assets. What about $1,000,000 a year in income and $50,000,000 in assets? Anything over those figures belongs to the whole society. That still allows some people to be rich but also ensures that the entire society functions well.

The problem with allowing a few people to amass astronomical wealth is that they can then buy political power thereby continually increasing their wealth by setting the rules of the game, the regulations or nonregulations on the economy. This ensures that the rich get richer, and the poor get poorer. This creates a true plutocracy, the rule by the rich.

Our country and the whole world are at a moment of crisis. The most fundamental questions are being laid bare. What is a human being? What is human society? What is our purpose on this planet and in the universe?

We are currently damaging and destroying the ecosystems of Earth – air, water, soil, plants, and animals. We are causing global warming with its mega storms, droughts, fires, flooding, food collapse, water shortages, migrations, blazing temperatures. Today in late October, it was 107 degrees Fahrenheit in parts of California. And this will only increase.

And as if this disaster is not enough, we have another mega-madness – the potential for nuclear holocaust. We could deal with both crises if we so choose. We could stop pumping carbon dioxide and other greenhouse gases into the atmosphere. And we could destroy all nuclear weapons. But will we? We currently do not agree on doing either of these to ensure the future of life on Earth. Such madness.

Are we an insane species? Are we suicidal? Are we a race of sociopaths and psychopaths? Are we so trapped in self deception that we cannot do what would protect and extend life on this planet?

Or can we wake up in time? Can we not see that protecting life on Earth and allowing it to flourish is in our own self interest and our collective interest? The over 7 billion of us must wrest control from the deranged few who would rather destroy everything than lose their fossil fuel assets or their nationalistic bravado and desire for world domination.

Yes, let us arise and with clarity of intention move life on Earth toward a compassionate civilization of sustainable development. It is now or never.

The Four Faces of MOM

(10 November 2017, Swannanoa, North Carolina)

What are MOM's four faces? The movement of movement (MOM) embodies and promotes 1) new mindsets and values, 2) new skills and behaviors, 3) new cultural norms and stories, and 4) new policies and institutions.

New Mindsets and Values
The individuals who comprise MOM have new mindsets and values. They think in whole systems. They know they are Earthlings. They understand that every living being is precious. And they exhibit compassion and kindness toward everyone.

New Skills and Behaviors
The persons who make up MOM manifest new skills and behaviors. They are group facilitators. They are social artists. They are servant leaders. And they are mindful activists.

New Cultural Norms and Stories
The organizations and networks that comprise MOM exhibit new cultural norms and stories. They promote norms of universal care for all beings. They tell stories of heroines and heroes who are building a world that works for all. They make

use of symbols of peace and cooperation. And they create rites of transformation and the "lure of becoming."

New Policies and Institutions
The movements that make up MOM generate new policies and institutions. They promote environmental sustainability and gender equality. They create socioeconomic justice and participatory governance. They manifest cultural tolerance and non-violence. And they catalyze a compassionate civilization.

Let us hear it for MOM!

Saving Life on Earth

(11 November 2017, Swannanoa, North Carolina)

The 200,000 richest people in the world do not need the rest of us 7.3 billion. They do not want viable democracies. They do not need too many educated, healthy, empowered people. They already control the money supply, corporations, the economy, the military, and the media. They can manage global society through autocratic rule of nation states and their masters, global corporations. And for political allies they are emboldening fascists, racists, and fundamentalists.

With climate chaos exploding around the planet, the super-rich will increasingly need to control the masses who will be fleeing rising waters and mega storms and railing against collapsed economies and unresponsive governments.

How do we the people right the ship of life? How do we hold the superrich accountable? How do we create caring communities at the local level? How do we forge a new common sense and new legal requirements? And how do we take care of ourselves in this moment of chaos?

Can we the people wake up the superrich to their own humanity, empathy, and compassion? Or is it not possible? Or is there enough time?

In any case, we must use the transformative tools of searing truth, mighty justice, and fierce love, as we empower the movement of movements to save nothing short of life on Earth by creating an ecological, compassionate civilization.

The Year to Defend Our Democracy: 2018

(26 December 2017, Swannanoa, North Carolina)

Remember, capital is global. The superrich and their corporations are preparing for a world of climate chaos. They are weakening democracies to control populations through propaganda and force. They are denying climate change so that they and their corporations will not be liable for damages and will not be called on to fund climate mitigation and adaptation strategies. They are forming alliances with neo-Nazis and religious fundamentalists, engaging in extreme gerrymandering, and suppressing the vote so that they can win elections and keep up a façade of democracy.

They are weakening multilateral institutions such as the UN and the EU so that they alone will be in charge. They are deregulating the economy so that they can continue increasing their fortunes through toxic investments, corrupt fiscal policies, and removal of liabilities against their corporations. They are withdrawing their tax support for public education and health. They are intending to weaken the safety nets of Social Security, Medicare, and Medicaid. They are governing through lies, fake news, and continuous propaganda. They are accelerating fossil fuel extraction to increase their wealth. They are building their luxury bunkers as places of refuge when climate and social chaos are in full force. They are creating massive armies, armaments, police forces, and prison systems to control populations.

I wish the above were paranoia, but this is what I discern. We the People outnumber the superrich, and they rely on us in so many ways. We the People must stand together in solidarity against the dangerous actions of the superrich and their allies. We must care for those in danger. We must remain calm, hopeful, grateful, and nonviolent. We must rehearse our vision of a hoped-for future for life on Earth. We must collaborate as a movement of movements using participatory leadership methods. We must care for ourselves and our colleagues. We must be ready for shocks and surprises. We must be flexible as we move forward. We must continue to move our democracies, economies, and cultures toward a compassionate civilization.

The next ten months leading up to November 6th, 2018, are utterly critical in defending and advancing a viable democracy, a just economy, and a sustainable environment. We must protect voting rights, register people to vote, support progressive candidates, and get out the vote in massive numbers. I am working with my local precinct to do that. I encourage everyone to do everything they can to help flip the House and Senate on November 6th and support progressive candidates in state and local elections. We must also speak out against propaganda, corruption, and bullying. We must support independent media and courts. And in our local communities we must care for the least, the last, and the lost. Onward!

Authoritarianism, Alliance,

Resistance, and Turning the Tide

(3 March 2018, Swannanoa, North Carolina)

M any of us are aware of powerful forces at work moving us toward authoritarianism. When I look for the patterns, I see the prime mover is big money – a few billionaires, especially the fossil fuel tycoons. They understand that climate change is real and yet their public story is that it is a hoax. The reason for this contradiction is that there are trillions of dollars of reserves that they are committed to extracting. Therefore, they must deny climate change, while extracting fossil fuels. And to have an authoritarian government that they control allows them to control the whole society on every policy issue. Most importantly they believe it will allow them to control a volatile society when the full impacts of climate chaos have hit.

Big money realizes, however, that they need allies for political cover. Therefore, they have formed unholy alliances with evangelicals, white supremacists, and the National Rifle Association (NRA). This allows them to use the energy of religious fervor, bigotry, hatred, and fear to further their purposes. The role the president is playing is one of distraction by focusing attention on himself as he moves ever closer to the desired authoritarianism.

The party of the rich, racists, and religious fundamentalist that is leading Congress is on board with all of this and is delivering the policies that the alliance desires – tax cuts for the superrich, an anti-climate change agenda, opening national parks and coastal waters to fossil fuel extraction, appeasing the religious right with Jerusalem and anti-abortion legislation, and holding steady with the NRA to keep the society flooded with weapons, killings, fear, and anger.

Furthermore, the alliance is using the Russians and voter suppression tactics with the intention to disallow voting to thwart their intentions.

Most Americans, however, are waking up to this strategy and are being energized to resist and fight back, especially women, and youth.

What we each need to think about is how to enable this push-back to become strategic and powerful to turn the tide against these mistaken, dangerous forces of environmental and societal harm.

Think my friends. What do we need to do and be in this moment of crisis?

March for Our Lives

(24 March 2018, Swannanoa, North Carolina)

I am deeply touched by today's 800 marches worldwide of March for Our Lives. Led by youth, albeit intelligent, articulate, compassionate youth, it is heartwarming and inspiring. When I heard one young person say "I just want to study math and play basketball not get killed" I had a deep realization. This movement is not based on some difficult to understand ideology or constitutional interpretation. It is simply choosing life. I choose to be able to live my life. Please take your boot off my neck or I will remove it for you. It occurred to me that all the great movements are equally simple. They each choose life:

I choose life; therefore, we must mitigate and adapt to climate change and protect the natural environment.

I choose life; therefore, women must have equal rights in all spheres and leadership of society.

I choose life; therefore, every human being deserves healthcare, education, and adequate income.

I choose life; therefore: We the People require a government by, for, and of the people.

I choose life; therefore, everyone has inalienable human rights to life, liberty, and the pursuit of happiness.

I choose life; therefore, we must use nonviolent means for resolving disputes.

It is now crystal clear how the movement of movements – MOM – will strengthen, and lead humanity to a compassionate civilization. We each must choose life.

Come with us and live your life. It is that simple.

Heartfelt thanks to our children for living their truth and leading us home.

Reinventing Society by
Transformational Thinking

(17 February 2019, Swannanoa, North Carolina)

Consciousness precedes everything for us humans. Drives everything. Invents everything. Everything is a thought. An experiment in thinking based on perspective, perception, and valuation. To reinvent human society, we must start a new thought experiment that goes viral, global, a mind hack, a systems breech, a revolutionary act. Our values: sustainability, equality, justice, participation, tolerance, and nonviolence. Our perspective: every living being. Our perception: integral, whole system mind. We will invent a new world. We will dream of a new way of being. We will reinvent ontology, and phenomenology, and epistemology.

Justin Whitaker will help. Ken Wilber will help. Naomi Klein will help. Robert Reich will help. Paul Krugman will help. Jean Houston will help. Joseph Stiglitz will help. Daniel Wahl will help. Scott Santens will help. Bill McKibben will help. AOC will help. Bernie Sanders will help. Elizabeth Warren will help. Nancy Pelosi will help. Greta Thunberg will help. Jane Goodall will help. Story Bridge will help. ICA will help. I will help. And millions more will help. We will form a Thinking Collective, to reimagine the world. We will toss our net out around planet

Earth through every available channel. We will capture the noosphere to think this thought. This thought will drive the new actions, the new mindsets, the new behaviors, the new cultures, the new systems. We will give our lives to this endeavor.

This is the new genesis, the reinvention of the world. In the beginning there was the Thought, the Logos, the Word, the shimmering of consciousness. Existence is not first. Essence is not. Thought is primal. We think therefore we are as we think. Not a new thought, but it is time for this thought to go viral, to transform everything. Otherwise, the crises will win, will destroy us: climate chaos, patriarchy, systemic poverty, plutocracy, bigotry, and perpetual warfare. This is the time for the new thought, the new thinking, the new action, the new being. It is already in motion. It has already won. Everything is in transformation. Everything is shimmering between the no-longer and the not-yet. Everything is transformed in a twinkling.

The call will go out today to all who would think these thoughts. In fact, the call has already gone out. These thoughts are already being thought by many. The movement of movements (MOM) is hard at work, with great ease, flowing, laughing, splashing, without fear, without dread, but with such peace, and happiness, and compassion, and understanding. The Buddha is at work. The Christ is at work. The Alpha and the Omega are at work. Teilhard is at work. These thoughts are more powerful than all the armies, all the money, all the political power, all the wealthy, all the confused, all the greed-bound, all the fear-filled, all the hate-filled, all the ignorant. These thoughts are awakening everyone and everything.

Everyone is joining in the movement, the embodiment, the swaying, the dancing, the raised hands, the Yes We Can and Are. There is no Separate Self. There is only the All in All. The Droplets making the Ocean. The Words making the Book. The Thoughts making a New Mind. A New Heart. A New Body. A New Way of Being. Now! It is accomplished. We will reinvent economics. We will reinvent sociology. We will reinvent politics. We will reinvent education. We will reinvent healthcare.

We will reinvent justice systems. We will reinvent every aspect of human society around our planet. Gratitude, infinite ineffable gratitude for this moment of sentience. Every living being will be valued. Every living being will be celebrated. Every living being will realize its ultimate purpose and genius. Yes.

Interactions among the Six
Crises Facing Humanity

(27 February 2019, Swannanoa, North Carolina)

Climate chaos and ecosystem degradation; patriarchy and misogyny; systemic poverty and social deprivation; plutocracy and corporatocracy; prejudice and bigotry; and a culture of violence and perpetual warfare – how are these six crises interconnected?

Climate chaos is harshest on the poor. The fossil fuel industry uses financial contributions to stop climate mitigation legislation. Patriarchal views produce few women in political leadership. Bias against women leaders is high. Systemic poverty is often hardest on women. The poor usually have little political power. There is prejudice against the poor with the misunderstanding that they are "lazy." Low-income people provide most of the soldiers that fight in armed conflict. Plutocracy and corporatocracy favor the continued extraction and burning of fossil fuels. The rich form alliances with racists and religious fundamentalists to gain political power. The armaments industry funds pro-war legislation. Prejudice and bigotry result in harm to women, and minorities. Fear and hatred of different races and religions can fuel armed conflicts, harmful policies, and support for authoritarian leadership. A culture of violence and perpetual warfare are most harmful to the poor, women, and minorities. Climate chaos can create the conditions for ethnic violence. Armed conflict becomes a means of authoritarian control. Every day violence is most harmful to women, minorities, and persons of different sexual orientations.

Agree? Disagree? How else are these six crises interconnected?

A Letter to Humanity and Life on Earth:

Time to Turn the Ship of Life

(15 August 2019, Swannanoa, North Carolina)

Date: August 15, 2019

To: The human race
From: A human
Re: The future

My dearest sister and fellow human,

I am writing to you out of great concern for our common future, "our" referring not only to humanity but to life on Earth. After much observation, analysis, and reflection, I, your fellow human, have concluded that not only are we (humanity and life on Earth) in danger of becoming by and large extinct, but that humans have been on a wrong track for a long time. When we evolved beyond the tribal stage and began agriculture and early forms of cities and empire, we became trapped in the illusion of separateness from nature and each other resulting in the creation of social forms that began to cause great suffering for most humans and other life forms. A few people, let us call them the "elite", saw that if they structured society in a vertical hierarchy then they could control the human population for their own benefit. Thus, they created mythologies and religions to support this hierarchy, educational systems to teach it, political systems based on it, economic systems that defined human beings as laborers, and health systems that were reserved for the elite. Life for most humans was "nasty, brutish, and short."

This form of social organization has continued up to the present times through the recent capitalist-industrial-fossil-fuel transformations. In our time it has resulted in the wholesale destruction of the life support ecosystems of air, water, soil, plants, and animals, leading to climate chaos, all of which are endangering the future of humanity and all other life forms.

We, humanity, now have a colossal choice to make between two futures: life or death. The correct choice would seem to be obvious were it not for the massive propaganda of the current elite. You and I, as the 99% of humanity, must now take control of history for the first time ever or at least in this most important moment, and not only turn away from the deadly path of hierarchical-capitalist-industrial-fossil-fuel civilization, but create a never-before civilization based on compassion and ecological regeneration. This will not only allow us to care for all of humanity but all life on Earth as we reinvent our social systems based not on hierarchy but on the care and wellbeing of all people and all life forms everywhere.

I am writing to you today to ask that you do everything in your power as an individual, family, community, organization, and network to seize the day and turn the ship of life toward compassion and ecological regeneration. Let us each henceforth vow to use our life in this holy endeavor.

May it be so,

R.

Now Is the Time

(13 September 2019, Swannanoa, North Carolina)

It is happening now. In the first six months of 2019, seven million people around the world were displaced by extreme weather. It is a climate emergency that will continue to swell – to 70 million, 700 million, and more. These people are you and me. They are us, our loved ones, our sisters, and brothers. They are my brother-in-law, nieces, and nephews in Panama City, Florida. It is time to reorient our economic, social, and political processes to respond to the suffering of people and planet.

In World War II, FDR shifted the domestic US economy to a war footing to build tanks, airplanes, guns, and other implements of war. It is time to shift the local, national, and global economy to mitigate climate chaos and ecological collapse and to adapt to and deal with rising seas, extreme weather events, mass migration, collapse of food production, water shortages, and more.

These crises are calling for radical, massive compassionate action. These crises are awakening humanity to its role of caring for all people, all species, and all natural resources for the sake of the future of life on Earth.

This radical, compassionate action must happen here in Swannanoa and Asheville, NC. It must happen throughout

North Carolina. It must happen across our great country. It must happen around this beautiful, suffering planet.

These crises are calling you and me to transform ourselves, to let go of fear, hatred, and greed, to come together to build a compassionate-ecological community and civilization.

Now is the time! We are the people!

Caring for Self, Loved Ones, Communities, Nation, and World in a Pandemic

(20 March 2020, Swannanoa, North Carolina)

Many, many people are suffering and worried. Will I get the COVID 19 virus? Will I die? Will any of my loved ones die? How can I ensure that I have food and supplies? How will I pay my bills if I have no job? Will my country fall apart from economic downturn and political incompetence? Is this merely the first of a seemingly endless series of crises that climate chaos will bring? In this moment, we must care for our self, our loved ones, our communities, our nation, and our world.

Caring for Our Self
Keep yourself safe. Be kind to yourself. Be aware of breathing in and breathing out. Enjoy moments of listening to music and seeing the bright colors of spring flowers. Be grateful for the gift of life.

Caring for Our Loved Ones
Keep your loved ones safe. Be kind to your loved ones. Invite them to do things that they enjoy such as listening to music or seeing the bright colors of spring flowers. Help them be aware of and grateful for the gift of life.

Caring for Our Communities
Keep your communities safe. Be kind to everyone you meet. Assist those in need. Invite people to enjoy life moment by moment. Help everyone be aware of and grateful for the gift of life.

Caring for Our Nation
Quickly create the structures and systems of testing, vaccination, and treating the virus. Practice physical distancing. Wear a mask. Wash your hands. Provide emergency financial assistance and other care for everyone. Invite all citizens to be kind to each other. Remind everyone to pay attention to the miracle of each passing moment. Call on everyone to be grateful for the gift of this life.

Caring for Our World
Provide equipment, personnel, vaccinations, and finances to other countries that are suffering from this virus. Urge other countries to practice physical distancing. Bring the international community together to plan and act together. Design global systems that care for all the people and all of nature on planet Earth. Invite all people to embody an ethic of compassionate action toward each other. Help people everywhere celebrate the miracle of living on planet Earth in harmony with each other and with nature.

   May it be so!

COLLECTION
Spiritual Transformations

This collection contains essays on demythologized Christianity, progressive Buddhism, and worldly spirituality. It does not contain essays related to Judaism, Islam, Hinduism, and other traditions because of the author's limited knowledge and practice.

THEME

Demythologized Christianity

These essays are among the earliest in this book. On the one hand, my understanding about spirituality and religion has evolved and deepened a great deal over these years. On the other, there are elements of continuity running throughout my life up to the present. I hope that you find these essays useful for your life-reflection.

Demythologizing: The Theological Method of Rudolph Bultmann

(14 November 1966, Chicago, Illinois)

Written in 1966, this is the second earliest essay in this book. I wrote it when I was twenty-one and a graduate student at Chicago Theological Seminary. It deals with Rudolph Bultmann's concern for interpreting the New Testament to contemporary people considering its seeming irrelevancy or impossibility of belief. Dr. Thomas Ogletree gave the paper an "A" and wrote: "This is an excellent paper, clear, well-written, precise. You have a good grasp of the issues and have demonstrated skill in exploring them independently." Some of the professor's suggestions were considered in the editing process, along with changing "man" to person or human.

Bultmann holds that Biblical times were mythological and modern times are scientific. By this, he means that the worldview of Biblical times included the objectification of the mysterious and uncontrollable into gods or demons which periodically broke into history to become part of the cause-and-effect chain of events. In this way, the mysterious was understood as the intervention of transcendent beings into profane human history. In opposition to this, the modern worldview holds that

there can be no break in space-time history, and every phenomenon can be finally understood in terms of a fundamental
cause and effect nexus which is part of history itself.

Because of this difference in worldviews, the message of the
Bible is distorted in modern times by its alien context – the
truths of the Biblical texts are hidden by their accompanying
worldview which cannot be accepted by modern people. To get
at and express these truths, Bultmann devised an interpretive
method which he calls *de-mythologizing* – that is, the drawing
out of the essential truths of a text and the placing them in the
modern worldview. Therefore, de-mythologizing is the attempt
to get at the deeper meaning behind any mythological framework and translate this for contemporary scientific humans.
In this way, the real stumbling block of the Bible may be made
manifest rather than the false stumbling block of one's own
inability to understand or accept a text intellectually. For the
New Testament in particular, this is possible because the message of Christ is *kerygma* or proclamation addressed not to the
theoretical reason but to the hearer as a self.

Since all interpretation is based on certain principles and
conceptions which guide exegesis as presuppositions, Bultmann
concerns himself with the discovery of that philosophy which
will best illumine the message of the Bible. Bultmann believes
that it is the task of the exegete to really hear what the Bible is
saying for our actual present, to hear the truth about our lives as
the Bible makes this known to us in confrontation. Therefore,
he comes upon existentialist philosophy, i.e., especially that of
Martin Heidegger, to use in interpreting the Bible's encounter
with us. The Biblical Word addresses us as persons in a particular time and place, and existentialist philosophy is concerned
with such encounters and the surrounding problems of freedom, responsibility, and decision. So, in answer to the question
of how human existence is understood in the Bible, we find
that a clarification of the appropriate questions for opening
what the texts are saying should naturally come from the philosophy which deals with the questions of human existence.

Through the application of such concepts, Bultmann discovers that the Word of Jesus Christ is that Word which calls a person from his search for security in the things of this world and directs her to God who is beyond this world. This is the understanding that everything of this world is finite and will pass away. This is the eschatological Word of Jesus Christ which proclaims the imminent end of the world and the final judgment of God. Beginning with the apostle John and the disciple Paul, this eschatological event was begun to be de-mythologized into an identity with the Christ-event itself. That is to say that for Paul, the turning point of history began with Jesus Christ and for John, Jesus Christ was the eschatological event by which all people are judged.

As individual persons are addressed with this Word of the passingness of all worldly things, they are faced with the awful freedom and responsibility for their lives. If someone says "yes" to this Word with her whole being, she understands that she is utterly free and responsible for her life and her death without any worldly security. It is in this situation of faith that the final security of God overtakes him, and he can live "in spite of" his loss of security. In this freedom, a person is left free to be obedient to the law of his own being – which is all the law of God as this is manifest through Jesus Christ. This faith is not a new worldview, however, but rather a complete openness to the future. It is a new understanding of personal existence which transforms the whole world as it moves into the unknown. In this way, God who is unknown and unknowable per se is experienced through his actions as he meets humans in concrete everyday life. Through faith, a person understands herself in relation to a final unknown and learns to rely on this unknown. A person experiences God as he comes to know his own limitation and creatureliness and the final insignificance of all that is. And by this act of calling the unknown final mystery "God the Father" rather than Satan or Fate, a person can live despite catastrophe, anxiety, yearning for worldly security, and her own imminent death.

What Bultmann has done here is prepare a concise, brilliant apologia for both his hermeneutics and the Christian Gospel itself. He has applied an understanding of the cultural myth and the epochal Weltanschauung, both got from modern sociology and anthropology to an interpretation of the Bible which is basic to any contemporary understanding of the message of the New Testament. And so, by addressing the Word to modern people in terms of their own scientific worldview, a modern person is given the opportunity to overcome the original worldview. Bultmann can risk losing the Word in this transference only because of this overriding faith in the universality and essential truth of the Gospel which can speak through any existential context.

Bultmann is aware that every age has its own picture of the universe, its commonly held modes of perception and its unique linguistic patterns. And once this is understood, we cannot help but see the necessity of interpreting any literary text considering the total cultural milieu out of which it arose. Human history is understood only in its particularity. And if there are any universal truths, they are to be found couched in a particular setting. The task of all literary criticism (in its broadest sense) is to discover that which is essential and universal about a particular configuration of words and characters.

And so even God's revelation to humans must be rediscovered and re-translated from era to era.

On first reflection, I find it impossible either to disagree with Bultmann's historical method or find fault with his results. He is simply too basic to my own understanding of history, culture, and the Christian Gospel. In other words, if it were not for the work of Bultmann and others like him I would have been able to disregard Biblical Christianity long ago. In fact, I had managed to do so until I discovered theologians such as Paul Tillich who use and go much beyond Bultmann's de-mythologizing. What concerns me, on second reflection, however, are the larger issues surrounding the concepts of worldview and interpretive philosophy. A statement of one aspect of the problem as I see it is this: if every people of every age operate out of a worldview, then what is the process (if indeed there is any) by which an individual rises out of (however partially or temporarily) his own "way-of-viewing-the-world" and doubles back on it critically and is able to compare it with that of another age. Bultmann is quite certain about the character of both the Biblical and the modern world-views, and he seems equally certain that contemporary existentialist philosophy is the philosophy which will best elucidate the message of the Bible, but what he does not deal with overtly is the ostensible circularity of, on the one hand, a man's being part of and separate from a culturally limited mode of perception and intellection, and on the other hand, one's understanding a historical document well enough to discover a philosophy which will best help him understand the document. It seems that for Bultmann the "commonly accepted ways of viewing reality" at any given time in history are mere fashions of thought and perception and are in no necessary correspondence with the objects of their attention and that humans are seemingly inescapably caught in these accidental limitations. For this reason, he comes down heavily on the eschatological message of the Gospel and its existential address. Only that Word which destroys any ultimacy about one's present world is the final truth. Only when a person comes to see that she is inexorably bound up in contingent time-space can she truly be human. Given this final Word, even the Christian theologian realizes that he is caught in his own present, but because he is is a Christian theologian, he realizes that he is free to live in and speak to his own time. This Word justifies her in her relativity, particularity, and contingency. In this way, Bultmann can speak to his own time on its own terms. But still, this does not fully answer the initial question raised. Let us briefly expand the other aspect of the problem, however, before attempting a conclusion about the notion of worldview.

If a theologian is aware that all interpretation is finally based in a philosophy and if he wishes to become conscious of the philosophy which will best interpret a document and if she chooses this philosophy based on her understanding of the nature of the document, how does she initially understand the nature of the document (prior to conscious interpretation)? Basically, the issue raised here is, again, how can one avoid beginning un-philosophically and caught-up in his own worldview so that he might then become philosophical and transcendent?

Bultmann calls this the hermeneutic circle and discusses this problem explicitly. On the one hand, my present situation enables me to understand the text; on the other hand, the text enables me to understand my present situation. Presumably, one moves little by little more deeply and understandingly into both directions of this "circle."

In part, we begin with the fact that humans seem to be able to transcend their own situation and enter significantly into other situations, and ask Why? What is there about humans that makes this possible? Currently, the response is that people are so constituted as to be able to "transcend" themselves and entertain other possibilities of existence. Thus, a human being is inherently capable of the interpretive process Bultmann advocates. Bultmann is simply refining this capability showing how it can be exercised with more precision and critical self-awareness.

In both instances, we see that Bultmann as an exegete (or one who is interested in understanding the Bible) begins as a modern, scientific man who because of his personal, existential confrontation by the Biblical Word then pursues in a systematic fashion the interpretation of the Word (which he has already heard in part) via existentialist categories and a knowledge of his own worldview. In other words, it seems that these issues can only be begun to be resolved if we accept that Bultmann the man was addressed by the Word (the Eschatological Word) as pre-requisite for his being able to develop a method by which other people could be so addressed.

If this is so, Bultmann's method is immeasurably strengthened and at the same time relativized into personal intuition formalized into theology unless it is finally based in an anthro-pology. Therefore, what seems to be faulty circularity might be more aptly called necessary inter-relation.

In conclusion, I see Bultmann's theological method arising out of his own confrontation by the Word and his own faith in the ultimacy and finality of the Word. It is only with fore knowledge of the power of this Word that Bultmann can posit an existential situation that otherwise would leave humans to utter despair in an absurd present from which there is no escape. Bultmann can begin his theology in search of a phi-losophy and in full knowledge of the limitations of every world-view because of his experience of God's grace and its liberating and redeeming reality.

Theological Activity among a Reality of Disciplines

(23 November 1966, Chicago, Illinois)

This essay was also written in 1966 in theological graduate school in Chicago. Prof. Thomas Ogletree gave this essay an "A" and wrote: "Excellent. Penetrating, insightful, carefully reasoned, with a vital rootage in your own quest for self-understanding in the context of contemporary culture." Some of Dr. Ogletree's comments were considered in the editing process for this publication as well as changes from "men" to human and so forth. This piece is both philosophical and theological.

Human beings are born into the world and then reborn out of the world into reality. The world is that which was before humans and from which they arose and found their being. Reality is what humans know of the world. Reality is developed by the human community into a given for each individual. It is the Life-context out of which the individual grasps meaning and significance for both himself and all that is non-self. When this Life-context is in radical transition due to massive changes in the environment, individuals experience varying degrees of meaninglessness or disorientation and must recreate for themselves a context to live in and out of. When this occurs on a wide scale, many variant contexts are created. As individuals encounter one another, they find communication a major problem. Even if they are natives of the same language tradition, they find that they do not always share the same referent for the same word. Certain words and phrases may have vastly different emotional associations.

The use of the languages of religious traditions is especially chaotic in these times. In fact, it is often questioned whether there was ever anyone in the tradition who knew and believed in what the words are now considered to have meant. Discontinuity between Ages and cultural epochs becomes highly manifest. The emphasis falls heavily upon the present moment, and the attempt is made to squeeze meaning and significance from the given of the now alone. Radical departures are attempted from known traditions of thought and expression. Persons forget that they themselves are part of many-thousand-year-old traditions of the human community on the Earth. Westerners disavow the Western tradition without being aware that they do so in Western modes of thought and language. Language itself is experimented with radically. New words are developed. Old words are used in shocking combinations. All words that are not distinctly "contemporary" come under severe suspicion. At the same time, established social and political patterns come under attack and disregard, and much experimentation goes on in human relationships.

Such a time as this is natural in human history, and for its contemporaries it is bewilderingly unstable and rootless but also may give rise to enormously creative possibilities. Out of conflict and dialogue emerge new patterns and new truths and new possibilities for and about human existence and the nature of the universe.

And to this I say: "Do not demand clarity of my Age! Let us be what we are, which is what must be at this time. Radical dialogue is taking place among disparate traditions of being and thought in the face of the fantastic changes in our material world. If you have faith in humanity and our history, then you will allow another, later Age to make clear our overwhelm-ingly rich and confusing present dialogue." And the moment this is understood I say to my partner in dialogue: "Now would you please make that statement clearer in light of…" Is it clear what I am saying? When one can articulate with simplicity and clarity what is happening, it can be enormously helpful indeed.

Today, we must make room for propositional (linguistic) contradictions and drive beyond the words themselves to the necessary contexts and traditions of thought that all words must carry with them to mean what they do. By "carry with" I do not mean anything different from "generate in the mind of the hearer and user.") As *one* statement of thoughtful belief I can say: "I believe in God the Father, God the Son, and God the Holy Spirit; I believe that God is dead; I am aware that God is not a vital issue in the Secular City; I recognize that God is a necessary metaphysical principle; I believe that God must be destroyed." But I cannot stop with that statement. I must go on to show that I am attempting to be responsible (responsive-able) to several traditions (from the most ancient to the one developed yesterday in a university professor's study,) and I must show that that which underlies each of my statements has a fundamental unity and integrity or makes them compatible with one another, and I must point out from which tradition each speaks.

What I am here concerned with is the present discipline-based approach to knowledge (and its consequences for our perception of the "reality of the world.") The evolution of aca-demic and professional disciplines can be understood simply in the following fashion: The more often more people looked at the world the more they saw. As they and other people tried to deal with what was seen, subject-matters and methodologies were differentiated for focus and emphasis. But along with this development, there evolved a gradual reduction of the whole world (at which any discipline looked only partially) into the reality that could be seen within any one discipline. Hence, the human being has at various times been reduced to an economic animal, a psychological being, pure spirit, etc. To confuse a disciplinary-context with the total life-context is to see and live a reduction of the full richness of a world-centered reality. Historically, disciplines became useful and necessary as individuals began to question and seek clarity for their given Life-contexts as they were confronted with new and threatening experience and ideas. But now, it seems as though we have a situation where it is impossible to re-establish the connections (or re-integrate the findings) between what, say, behavioristic psychology tells us about ourselves and who we are as social beings seeking acceptance and meaning. Sometimes it seems that we must either buy wholesale what a discipline offers us or reject it totally. Knowledge seems irrevocably fragmented, and it seems inevitable not to live a fragmented life based on various reductionisms.

In the light of such a predicament, I clearly see the need for a species of thought which has as its task the re-working of humanity's contemporary Life-context in terms of the uniqueness of our present moment, the movement of the past which we now represent, the movement into the future for which we are responsible, and the movement of what might be the next step beyond the human. This species of thought would need be based upon a thorough going faith in being human, although a relative faith because humans are not the whole Universe or the whole of Process. By this kind of faith in humanity, I mean the conviction that it is good and right (inevitable) for people to inject human-responsibility, human-reason, human-intuition, and human-centeredness into process. We need never be ashamed of being human. But as an individual human, we must also realize and accept that which we are not.

This species of thought would be based in the understanding of the movement in our human understanding of and relationship to Life as 1) total undifferentiated experience, through 2) rationalization, ending with 3) the possibility for responsible action in the world. Therefore, it would be experientially concerned, then rationally concerned (via disciplines), then metaphysically concerned (rational gestalt), and then politically concerned (responsible action in History.) In this way, humans participate in the Universe in its own reflective self re-creation.

As an aside, the process of rationalization could possibly avoid fragmentation as in Whitehead's cosmology or Tillich's use of Heidegger's ontology.

This species of thought would also deal with the bringing together of a comprehensive description of the human condition and the nature of the universe with the ultimate, yet specific, concerns, possibilities, and dreams of humanity. It is in coming to a knowledge of this latter aspect that the thinker of this species of thought (let us call her a "theologian" for need of a convenient label) will sometimes make radical appeals to such sources as "Holy Scripture," "God's contemporary revelation" and "religious experience" in general.

To use myself as an example in conclusion, as a "Christian theologian", I find myself part of a long-standing tradition of a certain kind of experience and belief. In the terms of my tradition, I believe that the one true God created the universe; that he sent his son Jesus Christ to die for the redemption of my sins; and that the Kingdom of God is at hand. In modern secular terms, I believe that all of history is of one substance, and that all people are siblings; that all that is is good, and that I am accepted and sustained in existence by the universe; and that I am free and responsible for society, the further humanization of humanity and history itself. Given these specific and ultimate concerns, possibilities and dreams for humanity and the Universe, coupled with my comprehensive description of the present human condition and state of society and the world, I engage in the theological activity of being relevant and responsible to my times, all time that has ever been, all time that will ever be, and even beyond time itself.

No other task is as presumptuous and as fully human as that of the theologian.

Authentic Existence in the Gospel of John

(1967, Chicago, Illinois)

*This piece is filled with much traditional language and also
many elements of an existentialist understanding of authentic
existence.*

God's Creation:

"In the beginning God created the heavens and the earth…
Then God said, 'Let us make humans in our image, after our
likeness…' So, God created people in his own image, in the
image of God he created them; male and female he created
them." (Genesis 1:1, 26, 27) "When all things began, the Word
already was. The Word dwelt with God, and what God was the
Word was. The Word, then, was with God at the beginning,
and through him all things came to be; no single thing was
created without him. All that came to be was alive with his life,
and that life was the light of all people" (John 1:1-4)

From the above, we see that just as the prologue to the
Gospel of John parallels and hearkens back to the Genesis creation story, the writer of the Gospel stands firmly within the
most orthodox of Jewish traditions: the Fatherhood of God as
Creator. John plainly understands that a human is the creature of God and that he (the human) has been made in His
image, i.e., through the Word. This is to say that God has called

humans into being out of nothing. He has shaped people as people – given them limits which define them as a particular creature as opposed to any other. And part of this particularity is a person's capacity to know her Creator, which is the same as to say that a person can known herself as the creature she is.

Pre-Existence of the Light:
Also in the prologue, we are told that the Word or Light was with God the Father "when all things began" and that "all that came to be was alive with his life" (the Word.) This is the Word that calls the name of everything that comes unto being – that shapes and forms and limits everything that ever exists. In the case of the human, this is the Word that makes a human the unique creature that he is – that informs him of his true relationship to his Creator. The Word is the light that has always been and that enlightens the true way for all of existence.

But a human was not only made according to this Light as other creatures were; rather she was also made so that she might know the Light that enlightens her.

Humanity's Rebellion (Inauthentic Existence):
Inasmuch as a human can know the Light, he can know Darkness. And it is the case that a human is first born into a world of darkness; for he fell away from his true nature in the Light as he acquired the capacity to know the Light. Humans became separated from their true way when they first came to know other ways. And as people fell away from the Light, they came to prefer the Darkness (3:19), because it afforded them the opportunity of not having to acknowledge their creatureliness.

Humanity's Rejection of the Light: The "World:"
"He (the light) was in the world; but the world, though it owed its being to him, did not recognize him." (1:10) Humans created their own world after they were separated from the Light; this then is the world not of God but of the Devil, for it is opposed

to God's truth. The essence of the world, therefore, is darkness: the shutting of oneself against the Light.

This darkness, then, is an illusory self-understanding which a person takes on in his revolt against the God revealed in the Creation, against the truth about himself: that he is a creature rather than self-sovereign. This human is, in his own darkness, blind to the Light, without knowing that he is blind or desiring to admit it.

The world is not only in darkness, but it is designated by falsehood as well. "Whoever does not acknowledge Jesus as the Messiah is a liar." (I John 2: 22) And just as it is that people prefer darkness so they also prefer falsehood to the truth, because if they were to acknowledge the truth – that Jesus is the final Lord of life – then they would have to radically alter their lives. And people do not choose to have this happen for they rather seek security and stability even if it means living death.

The world without the knowledge of God guiding the lives of people has fallen into bondage itself: it is cut off from that which is other than itself; it is closed in on itself, inverted, involuted, and in and of itself, it is not free to become transformed. The natural cosmos, then, is in essence existence in bondage.

Inasmuch as people love only this world, they are ruled by Death, for, in fact, the world is already dead. Everything passes away just as it came into being; it is the nature of things to do so – to pass in and out of existence. Thus, all that ever was, is, or shall ever be will at sometime cease to be. And if a person links her life with anything of this world, then it will be like building a house upon the sands for it will surely fall. Thus, the world is in bondage to Death; it is in fact the enemy of life because it destroys all that it creates. By disavowing God, the creator as its origin, the world falls into the hands of Nothing.

The world, then, is in Sin; it is separated from the One Reality: God the Creator and Sustainer of all that is. And because of this separation, Sin can only perpetuate itself; it can never break out of itself into union with that which brought it into being. The world is by itself hopelessly lost.

The result of this sinful state in the lives of humans is that they substitute their own selves for God; they believe that they are not creatures at all but rather that they are the lords and ladies of life. They worship themselves and one another and the institutions and traditions of this world in a desperate attempt to maintain the illusion that there is no power greater than the ones that they can acknowledge without endangering their own self-centeredness and self-justification.

For St. John, all the above are aspects of inauthentic existence. In a word, inauthentic existence is existence lived apart from the knowledge of God the Creator.

The Coming of the Light (Transition):

A human, then, escapes God by clinging to his old makeshift world; she hides in the face of harsh reality that makes demands upon her; he waits for a time in the near or distant future when he will be able to live his life; she abstains from taking a self-conscious life-stance under the pretense of waiting for more knowledge; he creates great illusions to buoy himself up as he floats in a sea of noncommitment. It is precisely into this world of inauthenticity that the Lord of life appeared.

When a person encounters the claims of this man Jesus that he is the Christ, he is seized with radical possibilities for his life. But coincidental with this seizure is an utterly irreconcilable offense to his past and present way of living. This is to say that she is suddenly judged by this awesome life possibility – that she could begin to live in the truth of Jesus the Christ. All his old, established ways of escaping affirmation of his creatureliness, his dependence, his responsibility are radically called into question. She then sees this claim of the man Jesus for what it is: a new possibility of human existence that by its very being judges to the quick all that is not of itself.

It is during this seizure-offense that a person is called upon, it is demanded of her, to decide for or against the life possibility that Jesus the Christ offers her. If a person decides for this Christ, then he must confess that he has been living in sin: in bondage to a world of darkness and falsehood ruled over by the Devil. He must repent of his past inauthentic existence.

As soon as she can make this confession, then she has begun to live in an utterly new and different reality than that of the world. This reality is faith. And it is here in faith that the offense-judgment is overcome; a person is redeemed by having decided for the judgment. Thus, what appeared to be only self-damning is a saving transformation.

This faith is a hearing of the Word in Jesus Christ and a responding in the affirmative to the Word: it is an admission that this Word is indeed the Word about Life. It is also a knowing faith; it has as its object an actual historical event. And faith itself is a personal, existential event. It is a knowing what it is that is heard.

Living in faith for a person is eschatological existence; life is no longer finally bound to that which is, but rather with that which always was and will be: the First and Last Reality that is apart from the created world altogether.

The Person of Faith (Authentic Existence):
Life for the person of faith is lived in the Kingdom of God come to earth. Whereas on the one hand, inauthentic existence is lived in the world ruled by the forces of darkness (the devil), on the other hand authentic existence is lived in the Spirit ruled by God. The person of faith is born again, this time into the realm of the Creator, i.e., the Creation. To live one's life in God's kingdom is to have exchanged one's origin and his essence for that of his true being, his creatureliness. (3:3 ff). it is to be in the world but not of the world.

The person of faith for the first time sees life as it really is, as it has been revealed by Jesus as the Christ. For John, the coming of Jesus is the eschatological event which makes known the truth about human life: its source and its destiny. The light which the world had been seeking is now present among all people, and all who have eyes to see now are offered the opportunity to see. God through his infinite love has revealed himself as the Creator by sending a man among men who perfectly fulfilled his creatureliness. And it is precisely this one life that lays bare the truth about all of life. It is toward the man Jesus that faith is directed, for he has shown the way – the way that people are to rightfully live before God.

So, it is in light and truth that authentic existence is lived. In this way, the person of faith gains abundant life as she escapes the hands of darkness, falsehood, and death. She is in fact free from the world and, therefore, from sin. It is in this freedom that a person is able to fully love the world, to work in an alien land by ministering to one's fellow human beings. But for the believer, her life is not lived in an alien land because everything has been transformed by the Spirit: death has been forever overcome and all she must do to fulfill herself is to love God and her neighbor.

The person of faith meets life with openness and assurance for she knows who the Lord of life is, and she seeks to be encountered by him within life. It is this liberating knowledge that allows her to see what is there and to hear what is there and to embrace every situation with love and creativity. Because of the absolute and final love that the believer has received from God through Christ Jesus, the believer is obligated to love other people. She accomplishes this in part by destroying all purely human standards and values and reinstating those of the Spirit. This transformation takes place within individual people; therefore, the person of faith must address the Word of possibility and hope in Christ Jesus to all people (preaching.)

In authentic existence, a person fully realizes himself as a child of God, and it is in this capacity that he lives in radical obedience to the Spirit. Her relationship to God is that of confident prayer, for it is mediated by the Revealed One, Christ Jesus. It is through this relationship that she can live her life with peace and joy, assured of her place with her Father.

My Soul Sings

(20 December 1987, Caracas, Venezuela)

This reflection was written in the Caracas House of the Order Ecumenical. I had recently encountered the sacred psychology and sacred theater of Jean Houston. I often attended mass in the Armenian Orthodox Church near our house. Soon after this, the global Order Ecumenical was dissolved along with the Caracas House – more about that in the collection on self transformation.

I feel like a member of the Royal Family as I look out the window of my room. I can imagine seeing our house from down the street. It looks like a palace, a mansion – with its white exterior, ivory trim, glistening black iron balcony railings, black iron lanterns hanging, huge white wall with black iron gate, tiled roof, arched entry ways, high steps. A palace of peace, a mansion for mankind. A Great House for the conscious ones, the awake ones, the grateful ones, the joyous ones, the humble ones, the servants of the servants of God. We are indeed a Royal Family, a noble family – of many races, religions, nationalities, cultures, ideologies, classes, educational levels, personalities, styles, gifts. A Royal Family in service to the Cosmic One – the One who is Love, who is Light, who is Consciousness, who is Spirit, who is Energy, who is God.

My soul sings. I dance. I am ecstatic. I worship with incense, with light, with gold, silver, crystal, marble, velvet, with bells, with song. I am enraptured. I weep. My soul is filled like a bowl with inexpressible feelings. I am in love. I delight in my Beloved – even Jesus, even Mary, even Joseph – the family of love, the Royal Family of God.

A light, cool breeze blows through our house; the bright tropical sun fills the courtyard; the goldfish swim in their random patterns; baroque music floats by; the green plants wave their leaves; the blue sky and white clouds peek at me from above the courtyard wall; the floor glistens; the white walls are adorned with paintings. My soul is full – saturated with sensory blessings. My life is a liturgy of colors, movement, sound, smell, touch, song, dance – rapture, magnificence, beauty. I am grateful to be alive, to be awake, to be in the service of the King of the Universe.

But I cannot stay and enjoy my palace, my life of beauty. I am called to go forth in battle, to ride forth in service, to fight, to risk all, to awaken others, to call others to dance, to live a life of worship. I am called to create sacred theatre, liturgy, movement of dignity, of honoring, of worship, of acknowledgement, of remembering our deepest identity, of sacred psychology.

An Easter Reflection

(3 April 1994, Garrison, New York)

This essay combines both traditional religious elements and personal reflections and could be placed in either the spiritual or self transformation collection. It is placed here because of the experience of the transparency of Christian symbols to everyday life and ultimate Mystery.

This morning at St. John's Episcopal Church in Garrison, New York, I was infused with a subtle energy that I would call grace. It was accompanied by several perceptions. First, I had arrived an hour late, forgetting about day light savings time. The Holy Eucharist was being celebrated. Sitting in front of me were three little children playing quietly in their Easter finery. The fresh radiance of their faces filled me with their innocence and beauty. At the front of the sanctuary depicted in the stained-glass window high above the altar was the risen Christ with his arms opened in compassion and victory. Surrounding me on all sides were banners and stained-glass windows of dark, rich colors and hues. Music delicately filtered through my consciousness.

When the holy sacraments were being distributed to others in the congregation and then to me, I was filled with such gratitude that my chest became constricted and my eyes began

to become moist. After the Holy Eucharist when the final pro-
cessional began moving toward us led by the cross held high, I
was overcome with a sense of history, gratefulness, and grace.
I experienced in a fleeting moment all the processionals over
the past 2,000 years in which people gathered to celebrate the
mystery of the incarnation, death, and resurrection of Jesus the
Christ our Lord. It was then that my eyes filled with tears and
the sweet pain in my chest tightened even more.

Upon reflection, I think that I had been prepared for this
experience by three other experiences prior to Easter Sunday.
The first experience took place over the two days of Good
Friday and Holy Saturday in a retreat of the Board of Trustees
of Wainwright House in Rye, New York. In this two-morning
exercise, we reflected upon and shared some significant events
in our individual lives and identified experiences which were
more in common and those which were not. We also discussed
the implications for Wainwright House and particularly for
the type of leadership that the House needs. During these six
hours, I experienced a powerful sense of awe at the profun-
dity and sensitivity of my colleagues, an acceptance of who I
am, and a newfound hope in people's capacity to grow in self-
awareness, compassion, and in the awareness of the Mystery
that is in and yet beyond our daily experience.

The second experience took place Saturday afternoon. I was
preparing a position paper for my fellow members of the Board
of Trustees following our retreat. After writing eight pages, I
felt that I had captured much of what needed to be said. I then
saved the file and took the diskette to another computer to
print. When I called up the file, it was blank! I was stunned. My
creation was lost. It was gone, evaporated. I must have made
a mistake when I saved it since I was using a new lap top computer with Windows and Word Perfect 6.0 with which I was not
entirely familiar. I returned to the laptop and began searching
desperately for back up files. Two hours later under great anxiety, I had still not found it. I called my youngest son for help.
He could not find it. I phoned my brother near Washington,

D.C., who knows much more about computers than I. He could not figure out how to find 1t. I began to think that perhaps I should accept the fact that it was lost and try to rewrite it. But for some reason, I kept searching. After four hours of anxious search and repeated statements to myself and others about how stupid I was, the file suddenly reappeared! It had been saved as a deleted file in a hidden directory with a new file name. I was able to find it by using the Microsoft undelete program and tracing it to where it had been tucked away for a few hours. Was I happy? I called out, "It is risen! It is risen indeed!" I then ran to my son and shared my good fortune. I called my brother and my parents and told them that what was lost was found, what had been dead was alive. I was so happy. I then transferred the file back into Word Perfect and saved it. But after doing a few more things to it, I lost it again. By this time, my oldest son had returned from Manhattan, and I called on his help. He could not find it. I then retraced my steps as before and found it a second time and for the second time transferred and saved it.

The third experience happened on the night of Holy Saturday when I took my youngest son Christopher for a drive. The purpose of this excursion was to talk with him about his future after graduating from high school this June and about his relationship with his girlfriend. He spoke about the possibilities he has before him – living in Brooklyn and working with a rock band, going to Korea to spend time in the land of his birth, going to Arizona to live in his Grand Father's cabin, or going to visit a friend in the Netherlands and exploring Europe. He said that he is clear that he is not ready now to attend a university. I affirmed that, although his mother and I would prefer that he go directly to college, we respect his judgement about what he needs to do. We also talked about other matters including his relationship with his girlfriend. He articulated some of his deeply held values and beliefs such as the importance of having good friends and living life as a gift. As we were returning home, we talked about his grandfather and the inevitability of death for each of us. Christopher said that he does not fear death. He said that he believes that death is the ultimate "chill" (teenage language) and that it is natural. He went on to say that although he will be sad when he loses someone he loves through death, he will know that they are where they should be. He also said that someday he will also be where he should be. He said that he knows this to be true, and that no one can disprove it. He knows what he knows. I was deeply touched by his sincerity and confidence. I had taken him for a ride to share with him my fatherly concerns about him, and in return he had addressed me deeply as a wise person.

When I walked out of St. John's into the overcast Easter day, I was filled with a strange sense of calm, an unusual feeling of confidence, a strong sense of hope, and an overabundance of gratitude for the mysterious gift of life and the equally mysterious gift of death.

Praise the Lord! Christ is risen!
He is risen indeed!

THEME

Progressive Buddhism

In 1986, I began to study Buddhist thought and to practice Buddhist meditation, both of which I found liberating and useful. I often called myself a Buddhist-Christian. In recent years, I more often understand myself as a Christian-Buddhist.

Buddha-Event, Christ-Event

(23 April 2004, Garrison, New York)

Awakening to deluded mind may also be awakening to enlightened mind.

The Christ-event reveals our delusion and releases us to our real life. The Buddha-event reveals our delusion, our ignorance about our own suffering, and releases us, unites us with our own perfect nature, our own mind, our Buddha-nature, of being awake.

Joseph Wesley Mathews loved to say that the essence of the human being is consciousness of consciousness of consciousness.

The Jews were waiting on a Messiah, someone to save them from their troubles, someone, a King, who would throw out the Romans, their masters. Jesus arrived on the scene. He said, "I have got good news! There is no Messiah! He is not coming! And I am it."

How was this Good News? People were waiting and complaining. They were not happy. They were disempowered. They experienced themselves as victims. Jesus said, "Don't wait any longer? Nothing is going to change your situation. You can live your given situation in freedom, in love, in happiness! Get up, pick up our bed and walk! You are free to live your real, given life!"

Shakyamuni Buddha woke up to suffering, his own and that of all existence. He said that to wake up to the reality of our suffering is the first step in releasing us from our delusion of believing that there is no suffering or that there should not be suffering. The second step, he said, is to identify the causes of our suffering. The causes of our suffering are three poisons in our mind – greed, anger, and ignorance. These poisons are manifestations of separation from the way life is (TWLI). When we become aware of these causes, then we can eradicate them as the source and ground that gives rise to delusion. This eradication is found in a path that has eight dimensions – right view, right thinking, right action, right concentration, right speech, right diligence, right mindfulness, and right livelihood. Thus, we ourselves, not waiting on anyone or anything, can transform our lives by waking up to our true nature, embracing it, understanding it, and transforming it. This is Good News indeed!

The concepts of sin and suffering both derive from the nature of separation or dualism. That which was One, has become separated from itself, has become two, is in a state of alienation, of delusion. Life itself wakes us up because life is Enlightenment Itself. Life is Mind. Life is Understanding. The event of experiencing being reunited with that from which you have become separated, Christians call grace, and Buddhists call enlightenment.

I am waking up to and from my deluded mind, my deluded action. I profoundly regret all the hurt I have caused other beings, especially those closest to me. I vow with diligence to take the sacred path of transformation, on behalf of all. As an act of repentance, at-one-ment, with all suffering beings. As I awake, all beings awake – because there is only one being – because there are no beings at all.

The demons that attack me, say "You can't wake up! You cannot be free! You cannot be happy! You are nothing!" These demons are negativity, paranoia, pride, anger, fear, confusion, in-discipline, laziness, greed, clinging and ignorance of TWLI – the way life is.

The Christ said, "Get thee behind me, Satan." The Buddha said, "The great Earth herself is my witness that I am awake because I am her child and she and all beings are awake."

Joe Mathews, the Dean of the Institute of Cultural Affairs, said that our campaign of Awakenment was more important than our campaign of Engagement. Awakenment will give rise to engagement.

I am awake. I am free. I am grateful. I am happy.

The Great Perfection

(2 May 2004, Garrison, New York)

Life is perfect.
Life is not a mistake.
Life has evolved to be exactly the way it is.

If there were no birth, there would be no possibility, no freshness, no innocence, no new beginnings, no radical discontinuity. If there were no death, there would be massive congestion, no room for the new, no open space for the young, no sense of the preciousness of life, no sense of the ultimate value of the present moment.

If there were no time, there would be no story, no movement, no memory, no anticipation, no change, no openness to possibility, no dance, no creation. If there were no space, there would be no movement, no dance, no beauty, no seeing, no touching.

Without evil, there would be no good. Without suffering, there would be no happiness. Without mind, there would be no world. Without a world, there would be no mind.

Everything is interdependent. Nothing is a separate entity or self. If things were truly separate, there would be no communication, understanding, or connectivity. By being empty of a separate self, everything is full of everything else.

This life is the Great Perfection. It is as it has come to be. It is us and we are it. Without it, we would not be at all. There would be nothing at all. But because it is as it is, all that is is.

Our task, my task is to come into harmony with what is, into union with what is, into understanding of, intimacy with, and compassion for what is.

Why do we spend so much of our life criticizing, denying, and fleeing from the way life is? It is quite useless and moreover it is impossible to achieve. Furthermore, it is tragic to try and trying makes us miserable.

What then is the only, the best response, to the way life is? Is it not love, compassion, gratitude, trust, understanding, and intimacy?

May it be so!

The Middle Way

(20 September 2004, Garrison, New York)

On 31 July 2004, I turned 60! What is the purpose of the rest of my life? It is not about security. It is not about status. It is not about stability. It is not about money.

It is about understanding everything. It is about compassion for all beings everywhere. It is about happiness for all beings. It is about peace for all beings. It is about transformation. It is about equity in the world. It is about a sustainable Earth. It is about participatory governance. It is about dancing. It is about social artistry. It is about daily spiritual practice. Be it so!

I am alive now! Yet I die every moment. Someday, I will die, and my body will be quite dead – cold, hard, still, silent, unmoving. What was my life about? What did I leave for this world? What were my thoughts, words, deeds, values, style, relationships, and creations? Was I generous? Was I loving? Did I make others happy?

Someday, everything that I love will pass away. Everyone I love will pass away. This is the nature of life. I must not succumb to fear, paranoia, clinging. I will be brave. I will be happy. I will love. I renounce guilt at this moment! I refuse to live out of guilt and fear. Be gone! Gone, gone, completely gone!

I am free, free to be this one – just this one – no other. It is good to be me. I can live my real, given life as a gift in gratitude and joy. Yes!

I renounce self-depreciation and self-doubt. I touch the Earth and stand my ground. I am awake. I am this one, no other, and it is good, accepted, received, and open to possibility. Yes!

Reality is like a drop of dew on a leaf, a flash of lightening, a cloud passing overhead. Existence is fleeting, here one second, gone the next. How live in such a world? How be happy? How accept and embrace this saha world?

Spirit is the really real. Appearance is an illusion – beautiful, but passing, like a flower, blooming and fading and dying in one day, like a wave on the ocean, like a fragile butterfly.

How live in this world? Identify with Spirit, Emptiness, the Ultimate, yet walk the middle way between Form and Emptiness, between the Relative and the Absolute, between Matter and Spirit, trusting in the Mystery of incarnate living, embracing the way life is, loving each moment and each being as perfect.

Practicing Compassion and Wisdom

(2013, Garrison, New York)

This first appeared in my book A Compassionate Civilization, *in 2017. It is the only piece in this current book from any of my earlier books.*

It has been said that compassion and wisdom are the two inseparable wings of the bird of awakening, allowing movement through life's often volatile currents. Compassion is "suffering with" and vowing to relieve another's suffering as one's own. Wisdom is the understanding of the fundamental nature of reality, its utter interdependence and continuous transformation.

As we negotiate the early years of this make-or-break century, we need to cultivate and manifest these two skillful means in mind, body, heart, speech, and action. Fortunately, there are many practices to help us do this including meditation, ethical studies, yoga, journaling, movement, art, reading, spending time in nature, volunteering, prayer, contemplation, liturgy and being part of a practice community. The most important practice, however, is to bring mindfulness and kindness into our daily lives moment by moment.

Please enjoy the beautiful faces and earnest voices of those you meet who are speaking profound words of compassion and wisdom, of love and truth.

What Is Compassion?

"What is the source of compassion?"

A colleague recently posed this question to me. Let's explore his provocative question together. How does compassion manifest itself and from where does it arise? It seems to me that its basis is a gift of our mammalian heritage.

All mammals have awareness of and empathy with others of their kind. This is true especially of our close relative, the chimpanzee, but it is also true of elephants and dolphins. Neurologically we know that the mammalian brain's mirror neurons allow one organism to literally experience what he/she sees happening to someone else. We warm blooded mammals have evolved to care about each other and to express affection for each other.

With human beings this capacity is both deepened and broadened. We feel each other's suffering and desire to help another relieve her/his suffering. We know what our own suffering is like, and we want to relieve it. In like manner we want to help others relieve their suffering because we know what it is like when it is our own.

But with us our compassion extends far beyond our own species. We also experience compassion for other animal species and for the Earth's plants, water, air, soil and minerals. This I believe is because we are essentially Earthlings and children of the evolving cosmos. Someone has said that we are a star's way of looking at a star. I would add that we are a star's way of loving a star.

Compassion arises from our basic nature of empathy, care and love, our basic goodness. This is one reason why we are shocked when someone harms another person. It is not expected; it is shocking and is not our usual way of being. We are communal beings. We love to be with others of our kind and to care for each other. The source of compassion is nothing more nor less than our very being. Compassion, then, is ontological as well as biological and sociological. We are the heart, eyes and hands of compassion itself.

But why then, you ask, do you and I harm others if our basic nature is compassion? Why is there violence, warfare, poverty, and injustice in human society? One answer is that our basic goodness becomes obscured and distorted by negative emotions of fear, anger, hatred, greed, ignorance, jealousy, and pride. Our attachment to what we mistakenly see as our separate self or ego poisons our mind and heart and creates confusion and harmful behavior.

Therefore we must continually *practice* letting go of self-attachment and *practice* cherishing others. We must wake up again and again from the nightmare of our confused mind to our true nature of interdependence. We must train our mind to follow its deepest impulse which is compassion and not be overtaken by negative emotions.

How Do We Know Compassion?

How do we know? How do we know that we know? How do we know what we know? What is required to convince us that we know? Is a statistic, experience, feeling, theory, reference, authority, measurement, experiment, or image that convinces us that we know something? Take compassion. How do we know compassion? We can read about it. We can ask others about it. We can experience receiving it. We can experience giving it to others. But what is it and how do we know that it is it?

Compassion is to be with suffering, either someone else's or one's own, and to help relieve that suffering. There are of course many forms of suffering including pain, anxiety, worry, fear, angst, disorientation, boredom, ignorance, sickness, abuse, dissatisfaction, anguish, loss, grief, humiliation, and on and on. What is involved in being with and relieving our own suffering?

Sometimes we can relieve our suffering by doing something tangible. If we are hungry, we can eat. But what if there is no food available? If we have a headache, we can take a pain killer. But what if it doesn't help? What if there is nothing tangible to be done to relieve our suffering? Then we can work with our suffering in the following ways. First, we can *acknowledge* our form or experience of suffering. Then we can *accept* this suffering. Next, we can be utterly *present* to it. We can *comfort* it and be *kind* to our suffering. We can then *recognize* its true nature of impermanence and interdependence, that is, it will not be forever. It will change when causes and conditions change. It will dissipate and become something else. Finally, we can *let go* of our suffering.

Once we have learned how to relieve our own suffering, we can help others relieve theirs. If someone is hungry, we can give them food. If someone is sick, we can take them to a doctor. At the societal level we can relieve suffering by creating compassionate policies and programs such as food stamps, universal healthcare, affordable housing, job training, a living wage, affirmative action, and environmental protection.

If another person's suffering cannot be eradicated by something tangible, however, we can help them alleviate their own suffering using the process we used with ourselves. We can help them acknowledge and accept their own suffering. We can help them be with and comfort their suffering. We can help them recognize that it is not forever and let go of grasping and being grasped by their suffering. We can help them liberate themselves from their suffering and experience gratitude and happiness inherent in being alive. The epistemology of compassion involves shining the light of awareness on the experience of suffering and letting that pure awareness begin to transform that experience and our relationship to it. May our compassion release and guide us to be there for others as well as for ourselves.

Daily Vows of Compassion and Wisdom

Fortunately, there are many wonderful religious and spiritual traditions that can help human beings live lives of love and truth. Every morning I bring my palms together, bow and make the following vows taken mostly from traditional Buddhist sources. (Following each section, I have provided my interpretation.) May this inspire you as it does me.

I take refuge in the Buddha, the Dharma, and the Sangha, until I realize enlightenment and bring all sentient beings to nirvana. (Interpretation: I find solace in the inherent capacity to wake up to a life of compassion and understanding, the teachings of compassion and understanding and the community of those who are continually waking up to compassion and wisdom, until I realize compassion and understanding and help relieve the suffering of every conscious being.)

Sentient beings are numberless, I vow to save them. (Interpretation: There are vast numbers of conscious beings, I vow to relieve their suffering and help them realize compassion and understanding.) Desires are inexhaustible, I vow to put an end to them. (Interpretation: Desires arise continually making their demands on us, I vow to place a limit to them and their influence.) The dharmas are boundless, I vow to master them. (Interpretation: There are vast numbers of phenomena, I vow to understand and work skillfully with them all.) The buddha-way is unattainable, I vow to attain it. (Interpretation: The pathway of waking up to compassion and understanding continues to unfold, I vow to realize it moment by moment.)

May all sentient beings realize peace, happiness, wisdom and compassion. (Interpretation: May all conscious beings realize the peace found in acceptance, the happiness found in gratitude and making others happy, the wisdom of understanding relative and absolute truth and the compassion of relieving the suffering of all beings.) May all beings in the six worlds realize peace, happiness, wisdom, and compassion. (Interpretation: May everyone who has died and those still living, realize the peace found in acceptance, the happiness found in gratitude and making others happy, the wisdom of understanding relative and absolute truth) and the compassion of relieving the suffering of all beings.)

I take the backward step to study the buddha-way, which is to study the self, which is to forget the self, which is to be awakened by the ten thousand things, which is to drop off body and mind, which is to let go, which is to let go of letting go. (Interpretation: I turn inward to contemplate and study how to continually wake up and live a life of compassion and understanding, which is to study the nature of the self, which is to realize that there is no separate, permanent self, which is to be awakened by everything we encounter, which is to dis-identify with my particular body and mind, which is to live in detached engagement, which is to live in detached engagement about living in detached engagement.)

Earth, fire, water, air, all dharmas manifest emptiness, impermanence, and suffering, thus realizing that all is good, the self is accepted, the past is approved, and the future is open. (Interpretation: All phenomena have the characteristics of interdependence and continual change and anxiety concerning these characteristics; and it is in the midst of this awareness that we can realize that everything that we are given in life is perfect, that this interdependent, ever changing, anxious self is perfect, that everything that has ever happened has brought us to this perfect moment and that the future is to be decided and created by those who live their lives.)

Om mani padme hum. (Translation: Hail, Jewel in the Lotus! Interpretation: I heartily acknowledge those who embody perfect compassion and understanding!)

Gate gate, paragate, parasamgate bodhisattva, prajna heart sutra. (Translation: Gone, gone, completely gone, everyone gone to the other shore, enlightenment, hail! Interpretation: May everyone realize perfect compassion and understanding!)

Mindful of Old Age, Sickness and Death
The Buddha began his spiritual awakening when, upon escaping the protected confines of his family palace, he encountered four phenomena for the very first time: an old person, a sick person, a dead person, and a monk. He suddenly realized that this life included suffering and impermanence and that there were ways to practice relating to the way life is.

After trying many spiritual paths and techniques and finding them all lacking, he finally sat down under a tree and simply became aware of his awareness. After some time, he fully awoke to the stunning realization that this life is indeed perfect and that there is a way to relieve all suffering. His realization was that by shining the light of mindfulness on suffering, impermanence, and interdependence, we could live this life in happiness, peace, compassion, and wisdom. What a staggeringly wonderful realization.

In a little over three months, I will celebrate living another year on planet Earth as this being. Every day I become a little more aware of the inevitability of sickness, old age, and death. I think about my legacy. What have I already done? Is it enough? What else do I need to do in this life? When will I die? How long do I have?

I know that I could die at any moment. Of course, that has always been true throughout my whole life. But now it seems more real, present, urgent.

Every day I dedicate myself to continually waking up to suffering, impermanence, and interdependence. I dedicate myself to relieving the suffering of all beings including myself. I dedicate myself to being compassionate and understanding. I dedicate myself to living a peaceful, happy life.

I dedicate myself to teaching, training, writing, consulting, and facilitating to awaken others to our time of crisis and opportunity, the possibility of an emerging civilization of compassion and strategies and methods of innovative, creative, facilitative, integral leadership.

Is this enough? Can I do more? Can I love more? Can I give more?

And then it is over. And I am gone. And it is finished.

Yet, it goes on – humanity, life, this Earth, this Cosmos. And I am part of it forever, flowing onward, changing, awakening, giving.

Gratitude.

Yes.

THEME

Worldly Spirituality

A Sketch of the Movement from Separation to Unification

(5 May 1966, Stillwater, Oklahoma)

When I was twenty years old and would soon graduate from Oklahoma State University, I wrote the following essay in May 1966, the earliest in this book. It was my term essay for a political science class taught by Dr. Bertil L. Hanson who gave my paper an "A" and wrote: "This is very fine. Coming from an undergraduate, it is extraordinary. The argument that nationalism and national sovereignty are harmful is commonplace. The suggestion that the solution may be found in an existential, religious reawakening is exceptional. . . This kind of essay is hard to write." Reading this essay now, I detect inklings of the trajectory of this young man's life which took him around the world serving villages, slums, cities, and nations. Due to my Buddhist training and practice later in life, I dropped theological language but am still focused on the movement from separation to unification. Thank you, Professor Hansen, wherever you are, for your affirmation of my young mind.

The simplest statement of the paramount problem in the world of nations can be put in the following form: nations do not act as though there were that which is wholly other, and which ultimately controls history; or in other words, nations do not make foreign policy based on a belief in ultimate reality or God. Regardless of the faith of a given citizenry in the goodness of life (as Tillich writes) and the God of history (as Bonhoeffer discusses), each nation makes foreign policy as though it were God. Each nation believes only in itself. Each nation believes that it alone can save humankind or at least that its own people deserve more than any other to live and to prosper. Nationalism as the predominant world religion places the burden of history on each ideological position that an individual nation assumes. Each nation has a body of presuppositions about humanity's place in the universe, its needs, and its goals; and each has a divine scheme for the attainment of these. What this does not consider is the larger scheme of things (the process of history) which is not in the control of any one nation, ideology, or culture. There are natural, external phenomena, worldwide problems including food, energy, shelter, and medicine shortages, population expansion, the dangerous effects of radiation fallout on the precious genetic code of humans, education, the effects of technology on humans and our environment, and the whole past and the whole future which no nation can realistically suppose to be able to comprehend alone.

In other words, the world has problems as a unit and those divisions which result in separate attempts at solution are in disregard of this. The awesome complexity of the inter-relatedness of each nation's attempts to survive and prevail economically, politically, and culturally are more than obvious.

A foreign policy based on an appeal to an absolute truth held by an individual nation is in disregard of the larger scope of history. That is to say that if a nation operates in the world with a foreign policy based on the economic, political, and cultural preferences of its people with concern for the rest of the world only where its own interests are inter-related with those of other nations, then it is not being responsible to the greater evolution of being. Here, it is suggested that a nation should be willing to sacrifice itself for humankind when a real opportunity presents itself.

This is the second point on which the problem of contemporary absolute nationalism is based: people not only do not believe in final mystery or God, but they do also not understand history or the evolutionary process of being (de Chardin.) This unawareness stems from others such as: the lack of a sense of the urgency over the problems resulting from people's inexorable separation from other people, as well as ultimate reality or God (Tillich.) Nations do not operate with the sensitivity of the givenness of humanity's existence, with an awareness of the basic pervading facts of life: the death of the individual; the necessary subjectivity of decision; the relativity of varying modes of being; man's separateness from all of creation; the necessity of institutions and structures for human life; the fundamental and ultimate goodness of the historic process; the necessity of change, variance, tension, destruction, and re-creation; and the necessity of the community to sustain and perpetuate human life. Without such an awareness, nations will continue to operate on the illusory assumptions that they individually are the embodiment of truth and their people above all others should live and prosper. This then is the problem of nationalism and ideological absolutism.

Beyond the separateness of the human condition as described by Tillich, we have unique manifestations of contemporary splits: 1) the eastern tradition versus the western tradition; 2) the "have nations" versus the "have not nations;" 3) idea versus being as elaborated by Erich Heller; 4) language versus idea; and 5) being versus language.

The resulting tension of the above is manifested in such phenomena as the threat of a worldwide nuclear holocaust and the cultural revolution taking place within American society as analyzed by Kenneth Boulding and Gabriel Vahanian.

The people of the world will be brought together as they become more concerned about their commonality than their separateness. Here the problem can be broken down into the theological, philosophical, sociological, psychological, and linguistic.

Movement toward unification must come within each of these while the people of the world become more aware of the world's problems and as they become increasingly fearful of the awesome possibilities for destruction of civilization and man's genetic structure that nuclear war poses.

At the same time, the unifying forces of technology including travel, cultural exchange, communication, the modern city, and secularization as elaborated by Harvey Cox, and the technical union of mankind for the conquest of space will work to create a common myth as elaborated by Etienne Gilson, and Nicholas Berdyaev, which will be the context in which the world's people will move and communicate. From this common myth will develop common symbols, common style, and common goals. Diversity will still exist, but it will be justified, functional diversity as in divisions of labor, discipline, and concern, rather than variation which consists of separate units which each attempt to either "live and let live" or impose its solutions upon the rest of the world. Each cultural group would contribute its wisdom and tradition to the world community so that all might be more enriched.

Therefore, it is seen that the problem of an artificially divided humanity and the sad consequences of separation can be approached only on multiple levels, that is, as the concrete, spatiotemporal problem it is. We must begin by accepting the separation that exists today so that we may understand it and therefore understand with how it can be dealt. We then must begin forging out models for a new world order which will be based on humanity's oneness and the world as a unit. This then is done by being responsible to the whole of the past and the whole of the future and the whole of being. The model will be created by a community of men and women who come together because of this common task. H. Richard Niebuhr among others would call this community the *Church*. These people must approach the problem of forging out a model and bringing it into being on three levels: the individual, the community, and the universal.

All the theoretical and practical disciplines must be employed with a self-corrective pragmatic method. All the existing structures of society and government must be respected for what they are while being utilized and changed into what they can be.

It is seen that the problem of people's lack of communication is grounded in numerous other problems. And, since it is, it is not a political much less a linguistic problem alone. The resolution of this problem will not be found at the empirical end of history when being reaches a static state of having arrived. Humanity will always be amid a seemingly insoluble complex of problems. What we must begin to do is experiment with the means of bringing about a more unified humankind.

If the leading citizens of the contemporary nation-states were to study seriously the works of Teilhard de Chardin including *The Phenomenon of Man*, and *The Future of Man*, they would be able to clearly see the possibilities for the evolution of consciousness and would then have the opportunity of choosing to take part in this struggle. Other works that should be studied include those of Paul Tillich, *The Courage To Be*, and *Love, Power, and Justice*; Friedrich Nietzsche, *The Birth of Tragedy*, and *Beyond Good and Evil*; the works of Søren Kierkegaard including *Fear and Trembling*, and *Sickness unto Death*; the works of Dietrich Bonhoeffer including *Ethics*, and *The Cost of Discipleship*; the works of Gabriel Vahanian including *The Death of God*, and *Wait without Idols*; Simone Veil including her *Notebooks*; and Nicholas Berdyaev's *The End of Our Time*. For then, we could transfer the intellectual and spiritual grappling with the problem of separation of these writers to the arena of national politics and continue the painful, uncertain struggle of humanity's evolving faith in our own goodness as well as the goodness of history itself.

Life Against Death by Norman Brown

(1967, Chicago, Illinois)

The Myth

In the beginning was Primal Unity. The God of the day was Dionysus. Humanity was a child. There was of yet no time to speak of; there was only play – the free play of the natural, primordial, unified instincts. We will call the play polymorphously perverse, for indeed people enjoyed all of life; there was a universe of sexuality. We cannot say that a person enjoyed his own body as well as objects in the world because there was of yet no such distinction.

So, people lived an eternally reoccurring life of innocence and pleasure. Everything was good; everything was right; there was no striving, no discontent, no progress. There was simply the all in all. And that was good.

But then it happened. From this Ontological Oneness, there appeared a split and the split was the psyche and through the psyche humanity fell. This split then was not in the Ontological Oneness itself but was in humanity. People fell into themselves. Or humanity became humanity as we know ourselves today. Thus, this split was psychological rather than ontological.

In the event of this split, humanity's primordial instincts were separated one from the other: the Eros (which had been all in all) was separated from the Thanatos. And this was the psychic conflict in and for humans. People were now made of two parts, seemingly at war with one another.

We shall call this state after the Fall from Primal Unity: Differentiation through Antagonism. Here there were two gods: Apollo and the Devil. In other words, because of humanity's fall, Repression came into the world and in so doing, established Reality; humanity's first principle of pleasure now came into conflict with his second principle of reality; Life was against Death. Here people developed a self as something separate from the world, a culture separate from nature, and a history separate from eternity. And each of these was the result of the coming of Repression; all of a person's life was neurosis.

Here people found that they were ambivalent toward these two instincts; they liked and did not like both. And it was in this Reality, with their unconscious desire for play repressed, that humans developed language, money, work, genital organization, and, in a word, all their cultural and historical devices, the most recent of which is technology. This process of diverting a person's sexual (play-full) energies into societal work, we will call Sublimation. So, all of humanity's cultures were sublimated because they themselves were first repressed. And the greatest of those things sublimated – Anality.

It is here that a person strives in time, forever discontent with what she is and has now, to reach a complete satisfaction such as she had known in Primal Unity, which even yet she carried with her in her unconscious as the most basic of her desires, wishes and purposes. But because of the coming of Repression, this can never be reached; and by the same token, the striving can never be let up. So here we see that humanity is caught in an absurd historicity called "progress" which is nothing more than people's endlessly frustrated attempt to regain their state of Primal Unity. Thus, people are prisoners of their own pasts, prisoners unaware of the nature of imprisonment.

But Nature did not set humanity a goal without endowing it with the equipment to reach it. And it is precisely the same equipment which came with the Fall that now acts as the beginning of people's redemption: self-consciousness. By making the unconscious conscious, people can objectify and there-fore overcome the results of Repression. And this making the unconscious conscious by projecting it into the external reality, we shall call Art. And the science which deals with humanity's original sin and its own salvation, we shall call Psychoanalysis.

So, through and with, psychoanalytical consciousness, a person can re-establish the source of every aspect of his life: the human body itself. By accepting that all of a person's social and cultural creation and his historical striving is grounded in and on the human body, everything comes into its proper per-spective for humans. That is to say that if we accept and affirm sublimation for what it is, we can return to the source of a per-son's adult life: his own childhood – the state of enjoyment-going-on. Thus, we have the possibility of reunifying ourselves with ourselves – the overcoming of the antagonism between life and death – the avoiding of repression and sublimation by affirming our animal natures, and therefore, our reaching the final and rightful state of humanity's becoming love's body.

Through the dialectical movement of psychoanalysis and art of affirming all that they discover and illuminate, a person can bring her own neurotic history to a halt, destroy time for eternity and re-establish herself as she ought to be – as she was. This final and third stage of humanity's life, we shall call Final Harmony. Here all is pure poetry; pure dance; pure play. All of life is imme-diate and sensuous. The body has been resurrected out of its own self-negation. The Eschaton has broken in and saves all who have eyes to see and ears to hear, who have a self-affirming body, a self-affirming self as what it is: natural, animal, excremental, pleasurable, and ending in death. Death now is seen as part of life itself; living is dying and dying is living. There is no false antagonism, no false striving after immortality, and hence, there is Eternity: time-less-ness. Pure present. Ripeness is all.

Aftermath
And so, we have Norman Brown's Poetic Myth which must surely take its place along side all the other great myths people

have created through the ages to explain humanity's deplor-
able state and offer the possibility of a New Order.

Commentary
For Brown, the real revolution is not taking place in history
(politics), but rather within humans themselves (their psyches
or better yet their bodies). Brown is a man possessed by a vision
of the way human life could be, and it is this vision that ani-
mates his commitment, zeal, and hope. In this light, Michael
Harrington would easily enough call him not only an artist, but
a good and great one at that. For indeed, Brown finds his concern within a realized eschatology – a utopia brought into ones
very present. Humanity need not wait on history and political
and economic revolutions to set things aright. Rather, we can
live life the way it was meant to be lived here and now. Only if
people will change their ways of looking at things (their modes
of consciousness) can human life be renewed. Otherwise, we
have only the continued and impossible task of unconsciously
striving after the kind of sexuality which the very means of the
struggle keep us from ever obtaining. This then is his judgment of culture and history: both are neurotic; both result
from repression and consequently from sublimation and both
are self-perpetuating. His solution is to destroy culture, stop
history, and begin to live life for what it is. His method is psychoanalytical consciousness.

    For the individual who has taken on for herself the psy-
choanalytical myth and worldview, everything is seen anew:
the world full of commodities and "modern conveniences"
becomes total, involving events of heraldic devices harkening
back to the human body itself; the body, then is discovered to
be the measure of all things.

    In this way, culture itself is resurrected, although this
time not as the result of sublimation but as the extensions of
the human (McLuhan), as symbolic of the body from which
we originated. And history too is resurrected, although this
time as no-time: Eternity; reoccurrence; renewal; revolution;

resurrection to pure dance, finding meaning and significance not from its goal but from the act itself. The dance is all.

This is, all of it, difficult stuff to sort out (in its parts) or to grasp (as a whole) since it is essentially a call to a new kind of understanding of life which cannot be known except from within. Let us then take Tillich as known with which we can compare some of Brown's thoughts.

Tillich and Brown

Is Brown aware that, as Tillich would say, all human culture is grounded ontologically in the Ultimate and the Unconditional? Brown does seem to give such a status to Nature, to Primal Unity out of which all things come. But for Brown there is not the ontological break between humans and Nature as there is for Tillich between humanity and God. For Brown, it is rather a psychological phenomenon which can likewise be overcome psychologically. Even so, it seems that what Brown has set up is an ontological distinction, since he admits that consciousness is a radical break with Nature in that humans can never know the unconscious per se but only its conscious manifestations. Even through psychoanalysis, people can, by retracing the process of repression and sublimation, only discover their separation from their source and then take this unconsciousness into account by giving free play to their emotions, dreams, art, and irrationality and accepting and affirming that which these make conscious as part of a person's inner most being. So, it seems that Final Harmony cannot be equivalent to Primal Unity, i.e., humans are only human because and through the Fall.

But still does humanity for Brown have any ultimate concern? Again, he would say that people are not aware of their ultimate concern because it is repressed. But through psychoanalysis, a person can regain this knowledge and can live according to its spirit and word. All of culture rests on this sexual energy, and it can be reached from any part of culture if there is self-consciousness. This self-consciousness seems to be

Brown's correlative to Tillich's concept of faith. For Tillich, a person must simply accept the fact that she is accepted (unconditionally) by God, and in this way, she is justified. For Brown, self-conscious affirmation of one's own animal origin and nature brings everything into proper perspective.

Tillich sees faith as a risk since its object cannot be proven. And for Brown, the unconscious has the same status since it is unknown and unknowable except through the eyes of faith.

Both men see culture as estranged, sick, neurotic as the result of humanity's separation from its ground.

On both parts, this is a profound ontological optimism: as faith in the goodness of being itself. Both men are willing to give their lives over to a reality which the world of culture and history does not recognize. For the world is in darkness and Christ and Freud have come to show us the light.

For both men, Eros, the energizing principle of the universe, has acted decisively in human history and has brought with it both judgment and redemption. From within the human envelope of sickness arose a saving and revolutionary principle: Self-Conscious Eros – the Christ. Eros takes all into itself and there transforms it. For a human, this transformation is that he can become the very incarnation of Eros itself: Love's Body.

Bibliography

Bien, Peter. Spring 1965. "Zorba the Greek, Nietzsche, and the Perennial Greek Predicament." *Antioch Review*, 25: 147-63.

Brown, Norman O. March 1967. "A Reply to Herbert Marcuse." *Commentary*.

_____. 1959. *Life Against Death*. New York.

_____. 1966. *Love's Body*. New York.

Cameron, J.M. May 4, 1967. "Rude Torso." *The New York Times Review of Books*.

Leary, Daniel J. January 1967. "Voices of Convergence." *The Catholic World*.

Marcuse, Herbert. February 1967. "Love Mystified: A Critique of Norman Brown." *Commentary*.

Neale, Robert E. April 17, 1967. "Brown's Body." *Christianity and Crisis.*

Nietzsche, Friedrich. 1911. *The Birth of Tragedy.* New York.

Tillich, Paul. 1966. 1964. *Systemic Theology*, Vol. I, III, Chicago.

_____. 1964. *Theology and Culture.* New York.

Choreographing Social Artistry

(9 December 2004, New York)

This piece is based on my sendout to the participants in the Master of Leadership in Social Artistry session held at the United Nations Headquarters that I had arranged for Dr. Jean Houston.

In times of chaos and terror, of confusion and suffering, many beings are called to awaken and take compassionate action. So, it is today. Evil rises to meet us everywhere. Events are soul-size. The enterprise is Sustainable Human Development.

This is the work of the social artist. With cool abandon, we stand our ground. With cool passion, we take the stage. With cool commitment, we dance as if our life and the lives of all beings depended on it. For indeed they do.

Others will choose to stay asleep. We love them still. Others will choose to deepen the chaos and terror, the confusion and suffering. We love them even so.

In our freedom, we can only choose our own mind and our own action. We are not in charge of the myriad forces of this world and of this universe. We are, however, players, and we have the right, even the necessity of playing our chosen roles. And as such, we can make a difference.

So, we dance on. We choreograph dances with other social artists. We awaken and train other dancers. Sometimes, we vacate the stage entirely to allow the larger dance to happen. But we never give up until our breath is finished.

So, I send you forth to continue your journey of being a social artist. May you dance with joy, with happiness, with abandon, but most of all with wisdom and compassion, remembering always that none are saved until all are saved.

Be it so!

COLLECTION
Self Transformations

In this collection are essays from 1986 to 2021 reflecting on transformations of my doing (mission and vocation), knowing (awareness and identity), and being (and presence).

THEME

Mission and Vocation

These essays concern my perspective on the transformation of my earliest missional and vocational vehicles – the Institute of Cultural Affairs (ICA) and the Order Ecumenical (OE.) ICA Venezuela, to which we were assigned as directors, was undergoing major changes, and the OE and its Caracas house (primary unit) where we were assigned as priors, were being dissolved. Next, there are essays celebrating the 30th anniversary of ICA and reflecting on some of my later and more recent commitments and actions.

Truth, Power, Lifestyle

(28 March 1986, Caracas, Venezuela)

From the original introduction: "This note was written out of an awareness of a deep and longstanding preoccupation of the Latin American continent with political processes – the realities of power in human society. It was also written as an attempt to place the Institute of Cultural Affairs' current concern with a "New Vision of Reality" in a more comprehensive context. This writing is also done in gratitude for the work our colleagues have done in collating and reflecting on writings in the genre of the 'New Vision of Reality.'"

Throughout our long evolutionary journey, humanity has been driven by, among other forces, a desire for truth – a clear, compelling grasp of human existence and our environment that would bring meaning to our ambiguous life, struggle, and death. Classically this has taken the route of either philosophy — the intellectual search for truth, or religion — the mythical and/or experiential search for truth. These two tracks are then expressed in sociological forms through the state, the family, the culture itself, or other institutions such as religious institutions.

Humanity has been and is driven by other forces as well, such as the desire for power, whether economic, political, or cultural — a comforting sense of control and security in the face of the uncertainty of our life, struggle, and death and therefore resulting in a fundamental mistrust of others who might take away our power and our security.

Human history has resulted in many expressions of truth as found in the great religions, minor sects, philosophies, cultures, worldviews (including the scientific), ideologies, etc. that are today coexisting on this planet. In the same way, there are today many concentrations of power on this planet where people have amassed economic, military, political, or cultural power for themselves.

What is now clear to virtually everyone is that the future of human society is endangered by the violent confrontation of these opposing concentrations of power and truth. Usually, we find both concentrations at the same time in a mutually supportive relationship, where a religion, ideology, or culture is supporting a major concentration of power of money, weaponry, or other assets. In the same way, the "power centers" may be supportive of the "truth centers." This is a mighty alliance indeed. The intensification of these two concentrations of power and truth results in an integrated lifestyle of a society, sector, or class which is self-fulfilling and self-justifying by its very nature.

However, due to the fact of multiple truth centers and multiple power centers on a single planet, two results are found: (1) as has been mentioned, conflicts between such centers become inevitable and (2) because there are still huge populations who do not share in this concentration of power or truth, there is inevitable conflict within each society.

Many people today are aware of the necessity of another model for social development than one based on concentration and confrontation. The themes of reconciliation, collaboration, detente, and redistribution of wealth are now commonplace as this "movement" expresses itself with increasing frequency around the planet. However, it is tempting but also naive to believe that it is inevitable that these social concentrations of power and truth are going to release their grasp easily, willingly, or quickly on what they have acquired.

The other two options seem to be in either violent revolution or slow, social evolution that works quietly from the bottom-up so as not to threaten the tops of the pyramids of concentrated power and truth.

The question then is how this can be done in a serious way beyond isolated instances of "doing good for the poor." The answer seems to hover around the concepts of "networking," "self-organizing systems," and "image transformation." Networking is a peaceful alternative to a revolutionary movement. A self-organizing system is an alternative to attacking the concentrations of power at their most fortified points — that is at the top. And image-transformation efforts can be an indirect alternative to attempts at outright conversion.

Where we must be careful is with naiveté – that a "New Vision of Reality" is inevitably sweeping away the concentrations of religious, cultural, and ideological truth which are well entrenched around this planet. Or that a "New Social Vehicle" is inevitably sweeping away the concentrations of economic, military, or political power that are well entrenched. Either belief is a form of "determinism" (not unlike Marxist "economic determinism") and denies human freedom and an open future. This may well be the direction of social evolution on this planet, but if so, it has been so for thousands of years, even millions of years. We need not be caught in the illusion of an imminent eschatology. We do not know the day or the hour. Perhaps another 5,000 years will be required for this process to "work itself into manifest form," perhaps 100 years or perhaps 1,000,000 years.

Our task is not to be prophets of planetary glory or doom. Nor is our task to be the evangelists of the "New Vision of Reality." If we do this, we are pushing one "truth" over against other competing truths, just as everyone else is doing. Our task is to help with the birth of the New Age as a participant. Our task is to keep dialogue alive, to keep social interaction deepening, to keep hope alive, to keep love alive, to keep the focus on the future of society and our planet, to honor the tops of the pyramids, and to work with them on their problems, to help "powerless" people to care for themselves as self-organizing systems and to live fully human lives within a structure of truth that is appropriate for them in their development, and to project more adequate images of humanness into the societal dialogue. Our task is also to create a movement-service-core (an Order) that will continue to help network and link people and organizations of common concern and will by its own lifestyle project an alternative self-organizing system of humanness.

A New Paradigm for the 21st Century must not only embrace an analysis of truth (such as the three types of knowledge of Ken Wilber's analysis.) It must also embrace an analysis of power and an analysis of lifestyles, both entrenched and experimental. Our Order's strategies must be created with a comprehensive analysis not only of nature but of human history.

Reflections on the
New Vision of Reality

(29 March 1986, Caracas, Venezuela)

From the original introduction: "These few notes were written after reading the last two pages of the document of the Foundational Underpinnings of the Order Ecumenical from North America, 20 February 1986. They are written out of a perspective of eighteen years of Order life. They are also written in gratitude for the incredible work of collating and reflecting on hundreds of 'New Age' books which our colleagues have done over the past one-and-one-half years. These remarks are intended to be constructive."

1. The "New Vision of Reality" (NVR) is not new to humanity. There are strands of the NVR that can be traced back 2,000 – 5,000 years in human history, especially in India, China, and Africa.
2. The NVR is not new to our Order. Our thirty-two-year history is a journey to clarify and articulate "The Way Life Is" or the "Truth About Life." Cultural Studies 1 (CS-1) and Religious Studies 1 (RS-1) are pioneering efforts in this regard.
3. A steel door has not dropped down over our past (as we are asked to imagine in the Foundational Underpinning's

document, final page). Or if it has, we would be psychotic; we would not know that we are the body we are; we would not know why we ever came together as this unique body; we would be a-historical; we would not be on a journey "from-to."

4. In a moment of transformation, great care must be taken that amnesia does not set in, that we forget who we have been called to be.

5. In a moment of transformation great care must be taken that searching for another spiritual guru to lead us out of the darkness does not short-circuit our authentic struggle to be who we are becoming as the unique historical body we are.

6. If a steel door has dropped over our past, why should we bother to quote from CS-1 "that our roots are in the future." Is this a justification based on a selective use of a past that has been judged irrelevant?

7. Foundational Underpinnings have to do with past-present-future: a journey. Not just the present or not just with future. Such efforts result in superficial, truncated seeing of reality.

8. We must be careful that "non-verbal, sensual, non-rational" methods are not moving us forward into the Transpersonal realm but back into the archaic, sub-human dimensions of our evolution as a species.

9. As Ken Wilber points out (and as F. Powell has pointed out) most of human society on this planet is in grave need of rationality and development of the ego-self. Small parts of very few societies are ready for the journey into the Transpersonal. This is a helpful analysis for our Order's creation of societal strategies.

10. We must acknowledge that much of the NVR is a new worldview formulated by and for Americans. Marilyn Ferguson says that California is the promised land for the planet.

11. We must analyze each society we are working in in terms of the economic, political, cultural, and spiritual patterns before we create a global campaign of worldview transformation.

12. Making a skit or drawing a picture is not a superior mode of response to an intellectual study or a reflective, rational, verbal response.

13. We will find the NVR not only from reading two hundred books and meeting with twenty new gurus, but also from analyzing our own personal experience (past and present), analyzing the societies we find ourselves part of, and analyzing human history in its complexity, not just the history of ideas, as important as this is.

14. Metamorphosis assumes that there are interior, latent structures that are becoming manifest. Being beings of consciousness requires us to be conscious of our interior structures as an Order that were enfolded in our past and are now being unfolded. Otherwise, we may be doing massive surgery rather than metamorphosizing.

15. The NVR will not only emerge through wild experimentation but through careful study, analysis of our societal settings, and reflection on our own personal learnings as self-conscious beings.

16. There is an unfounded belief that that which is new is superior to that which is old. This is certainly not the case and is a dangerous (and very American) frame of reference.

17. Transformation is happening all around us at every moment. How do we reflect on this very real transformation in society and nature?

18. Transformation is happening to each one of us at every moment. How do we reflect on this very real transformation and not just engage in stimulation?

19. Where is compassion for the other in the NVR? How do we not fall into psychologistic, self-analysis, and self-realization when the world is crying out for help?

20. Consciousness is a phenomenon of KNOWING and is not synonymous with the BEING MODE. We must clarify how we use words such as SPIRIT, SELF, SOUL, CONSCIOUSNESS, BEING. Wilber has clarified nine uses

of the word RELIGION. Each of these words may have as many uses.

21. We must not cloud the realities of volition (will), covenant, discipline, or free-obedience-responsibility as we have a love affair with the dynamics of consciousness.

22. We must not let our excitement with holistic thinking dull our analytical powers. Even if all is one, there is still diversity (the Many) that constitutes that One. We must continue to clarify the one reality of the "OE/ICA-Movement" while at the same time we clarify the unique reality of each dynamic. The margins may be getting leakier, but they are also getting clearer.

23. A Time of Transformation is a time of great possibility and a time of great danger. Let us be prudent while being wildly open and creative.

24. We must acknowledge that each society we are part of is at a different place on a different journey just as each member of our Order is at a different place on a different journey. This makes having one, neat NVR a bit more complex and subtle.

25. Let us remember that the NVR for 1986 will be overwhelmed by the NVR for 2586 just as the NVR of 1986 has overwhelmed the NVR for 1686. We human beings are always having NVR's. But what of faith, hope, and love? These are forever.

26. Let us not turn our NVR into simply one more "worldview" in competition with all the other myriad worldviews, religions, etc. in the marketplace or the cafeteria.

27. Let us remember that once we are transformed either as an Order or as an individual that we will still have our life, struggle, and death on our hands. And that the Creative Mind or God or Whatever will not love us any more than we are loved now.

Conclusion

Please do not take any of the above too seriously.

A Witness: Commemorating the Death of the Caracas Primary Unit of the Order Ecumenical

(30 July 1988, Caracas, Venezuela)

As I recall, this was my witness at our final house church. Lyn Mathews Edwards and I were the hosts. I called us to grieve our losses but also to celebrate our new challenges and possibilities of service.

We need to call the panchayat and tell them that there are now seventeen primary units of the Order Ecumenical, that the Caracas primary unit (P.U.) has died. But I think that they may already intuit it. They made a global announcement of the going-out-of-being of our local structures: no more stipends, no more corporate living requirement, no more priory, no more spirit life for the house, indeed no more house.

And the poet D.H. Lawrence said it this way:

"At last came death, sufficiency of death,
and that at last relieved me, I died.
I buried my beloved, it was good, I buried myself and was gone.
And I am dead, and trodden to nought in the smoke-sodden
    tomb;
Dead and trodden to nought in the sour black earth

Of the tomb; dead and trodden to nought, trodden to nought.

"God but it is good to have died and been trodden out,
trodden to nought in sour, dead earth,
quite to nought,
absolutely to nothing,
nothing,
nothing,
nothing.

"For when it is quite, quite nothing, then it is everything.
When I am trodden quite out, quite, quite out,
every vestige gone, then I am here
risen, and setting my foot on another world
risen, accomplishing a resurrection
risen, not born again, but risen, body the same as before,
new beyond knowledge of newness, alive beyond life,
proud beyond inkling or furthest conception of pride,
living where life was never yet dreamed of, nor hinted at,
here, in the other world, still terrestrial
myself, the same as before, yet unaccountably new."

And Oliver Wendell Holmes said it this way in his poem "The Chambered Nautilus:"

"Build thee more stately mansions, O my soul,
As the swift seasons roll!
Leave thy low-vaulted past!
Let each new temple, nobler than the last,
Shut thee from heaven with a dome more vast,
Till thou at length art free,
Leaving thine outgrown shell by life's unresting sea!"

And the New Testament speaks of death and resurrection; the song "The Lord of the Dance" sings of being cut down and springing up. The truth of life is still that to die is to live, to let go is to receive.

I remember twenty-three years ago, sitting in a Chapel basement in the Black ghetto of Chicago's westside, when I was quite unexpectedly struck by Grace. When I returned to my university in Oklahoma, I felt that I was levitating across campus for weeks. Again, as Lawrence said it:

"Ha, I was a blaze leaping up!
I was a tiger bursting into sunlight.
I was greedy, I was mad for the unknown,
I, new risen, resurrected, starved from the tomb,
starved from a life of devouring always myself,
now here was I, new-awakened, with my hand stretching out
and touching the unknown, the real unknown,
the unknown-unknown."

I was on fire with Acceptance. I was electrified with possibility. I had been captured by The Spirit that over the deep world broods.

There are millions of human beings across this planet who have also been graced, who have been touched by the Beloved of the Soul, who are in love with the Earth, and who are driven to manifest this being, this consciousness in their daily work and service and in their style of living.

This is the planetary network of awakened, compassionate souls who long for a profound transformation of the human psyche, society, and our planetary home.

These people are villagers like Domingo Rodriguez of Caño Negro, political scientists like Jose Antonio Gil, educators like Beatriz de Capdevielle, business leaders like Gustavo Roosen, religious leaders like Bishop Pio Bello, people in service clubs like Jamil Dunia, people in government bureaucracies like Mercedes Pulido, consultants in professional service organizations like Tony Beltran.

They are also people like Jean Houston, Willis Harman, and Robin Van Doren, Kang Byong Hoon, Bob Vance, and Frank Hilliard, Bill Edwards, Anne Yallop and Cyprian D'Souza, Peter Fry, Joyce Williams, and Linda Todd.

The Earth Herself has given birth to this "noosphere," this envelope of spirit-consciousness. This network, as it were, is a cosmic event, a divine intervention in the life of the universe.

The challenge now before us is HOW to give form to this diverse network of people. Or better yet, how to give a clear, compelling missional focus, a CENTRAL PROJECT, that will channel these incredible energies into a transformative force on the planet.

And the planet is ready and yearning; she is already transforming. Everything is swirling and changing.

The Soviet Union has issued Visa credit cards and Gorbachev is calling for free elections of a new people's congress. China is now more concerned with marketing than Marxism. Japan is now the number one financial power in the world. The U.S. is almost ready to elect such socialist groups as the ICA. The "New Age" is so commonplace that a globally circulated comic strip regularly pokes fun at its funnier side. A French Archbishop has defied the Pope. South Africa allowed "Cry Freedom" in the theaters, then later the police pulled it out, but it had gotten in! Venezuelans are demanding direct elections of representatives at the state and municipal levels. There is increasing awareness of the global crisis of the ozone layer and the destruction of the tropical rain forests. And on and on.

The planetary network or the spirit movement is growing and will continue to grow. I call each one of us to play our appropriate part.

And what of the Order Ecumenical. Those few of us who have been so blessed and privileged to have been part of this great experiment these fifteen to thirty-five years, each one of us must decide where and how to put our light, our energy, our talent, our life and death into the fray. We are being sent out like a shower of stars into the night sky to light the way, to coalesce, to converge with other historical and evolutionary forces. Some of us will be part of an ICA somewhere; some of us will be part of a Center of Human Development somewhere; some of us will be part of educational ventures; others will help develop their villages; others will be part of groups dealing with peace and ecology; others will be part of groups concerned with women and spirituality; yet others will be part of business or government.

But wherever we go and whatever we do, we have been marked for excellence – excellent service for our planet, and our fellow person.

We will miss the old structures. We will grieve. We will doubt if we can go on. But we can always remember and reminisce. We can always visualize and relive our past and continue to cherish it and enjoy it and learn from it. We will now rediscover once again, our relationship to ourselves, others, and the Ground-of-Being. We may be resurrected once again from the death-shroud that pre-history and history have thrown over all human institutions over the past two million years. And most important, our Spirit, no not our Spirit, the HOLY SPIRIT – or the Spirit of Wholeness and Unity – will be reincarnated in new flesh, in new sociological form, but this time a million-fold more powerful than our tiny band of 500.

"Build thee more stately mansions, O my soul,
As the swift seasons roll!
Leave thy low-vaulted past!
Let each new temple, nobler than the last,
Shut thee from heaven with a dome more vast,
Till thou at length art free,
Leaving thine outgrown shell by life's unresting sea!"

The Vigil

(30 July 1988, Caracas, Venezuela)

This was written when the Order Ecumenical (OE), the staff association of the ICA, was being taken out of being. I wrote this during a twenty-four hour fast commemorating the death of the OE and the Caracas House. In it, I briefly reflected in honesty and gratitude on my past twenty-four years. Happily, in 2021, I am still part of the OE/EI/ICA network of colleagues, with most of us in our seventies and eighties. Gratitude.

I saw a doorway in the black-draped Order cross, a doorway into the future. But for now, what is the grief? Where is the sense of loss, the disorientation, the pain, the loneliness, the sobbing? What, who is dead?

It is part of me, for it is my relationships, and I am constituted by my relationships and my relationship to my relationships. Therefore, part of me has died: my self-righteousness, my martyrdom is over. The Earth will go on for another million, another billion years. What I give is my own gift not a sign of my being chosen. Bonhoeffer was right after all: the twilight of history (and evolution, I would add) obscures our seeing our own action as either right or wrong, either good or bad, either just or unjust. We can but do the deed and render it up to history.

My identity as a prior is gone; my identity as a monk in a monastery is gone; the poverty of my monk cell is gone; the obedience of my global assignment is gone; the chastity of adhering to a global strategy is gone; my humility of receiving my equal and inadequate stipend is gone; my relationship to a global panchayat is gone; my relationship to global commissions is gone; my relationship to a global budget is gone; my waiting for someone else's child to get out of the bathroom is gone; my having to listen to people at 10 pm in my bedroom is gone; my having to play moral-policeman is gone; my status as 1st-Among-Equals is gone.

And more: no more fantastic global campaigns like the Local Church Experiment (LCX), the Primal Community Experiment (PCE), "Golding the Counties" with town meetings, the International Exposition of Rural Development (IERD.) Can this be true? Or, will there actually be more of these, with more groups, where we play different roles? What is our role now? If not the messiahs, then what? If not the ones with the true spirit and true method, then who?

WHO ARE WE? WHO AM I?
WHAT DO WE? WHAT DO I?
HOW BE WE? HOW BE I?

These are the questions of thirty years ago, but now new, newly pointed, and relevant.

But I really do feel freer already. It is not that I do not grieve. I, we have been grieving for ten years – since Joe Mathews died. He was our charismatic leader. We never did recover, and we did not want another charismatic leader. So, we kept going. And, we did some fantastic things over these ten years. But now, we must once again change, transform, resurrect, re-incarnate, develop, evolve.

There was security and self esteem attached to our old poverty, obedience, and chastity. I felt my life was charmed, that I was protected by an invisible shield against all harm, that my plane would not crash, that I was called, and needed by the planet.

But wait, I still feel called and needed, so what is the difference? The difference is now I must make my own way. I must decide to master Spanish. It is not enough to be assigned to Venezuela by the global order. Now, I must assign myself, and I must change, grow, develop, evolve, transform. And this is painful and full of uncertainty. This is the pain of the death. It is the pain of living my own life and dying my own death.

And, what of corporateness, what of community? I do not really know. It too must evolve, emerge anew, out of new relationships, new encounters, new struggles, new covenants locally and globally, new opportunities for service, new adventures, new projects.

Oh yes, I remember the last twenty-four years:

1964: a university student struggling with his identity, his calling, his motivation, his future, his relationship to his family.

1965: the year of being struck by grace, of experiencing acceptance, and accepting my acceptance, of encountering impressive adult models, of encountering high intentionality and intellectual clarity.

1966: encountering comprehensive, rational models – the life triangles, and effective methods – intellectual, social, and spiritual; also encountering master pedagogues, and a movement of people concerned with social change; graduating from university and going off to Indiana to graduate school in English literature.

1967: not being happy studying English and transferring to Chicago Theological Seminary (CTS) to be near the Ecumenical Institute (EI) and to study theology, but not to become a minister; meeting my future wife, Mary Elizabeth Avery.

1968: not really enjoying seminary classes filled with abstractionism and sensitivity-training; becoming a university-sojourner with EI and moving to the westside; Mary moved first; I worked in the print shop, attended evening studies of Kazantzakis, early morning lectures and worked on the new religious mode charts, taught the Academy, did not enjoy pedagogy classes; became an intern and married Mary.

1969: had a thyroid operation; moved to the editorial office, worked on the Institute's publications – IMAGE, the 5th City Voice, I.E., etc.; studied the *Warriors of God* by Walter Nigg and St. Teresa's *Interior Castle*.

1970: the year of the Global Odyssey – around the world in thirty days, delighted with Japan, blasted and shocked by India; received a call from Joseph while he was in Singapore asking us to go to Malaysia; we said yes and dropped our plans to return to CTS and move to the north-shore house; after a three month wait, we arrived in Kuala Lumpur and began the work of the movement; Joseph had said, "build iron men", but we didn't have any idea how to go about it; we communicated with our colleagues in Singapore and Jakarta; we visited International Training Institute (ITI) grads and taught Religious Studies 1 courses (RS-1's); Mary taught at an international school; we had many students in our beautiful house in Petaling Jaya; we could not have a baby and sought medical advice but nothing worked.

1971: We continued teaching RS-1's, visited Thailand and Indonesia to recruit an ITI and set up RS-1s; I went to Manila and taught and managed an ITI; got a call from Chicago to return to the USA; we stopped in Taiwan on our way and got another call to go to Kobe, Japan, and await further instructions; there we taught English and received an assignment to Korea.

1972: We began our work in the ''Land of Morning Calm'' by getting very ill on yontan gas poisoning; we lived in a little house near Rev. Kang Byoung Hoon, the EI director; we taught many Parish Leadership Colloquies (PLCs) and RS1s; I went to

Hong Kong to setup and teach an advanced ITI; and I went to Tokyo to an Area Tokyo meeting.

1973: We moved into a large, beautiful religious house with a garden and fountain, still in the neighborhood near Rev. Kang; we continued to do many PLCs and RS-ls; we also taught Leadership Effectiveness and New Strategies (LENS); more Koreans joined the House; I helped setup and teach an ITI in Seoul.

1974: We continued to do many PLCs and RS-1s, also Women's Forums, and LENS.

1975: We asked Rev. Kang and Joe Mathews for their permission and blessing to adopt a baby; they said yes, and we adopted two-year old Benjamin; Mary also got pregnant with Christopher; after Christopher was born, I was in great stress and was assigned for a short while to Japan to help teach a Global Language School (GLS) in Sendai; I enjoyed this very much; when I returned to Korea, I helped do another GLS there; we continued doing many PLCs and RS-1s; we started the Primal Community Experiment in Nok bun dong in Seoul; our house-life was very meaningful.

1976: This year, we returned to the states because Mary needed an operation on her eye lid for cancer; we took our two sons with us and also attended the Institute's global research assembly in which we created the three global campaigns and launched the social demonstrations and the town meetings; I returned to Korea and went directly to Jeju Island with Rev. Kim to set up and teach an ITI which was to help launch the first Human Development Project (HDP) in Korea; during the HDP consult, held in a 5-star hotel, we thought that the project would deal with the entire island province of Jeju; but Joseph Mathews (JWM) said we needed to find a pilot village so we found

Kwang-yung- Il - ri; I moved my family into this village of mud, rock, and thatched roof houses; it was a great cultural shock.

1977: The project went along; it was fascinating and very difficult; I was on the agricultural guild; the village was perched on the side of volcanic Mt. Halla, and overlooked fields of bright yellow flowers leading down to the sea coast of black volcanic rocks and white-foaming waves; we got a USAID grant; we were reassigned back to Seoul, and Mary and I were for the first time designated as the House priors with Rev. Kang Byoung Hoon as the Area Tokyo prior; I broke open the fund raising effort with several large donations from oil companies and manufacturing companies; we held more LENS and forums; we setup and held the World's Fair of 24 Human Development Projects after much soul searching about whether we really could do such a thing; JWM died, and Mary and I flew back to Chicago with Rev. Kang and Rev. Park to attend his funeral. Kang deeply missed Joseph.

1978: We conducted an ITI in Kang-won-do to prepare for a new project in the north, near the demilitarized zone; we held a consult and launched the Koh du I ri HDP north of Seoul; the Works and the Parks moved to the village; that summer the Works decided that it was time to leave Korea for a new assignment; we felt that if we stayed longer we would never leave because we loved Korea very much and enjoyed working with Rev. Kang; but we decided that we were part of a global order and that we must move on; that same summer we attended the global research assembly and council in Chicago; Kang did not come; new staff went into Korea; our perception was that things were difficult for everyone; that fall, we were assigned to Salt Lake City and traveled to San Francisco, and Salt Lake City, finally settling for a short time in Denver.

1979: We were re-assigned to Dallas and lived in a big two-story house that our colleagues had purchased; we had a great group of colleagues and had fine house churches and round tables; I traveled around the region doing "saturation maneuvers" with many forums.

1980: We were re-assigned within the Dallas-Oklahoma City region to the Indiahoma HDP in southwestern Oklahoma, my home state; I enjoyed working there after being in Asia for almost eight years; I was the project director of our local VISTA project; we did an evaluation and published a report on the project and held an exciting Fair of Hometowns, to which both sets of our parents attended; the town built a water tower and applied for a national environmental improvement grant.

1981: We got a call in February that we were needed in Jamaica within two weeks to be the Caribbean Area Priors, lead the Woburn Lawn HDP, conduct a national symposium, and "do the Caribbean;" with much effort we uprooted our family and moved to Jamaica, living in the village of Woburn Lawn in the Blue Mountains; the Jamaican Potential symposium was a great success; we managed an Interamerican Development Bank (IDB) loan and grant of US110,000 for the Woburn Lawn cooperative; we facilitated the first three LENS seminars in Jamaica, applied for Rotary and Canadian International Development Agency (CIDA) grants, and I went to Curacao to attend the Caribbean Conference of Churches convention.

1982: We launched the Blue Mountain Cluster with a CIDA grant of US50,000, conducted one more LENS, made a LENS marketing trip to Trinidad, visited Barbados, conducted many forums and mini-consults, and enlarged our staff; I also registered ICA Jamaica as a Jamaican organization with a multi-sectoral board of directors.

1983: We launched the Human Development Training Schools with the Rotary 3H grant of US$240,000 and held a national

Rural Development Symposium as part of the IERD process; Mary and I moved to Kingston and established the first urban ICA house in Jamaica; we also launched other clusters in the eastern end of the island.

1984: I took a delegation of fifteen to New Delhi for the International Exposition on Rural Development (IERD) including the Jamaican Cabinet Minister of Youth and Community Development; we raised US$60,000 for our delegation including $20,000 from USAID and a grant from the Canadian Embassy; we continued the Rotary funded HD training schools; I took a team around the island visiting potential sites for consultancies, such as on the Appleton Estates; that summer we left a confident team of young Jamaicans in charge and participated in a "council of a life time" in Chicago with a strong Jamaican delegation; we were reassigned to Caracas because the directors had left and the Order was concerned about our oldest location in Latin America; another family was assigned to Kingston but had a difficult time and left the next year; when we moved to Caracas everyone was living in Caño Negro in Barlovento except Fr. Bob Rank who was living in Fr. Marcel's community center in Las Minas in Caracas; we rented two apartments and moved most of our staff to Las Minas; I went on the first consultancy trek to Zona Zuata for Maraven oil company with Antonio Beltran and Jacobo Pacheco; I became excited with learning Spanish and reading *Cosmos*.

1985: We continued the treks to Zona Zuata and applied for a Rotary 3H grant with Jamil Dunia, a well known Rotarian; we got an additional contract with Maraven to work in Zona Zuata; I went to Rio de Janeiro and met with the Rio House which was part of the Caracas Primary Unit; then Kit Kraus and Bill and Nan Grow came to Caracas for a Primary Unit council; I went to Brussels to the global check signals meeting where we discerned the "doorways and the crunch"; we experienced our own local crunch as Rio had little money and Caracas had few trained Latino staff; in our planning, we used the four global communities or networks as our primary screen.

1986: We got an additional Maraven contract and also a Corpoven oil company contract to work in Guasdualito; we struggled to get the Rotary project launched; we moved all of our staff to one large house in San Bernardino and hosted a global think tank; Mary and I attended the ICA's Planetary Vision Quest in Chicago in which we encountered Jean Houston for the first time; we had a sizeable delegation at the global council in Bilbao, Spain; we were all shocked and saddened with the death of Rotarian Paul Bosch; we got an in kind office in Altamira in Caracas through Paul's help; we got a contract with Sismoven oil company to work in El Nula; we began to talk about marketing, research, and strengthening our finances; we launched an advisers' luncheon and began to create new statutes and a strong Board of Directors for ICA Venezuela. Tony Beltran and I went to the Continental Council in Aspitia, Peru. Money became very tight. We invited Jean Houston to Caracas to conduct a seminar. We had a Primary Unit meeting with both Kingston and Rio representatives in Caracas.

1987: This was an incredible year; it began with no money and the Rotary project on the rocks; our landlord got a court order instructing us to move out; we had two fantastic seminars with Jean Houston; Jean greatly affirmed and challenged us; we located and bought the Quinta Los Bosquecillos property with two mortgages leveraged by our Board President Alejandro Lara; we moved into the building the day after Jean left; the building was in bad shape and we began renovation; while Jean was in Caracas, we got official word that the Rotary grant was cancelled; we began to intensify our program marketing; we sold a seminar series to Colgate-Palmolive; I decided not to go to the Brussels check signals meeting in order to stay and lead the team in conducting the Colgate Palmolive seminars; this was a real learning experience; we discovered that our team was not perceived as adequate although the seminars went relatively well; we spent much time and money renovating the Center of Human Promotion; we began to do seminars with the ICA team in Kingston for Citibank in Jamaica, Miami, Colombia, and Trinidad; we hosted Willis Harman and Robin Van Doren in our house while they were here conducting public seminars with us; we greatly enjoyed their colleagueship; we invited the Long Term Investment Team to Caracas to work with us in a Whole Systems Transformation experiment; we had another Corpoven and Sismoven contract during the year; we also did seminars with VenAmCham, Fundacion Senior, AVAA; we did a series of modules for Colegio Internacional de Caracas for Bs110.000 to pay for our son Benjamin and Teresa Jones's education; the Board met monthly, and we kept a book of minutes for all meetings; at the beginning of the year the Board had approved the new statutes; this year I was particularly excited about my experience in private sector seminars and my conversations with Jean Houston.

1988: We began the year with a Retreat in January in which we focused on individual initiatives and income generation; we then received the global panchayat on a trek in which we objectified our shared values; I went to Mexico early in the year to help plan the ICA global conference in November; this is where I first heard a colleague say that "the Order is dead"; this sent me into despair; in April we held an "Advance" (not a Retreat) to launch the Whole System Transformation experiment, and we identified three pathways of transformation; this event greatly motivated me as did the business game which formed the ICA Associates proforma for the next two years; my self-image began to change; I saw myself as a private sector consultant; I bought new clothes; we began to improve the image of our office with new plants and equipment; I was excited to help conduct the Household Mortgage program in Chicago, visit my parents, and attend the Latin American check signals meeting in Oaxtepec, Mexico; I was also excited to go to Trinidad to do a design conference with Amar Holdings and to Curacao to do a seminar with ALICO; I am now selling the Cultural Research Project and working on selling to Citibank; I will be challenged to conduct the seminar in Tampa in August with Household; the creation of the third pathway of transformation is once again changing my self-perception, style, and action; we have now created ICA Associates, ICA Development, and ICA Network; I am beginning to sense the responsibility of being the Executive-Director (rather than prior); My family and I are moving to an apartment, and I will be earning a professional salary beginning in August; John Lawton, ICA Venezuela Vice President, and I are interviewing our staff for jobs with ICA Venezuela; we are launching new programs for the Center of Human Promotion; residency is no longer a requirement for being in the ICA, or the Planetary Spirit network; tonight I am reliving the past twenty-four years; tomorrow, I celebrate my forty-fourth birthday after a twenty-four hour fast commemorating the death of the Order and the birth of the planetary spirit network; what a full life I have lived. Gratitude.

Practicing the Fine Arts of Culturally Based Transformation: A Vision for the Instituto de Asuntos Culturales de Venezuela

(1989, Caracas, Venezuela)

This essay is based on a brochure I created for a reformulated ICA Venezuela following a whole system transformation process in which the Caracas House was dissolved.

The vision of the new ICA Venezuela is to be a catalytic force of individual and collective transformation.

Our mission is to release the human spirit within organizations, communities, networks, and individuals through actionresearch, leadership training, participatory planning, and catalytic implementation.

In our philosophy of change, we believe that human culture is the ground of development. To develop any corporate structure or person their *unique culture* must be honored, understood, and transformed. We believe that people can become aware of the very dynamics of transformation and thereby co-create change toward greater productivity and quality.

By becoming conscious of their values and assumptions, people can begin to manage change through their own myths, rites, and symbols. The fundamental assumption in this approach to managing change is that consciousness affects action – that consciously held perceptions result in concrete action, and that to change a person's perception is to begin to change the form and activity of an individual or collective structure.

We believe that the macro-context for social transformation is the Earth as an ecosystem. The micro context is the individual human being as a mind-body-spirit system. Communities, organizations, and networks are the middle level, structural contexts for transformation.

ICA Venezuela's programs of the fine arts of culturally based development include:

Action Research: Through depth interviews, we analyze trends, values, assumptions, dilemmas, and successful approaches of managing change.

Leadership Training: Through imaginal seminars, we stimulate learning about personal growth and development, inclusive thinking patterns, depth reflection, and the personality and style of leadership.

Participatory Planning: Through interactive workshops, we facilitate the creation of organizational philosophy, strategies, problem-solving, and systems of change.

Catalytic Implementation: Through onsite interventions, we enable taskforce creation, project design, self-organizing systems, and self-evaluation.

We are structured as a not-for-profit, civil association, registered in Venezuela since 1978. Our human resources include 11 directors, 25 advisers, 12 staff, and many volunteers. Our consultants have work experience in over thirty nations around the world and operate in three divisions out of offices in Altamira in Caracas with residential training centers in La Florida in Caracas and in the village of Caño Negro in Barlovento. Our income comes both from professional honoraria and donations.

ICA Venezuela is an autonomous member of ICA International, a world-wide federation of 35 national institutes with its coordinating center in Brussels, Belgium. ICA International has consultative status with the Economic and Social Council of the United Nations as well as with UNICEF, UNDP, FAO, WHO, and is a member of the International Council of Social Welfare.

Three Angels: A Planetary Spirit Association

(1989, Caracas, Venezuela)

This essay provides a vision for a Planetary Spirit Association (PSA) following the dissolution of the Caracas Primary Unit. It is included here to spark ideas and creativity.

"SONG OF A MAN WHO HAS COME THROUGH" (D. H. Lawrence)

Not I, not I, but the wind that blows through me!
A fine wind is blowing the new direction of Time.
If only I let it bear me, carry me, if only it carry me!
If only I am sensitive, subtle, oh, delicate, a winged gift!
If only, most lovely of all, I yield myself and am borrowed
By the fine, fine wind that takes its course through the chaos
    of the world
Like a fine, an exquisite chisel, a wedge-blade inserted;
If only I am keen and hard like the sheer tip of a wedge
Driven by invisible blows,
The rock will split, we shall come at the wonder, we shall find
    the Hesperides.

Oh, for the wonder that bubbles into my soul,
I would be a good fountain, a good well-head,
Would blur no whisper, spoil no expression.

What is the knocking?
What is the knocking at the door in the night?
It is somebody wants to do us harm.

No, no, it is the three strange angels.
Admit them, admit them.

Context

In the global council in Bilbao, Spain, in 1986, we sent ourselves out under the Three "Rs" of Residue, Resources, and
Research. Prior to and during the council, we had discussed
the possible forms for these three dynamics as a Business to
market our residue, a Foundation to amplify our resources,
and a Think-tank through which to conduct the socio-spirit
research needed. This model for the Caracas Primary Unit is
based on these "three angels."

Mission of the Planetary Spirit Association (PSA):

The mission of the PSA is human development in its most
profound and inclusive sense, both societal and personal,
both spiritual and practical. This mission is to be a "network
of transformation" of awakened, compassionate individuals
around the planet.

Study and Symbolic Life of the PSA:

Members of the PSA will gather for a Planetary Roundtable
luncheon each Wednesday from 12 to 3 pm. Each roundtable
meeting will have three dynamics: spiritual activity, intellectual study, and a practical workshop. The spirit dimension will
take various forms such as reflective conversations, psycho-
physical exercises, meditation, visualizations, rituals, etc. Each
member of the PSA will be presented a blue Earth-pin and a

silver ring as symbols of participation in the planetary circle of human development. The studies will consist of a variety of speakers, book studies, seminars, reports on personal projects (each member will have one project), etc. (*Global Mind Change* by Willis Harman is one book which will be studied.) The practical workshops will be focused on topics of vital interest to the members such as social change, new modes of learning, organizational development, community development, social research, etc. The Planetary Roundtable is the Think Tank dynamic of the PSA. Initially these luncheons will be held at a hotel, such as the Tamanaco. Later, after much renovation, they will be held at the ICA Center in La Florida.

Economic Life of the PSA:
The partners of the business will be salaried (initially at US$1,000/month each). The business will have a pension and health plan for all partners. Professional training will be covered by the business, but individual education for adults and children will be covered out of salary.

The "In-Service Trainees" of the foundation will receive a stipend from funds raised and from fees of programs at the ICA Center in La Florida.

The members of the Planetary Roundtable will each pay a membership fee as well as cover the cost of each weekly lunch. They will select a treasurer to coordinate their finances. There will be a sliding scale of membership fees to allow anyone to become a member.

Time Discipline:
The business partners work at least a forty-hour week. They also attend the weekly roundtables.

The "In-Service Trainees" also work a forty-hour week and attend the weekly roundtables.

The other members of the PSA attend the weekly roundtables and volunteer to participate in various committees, taskforces, program marketing, and delivery teams.

The ICA Center in La Florida and Residency:
The salaried business partners will live in their own apartments in Caracas near to the La Florida Center. The in-service trainees will live in the La Florida Center to coordinate and conduct the residential training programs there (for international volunteers and youth, etc.) The function of the La Florida Center is to act as a symbolic node for the PSA and to provide space for various programs of research, personal development, training, roundtable, cultural activities, etc. In this way, the La Florida Center will generate income from program fees, roundtable fees, and the 10% royalty paid to the ICA Venezuela by ICA Associates. This center will be completely renovated to achieve first class conditions. Other members of the PSA will live in their own housing.

Organizational Structure of the PSA:
ICA Venezuela will be guided by a strong representative Board of Directors. ICA Venezuela will have three divisions of the one legal entity. These are:

The Business: This is a group of partners who will market and deliver our 35 years of creative "residue" in organizational development and new modes of learning, primarily to the private sector. This is currently called ICA Associates. To be a partner of this business a person must have at least a high school degree and at least four years experience with the ICA.

The Foundation: This is a group of "in-service trainees" who will do fund raising for human development projects, coordinate the educational programs of the ICA Center in La Florida, and do field work in the community development projects or programs which are funded. The aim of the foundation is to accumulate massive financial "resources" both for ICA projects and for non-ICA projects.

The Think Tank: This is the group of all members of the PSA who have paid their fee and attend the weekly Planetary Roundtable luncheon-meetings. This group of colleagues will select a president and have membership in various committees which will ensure that the Roundtables are prepared for, conducted, and followed-up in an excellent manner.

Global Relations:

ICA Venezuela will sell, distribute, translate, and write articles for the new global ICA magazine published in Toronto, Canada. ICA Venezuela will send representatives to global meetings of ICA International, from ICA Business, ICA Foundation and ICA Think-Tanks. ICA Venezuela will also help establish other national ICAs in Curacao, and in Trinidad as well as assisting ICA Jamaica. ICA Venezuela will publish a newsletter with national and international distribution. ICA Venezuela will also participate in continental ICA meetings and activities.

Transformational Seminar Designs

(1989, New York, Caracas, Venezuela)

After we took the Caracas Primary Unit out of being, we rede-
signed ICA Venezuela, and empowered the local staff and board.
Before my family and I moved to New York City, I began thinking
about transformational seminars. What follows are my reflec-
tions and the design of a seminar. These might spark design
ideas for a reader. This reflection led me to create in New York
and facilitate in Caracas a seminar in 1991, "Orchestrating
Organizational Energy in a Whole System Transition of Self,
People, and Planet" found in this book at the beginning of the
Whole Systems Change theme of the Societal Transformations
collection.

What is my contribution, my product?

My contributions and products include reflection-in-action, seeing and articulating the interrelationships of the whole, transforming perception from reductionistic to systemic holism,
creating alternatives, linking and honoring people, binding
together that which has become separate, and clarifying the
meaning of trends.

What is my field?

My field is systemic epistemology – knowing within a system of knowing beyond the consumption-production system toward the Learning Society and the transformation of consciousness resulting in socio-economic-cultural development.

My question for Venezuela:

My question for Venezuela is how can Venezuelans create a "culture of learning" for their nation as a model of development for the world?

What did I say in New York at the Whole Systems Transition Think Tank?

I said that transformation is taking place at the personal level, the social level, and the planetary level. At the personal level, we are dealing with a matrix of body-mind-spirit (Ken Wilber). At the social level, we are dealing with an economic-political-social-cultural matrix. And at the planetary level, we are dealing with a matrix of the physical environment, the Global Brain (Peter Russell) and the Gaian Mythos.

I talked about the three major global cultural dynamics of the West, the East, and the South. In the West, there is a cultural source-image (UR) of rationality and dualistic consciousness. In the East, the cultural source-image (UR) is that of intuition and unity consciousness. And in the South, the cultural source-image (UR) is that of energy and space-time consciousness.

Finally, I spoke about the primacy of consciousness. There is a third metaphysic that posits consciousness preceding matter (Willis Harman). This metaphysic supports our urgent need to transform our external reality through our interior processes (awareness, will, decision, intuition, rationality, value, assumptions, imagery, perception, and cognition.)

Paradigms: toward a meta-paradigm

The authors helping us move toward a meta-paradigm include Ken Wilber – body, mind, and spirit; Pierre Teilhard de

Chardin – cosmogenesis, geogenesis, biogenesis, and noogenesis; Erwin Lazlo – cosmic evolution, life evolution, and social evolution; Jean Houston – dimensions of the sensory, psychological, mythic, and unitive; and Joseph Mathews – dynamics of knowing, doing, and being; and self, world, and mystery. There are also the dimensions of space – micro (sub-atomic), meso/human, and macro (cosmic.) And, there are the dimensions of time – past, present, and future.

What am I intending with a seminar?

In this seminar, I am intending to take people on a journey from observations, to reflections, to interpretations, to decision and action; to raise the two questions of What is humanness? and What is development?; to allow people to see the relations amongst knowing, doing, and being; to allow people to experience that "if they give each other the space to exist that they are bringing forth a world together." (Maturana, Varela); to allow people to see the relationship between assumptions and behavior; to combine theory and practice into one fabric; to provide useful models, screens, and methods; and for the individual to move to the "higher self" or transpersonal level of experience.

Designing a seminar for Venezuela:

What is the depth spirit problem of Venezuela? The depth spirit problems of Venezuela include mistrust of others (*desconfianza*); a centeredness of self and family to the exclusion of the community; the assumption that corruption and taking advantage of others (*aprovechar*) is a way of life; and being trapped in space-time immediacy with little reflection or transcendence; in summary – a reduced context of responsibility in space, time, and relations.

What is the great gift and genius of Venezuelans?

The great gifts of Venezuelans are a high level of energy, a common-sense of social care (socialist) – few homeless, the barrios, distribution of oil-wealth, and human relationships transcend legalities; in summary an energetic, human-centered society.

What are the problems Venezuelans managers face?
Venezuelan managers face low productivity, weak marketing, corruption, unstable socio-economic conditions, over reliance on oil income, expectations of subsidies and protection, and a weak, participative culture.

Therefore, the tension between problem and gift is a reduced context of responsibility in time, space, and relations vs an energetic human-centered society.

Therefore, the strategic question is how to release and channel the energy of Venezuela's human-centered society to a larger field of responsibility for community, organization, nation, continent, and world?

Possible Answer is to make people self-conscious of what is happening, make people aware of their own and other people's life energy, and offer practical channels for its flow through methods and structures.

Brainstorm of Elements for the Seminar:
Elements of the seminar would include a presentation of the ICA Organizational Energy model, a presentation of Mary Work's human energy model, a conversation on energy, a workshop on methods and structure for energy flow, an experience of spiral balancing or energy meditation such as dancing with the tambor of Barlovento (followed by a reflection), teaching techniques of reflection-in-action, a presentation on Contextual Ethics, and workshops on the contextual ethics image of a comprehensive story of the planet, the history (past) of Venezuela, the future of Venezuela, and personal consciousness.

Title of Seminar:
"PRODUCTIVITY   THROUGH   RELEASING   PEOPLE
ENERGY: A VENEZUELAN CHALLENGE"

Seminar Outline: Day One
8am   Opening
8:15   Conversation: Personal experiences of energy
8:45   Presentation: Model of Personal Energy flow
9:45   Study: paper by Donald Schon on "reflection-in-action"
12:00   Lunch
1:30 pm   Conversation: Corporate experiences of energy
2:00   Presentation: Model of Organizational Energy
3:00   Workshop: Methods and structures of energy flow
5:00   Closing

Other Intellectual Products that can be used in the seminar
include "Managing Systems", "Contextual Ethics", "Consciousness
Transformation", "Re-articulating Organizational Philosophy and
Mission", "Creating Flexible, Responsive Strategies", "Educating
Through Images", "Technology of Participation", "Social Change:
Theory and Practice", "How to Conduct a Practical, Profound
Conversation", "Methods of Community Development", "A
Comparative Study of Paradigms and Assumptions", "Transpersonal
Psychology", "Eastern and Western Models of Psychology",
"Approaching the Questions of 'What is humanness?' and 'What
is development?'", "Knowing, Doing, and Being", "Bringing Forth a
World Together", and "The Paradigm of Evolution."

Design of a five-session seminar:

Sessions I, II, III
PERSONAL DEVELOPMENT IN A NEW PARADIGM
CONTEXT

INTENT:

This seminar will present a theoretical framework for personal development within holistic, ecological consciousness. The seminar will utilize state-of-the-art mind-body techniques to allow the participant to experience a new way of perceiving and a new way of being.

APPROACH:

Participants will be exposed to cutting edge theories from the sciences of psychology, biology, chemistry, and physics and the implications for personal awareness will be made explicit. In addition to stimulating talks, the seminar will make use of workshops that ensure the participation of each person with his or her insights and questions being put forward.

BENEFITS:

Each participant will gain a new sense of self as a creative agent within his or her organization and society. This new consciousness may be called "systemic" – for the self is experienced as the very author of the various systems in which one finds oneself as "we bring forth a world together." In this very act of knowing what we know and how we know it, we dispel the "ignorance of knowledge" which is at the root of many of our personal blocks.

WHO SHOULD PARTICIPATE:

This seminar is for Human Resource directors, managers, teachers, and persons in the "helping professions" such as doctors and psychologists. It is also suitable for anyone with a deep concern for self-awareness and personal and social development.

TIMING:

The seminar begins at 8 am and ends at 5 pm. Longer seminars with more content and experiential activities can also be arranged for two or three days with even greater benefits.

Session IV
FUNDAMENTAL TENSIONS WITHIN VENEZUELA
CULTURE AND A STRATEGY FOR MANAGING THEM

INTENT:
This seminar will explore the fundamental tensions which
constitute Venezuelan culture and will co-create with the participants a strategy for managing these tensions creatively. The
seminar will utilize state-of-the-art body-mind techniques to
allow the participant to experience a new way of experiencing
his or her culture.

APPROACH:
Participants will investigate the dynamic relationship between
the depth problems of the culture and their corresponding gifts
to come to appreciate the unique genius of Venezuelan culture
in the context of a global ecology of cultures. Participatory workshops will then involve the participants in designing a strategy for
orchestrating these tensions within one's organization and society.

BENEFITS:
Each participant will gain a radical awareness of the inner work-
ings of Venezuelan culture in a way that releases pride and new
resolve to manage these dynamics toward greater effectiveness
and satisfaction. The participant also can understand where
Venezuelan culture "fits" within the emerging planetary culture.

WHO SHOULD PARTICIPATE:
This seminar is for managers, psychologists, human resource
directors, teachers, doctors, and anyone who has a deep concern for the future of Venezuelan organizations and society.

TIMING:
The seminar begins at 8 am and ends at 5pm. Longer seminars with more content and experiential activities can also be
arranged for two or three days with even greater benefits.

Session V
RELEASING   CREATIVE   ENERGY   FOR   INCREASED
PRODUCTIVITY

INTENT:
This seminar will release and channel the energy of Venezuela's human-centered culture to a larger field of responsibilities for self, family, community, organization, nation, and world.

APPROACH:
Participants will become aware of their own and other people's energy. Various types of energy will be explored – biological, emotional, psychological, archetypal, ontological, and historical. This awareness will then be followed by the discovery of practical channels for the creative flow of this energy through methods and structures.

BENEFITS:
Each participant will gain a deeper and broader consciousness of the high level of energy that propels him or herself, one's organization, and the national culture itself. This consciousness will provide a "pattern of connectivity" which will then illuminate several practical ways of turning this seemingly chaotic energy into a "dance" of productive work and behavior.

WHO SHOULD PARTICIPATE:
This seminar is for executives, managers, human resource directors, industrial psychologists, teachers, doctors, and anyone who has a concern for stimulating a more productive individual, organization, or society.

TIMING:
The seminar begins at 8 am and ends at 5 pm. Longer seminars with more content and experiential activities can also be arranged for two or three days with even greater benefits.

Leadership: Skillful Means

in Balancing and Dancing

(1 January 2004, New York)

I wrote this essay at the request of ICA USA for their website to help celebrate the ICA's 30th anniversary.

It is indeed a pleasure to help celebrate the 30th anniversary of the Institute of Cultural Affairs (ICA). What an extraordinary organization ICA was, is, and continues to be! It has done so much for human development around the world, has trained so many people in effective leadership skills and styles, and has been a strong beacon of hope and courage.

Leadership – how do you know it when you see it? How do you do it? How be it?

In university, leaders of thought and action were my heroes, my role models, often encountered through books. There were Albert Camus and Jean Paul Sartre, calling me to authenticity and angst. Fr. Pierre Teilhard de Chardin inviting me to see the universe as mystical and magical. There was Mahatma Gandhi leading with great gentleness and yet with iron will. Dr. Martin Luther King, leading me into a new world of hope and nonviolent love. There was also Dag Hammarskjold, the world leader and UN chief with a secret poetic and spiritual life.

Then, there was Joe – Joseph Wesley Mathews – my first spiritual master and the founder of the ICA. Joe was powerful, brilliant, and charismatic. Joe shared with me (and with everyone he encountered) his clarity, his passion, and his resolve. "You can bend history!" "Let's transform the world with human development!" "You must take care of yourself." "What the world needs are social pioneers."

When Mary and I were going to Malaysia in 1969 on our first international assignment with the Institute, Joe sent us out with the exhortation: "Go out and raise up Iron Men!" This of course included Iron Women and Iron Children as well. We did as Joe said – everywhere we went, we tried to enable others to stand tall, to be their greatness, to trust their intuitions, and to create history.

I will never forget the electric excitement of experiencing for the first time the Technology of Participation (ToP) (although we did not call it that at the time.) Brainstorming, gestalting, naming, ORID, strategic planning – this was the way to be a leader, a facilitator of other people's wisdom, decision-making, and action. What a great time I have had with these methods, trying to be of service to other people, whether in CitiBank, Colgate Palmolive, the Girl Guides, Kwang Yung Il Ri, the Government of Jamaica, or wherever. Long live ToP!

Over the past thirteen years, I applied ICA's social, intellectual, and motivational methods in my work at the United Nations Development Program (UNDP). I charted, facilitated, problem-solved, strategized, designed, and reflected on events, projects, programs, and policies. I have tried to provide a profound and practical style of leadership in my work as a policy advisor in decentralized governance as I have worked in over fifty countries.

New methods of leadership have also come my way and have been put into practice – Whole System Design, Chaordic Processes, and Emotional Intelligence. We have used these, in just one example, with great effectiveness in our work on Decentralized Transformative Approaches to HIV/AIDS in Nepal, in a partnership with ICA Nepal.

A leader must understand whole systems not just single issues or sectors. As Ken Wilber has elaborated, every reality has both individual and collective dimensions as well as external and interior ones. Dee Hock, the founder of Visa International, adds another dimension to this understanding, and that is that systems are self organizing, or as he calls them "chaordic" – the intersection of chaos and order.

A leader must not only be intellectually intelligent, but also emotionally intelligent. Daniel Goleman has written beautifully about Emotional Intelligence. The leader must be aware of self, of who he or she is, both strengths and weaknesses, as well as able to manage that self as needed, ego and all. The leader must also have prowess in social awareness and relationship management.

Now, what is emerging? What is on the horizon as the next burst of profound leadership? Jean Houston is working with us at UNDP to develop a global program to train young developing country leadership and UN leaders in the skills and style of what Jean calls "Social Artistry." The social artist can move between cultures, with the ability to enter other's belief systems, cultural styles, energizing stories, and rituals.

We will pilot test a seminar on "Human Development, Decentralizing the Millennium Development Goals (MDGs) and Social Artistry" in Tirana, Albania, in February 2004. We will then offer the basic course in other regions and countries and at the global level, both informal as well as graduate level courses.

I would like to conclude by thanking three other leaders who have awakened and nurtured my own leadership style and skills. These are – His Holiness the Dalai Lama – for his authenticity and kindness to all beings, Nelson Mandela – for his great heart and transcendence of all bitterness, and Mother Teresa – for teaching us what it means to be married to the beloved of the soul.

This suffering world is sorely in need of authentic leadership. We must be willing to give everything we have and are, our very life and death. Leadership is very much about balancing and dancing. It is a movement that is both inner and outer, local and global, individual and corporate, responsive and guiding, direct and indirect, listening and talking, beckoning and enabling, risk and stability, self and other, visible and invisible, humility and self confidence, strength and weakness, wisdom and compassion.

May it be so.

Celebrating ICA's 30th Anniversary

(2004, New York)

This essay was written as a foreword to a book of stories published by ICA to celebrate its 30th anniversary.

O the memories – painful and sweet. These vignettes unleash a flood of memories of the twenty-three-year journey that my wife Mary and I enjoyed with the Institute. Thank you for reminding us of the glory of that time and indeed the wonder of our lives on this mysterious planet. These stories would have provided Lyn Mathews Edwards with many a chuckle, wry smile, or surge of motherly pride.

It is a privilege to have been part of the journey, part of the story. We were so young, naïve, and invincible, so full of hope – perhaps blinded by the brilliance of our own vision of human development. We survived and grew up. We had our eyes and minds opened wide to the ways of the world. It is humbling to remember how many villagers all over the world forgave us and supported us in our naiveté and enthusiasm to change the world.

Last week on a UN mission, I visited a village in Nepal, a country I had last visited thirty-two years ago on a global odyssey with the Institute. Reading these wonderful recollections connected past, present, and future. For this I am grateful. These stories remind us that much of our own awakening comes through cross-cultural encounters. Anyone who is on a journey of awakening will take delight in these little stories. They will entertain, amaze, and challenge your assumptions about yourself and the world in which you live. Through the lens of personal experience, this book provides the reader with a rich array of knowledge concerning social, political, economic, and cultural change – the nitty gritty of human development. And as for the future, the world is more in need than ever of the bold deeds of "those who care".

For us human beings, an external event creates an interior response. In fact, some would deny a separation of these two because each happens and is known only in interdependent co-origination. In these stories, we hear the voices of people who were by and large outsiders being deeply touched by their external surroundings be they cultural or physical. Amid the ordinary, secular world, another world appears, a world of mystery, consciousness, care, and tranquility. Many of these shared reflections convey this transparent connection between inner and outer reality.

Service is a strange concept. Who is served and who does the serving? Sometimes it is the served who are of greatest service to those doing the serving. Some of us try again and again to be of service in situations of suffering whether from poverty, war, disease, or ignorance. But it is not a simple task. Sometimes the people we attempt to serve have their own agendas and our service is thwarted. Sometimes our service is inappropriate or ill conceived. But should we stop trying? Finally, we must each do what we believe we must and leave the judgment of our deeds to history.

The Merry, Merry Month of May

(1 June 2008, Cold Spring, New York)

June 1st, we made it! We lived May to the full and it is gone, partly to memory, some to history. What a month . . . unrepeatable. We moved! I had dreaded moving, as usual, but with a difference. This had been my home for ten years – four lived with my late, beloved wife Mary (sometimes with our children), three as a widower, and three with my new beloved wife, Bonnie Myotai Treace. I loved that house, and still do. I owned it, and still do. It is beautifully sited in solitude overlooking the Hudson Highlands and Hudson River at a distance. But it was time for a change. I had remarried. I had a new life. It was time to symbolize that new covenant, love, and life in space and homemaking. So, we looked for another home, chose one, packed up, moved, and unpacked. Now, we are home in a two-story apartment on the beautiful Hudson riverfront in Cold Spring, New York, across from Crows' Nest Mountain, a five-minute walk to catch a train to Manhattan.

Within days after moving, I went into New York City and taught a four credit/twenty-five-hour grad course at New York University (NYU) Wagner Graduate School of Public Service on innovative leadership for sustainable development. Bonnie immediately began finalizing negotiations to lease an historic gristmill as the central hermitage for her non-profit,

Hermitage Heart and its Bodies of Water School. Immediately after teaching, I returned to planning a global conference on climate change to be held later this year in Washington, D. C., preceded by a Preparatory Committee (PrepCom) meeting in Brazil. I also began planning my presentation for a global symposium on local governance to be held in Saudi Arabia later this year but decided not to go because of the country's gender policies.

While putting up art and buying things for the apartment, I am grading papers from the NYU course. I am also anticipating the publication of a book by the East-West Center that includes my chapter on innovative leadership. At one and the same time, Bonnie and I are anxious to return to our cabin in Asheville, North Carolina, to be near our children and only grandchild, Phoenix Orion Work. And all the while, I am grieving the recent loss of my precious mother. Fortunately for me, I am learning many new lessons about being an Earthling, as a husband, father, grandfather, son, brother, friend, writer, facilitator, educator, spiritual practitioner, and lover of life.

Life is so very full. Global climate change, global pandemics, and global economic meltdown overwhelm, hurt, and frighten us. Will I, will humanity wake up in time? Isn't it already too late? Nevertheless, we do what we can, believing that we can do what we must.

Old age is just around the corner. Then comes death, sufficiency of death. And it was all good, all of it. And it will always be good, all of it – the joy and the sorrow.

Oh, sweet Mystery of Life, at last, I have found you!

Possibility

(2010, Garrison, New York)

This piece was written four years after I retired from UNDP. It contains some of what I was doing at the time, flowing out of my mission and vocation.

I am deeply concerned about this moment in world history along with my own "old age, sickness, and death." I believe that human society has entered a critical period of environmental, energy, economic, and governance crisis and transformation. We have entered the birth canal to a new civilization of sustainability, equity, and participation, *or* to a tragic world of chaos and destruction. The entire future of life on Earth is being created by each choice you and I make moment by moment.

Recently, a colleague wrote to me asking "what are you doing to advance sanity?" I wrote to her concerning my small offering as follows:

"In the past six months, I facilitated an international workshop in Honolulu on long-term policy-making for sustainable development sponsored by the East-West Center and UN University. At New York University Wagner Graduate School of Public Service, I taught a course on innovative leadership for sustainable development. My chapter on leadership innovations from civil society appeared in a new book, *Engaging Civil Society: Emerging Trends in Democratic Governance*, edited by Cheema and Popovski, and published by UN University Press. I participated in a UNDP high-level event on biodiversity, climate change, and localizing the millennium development goals (MDG) as part of the UN MDG Summit in NYC.

"At an interfaith conference on climate change and ecological civilization sponsored by the Temple of Understanding in New York City, I served as an environmental advisor. The Fulbright Specialist Program of the Council for International Exchange of Scholars and the Bureau of Education and Cultural Affairs of the US Department of State has appointed me to their global roster through which overseas institutions of higher learning can request my services with support from Fulbright. At a think tank on international development sponsored by the Institute of Cultural Affairs USA, I made a presentation on the critical decade we have just entered."

I have tried to be a good man, husband, father, grandfather, and friend. I fail everyday and do little. Nevertheless, I am grateful for the unparalleled possibilities of being alive at this moment of crisis and opportunity.

May we each in our unique ways offer ourselves to the unfolding of the possible human and the possible society. For the sake of my two grandchildren and indeed all of life on Earth, I rededicate myself to respond to these challenges as best I can. May it be so.

How to Save Life on Earth Today

(20 February 2019, Swannanoa, North Carolina)

From the instant my father's sperm found its way to my mother's egg, penetrating, becoming one with explosive unfolding, until now, seventy-four-Earth-years later, what is the news, the revelation, the insight into being conscious with one hundred billion brain cells, with 13.7 billion years of cosmic evolution, with 7.3 billion other humans alive at this instant, with this moment of crisis in which once again life on Earth is imperiled, when once more the awakened ones are called to save all sentient beings? What is it? What is called for? To orchestrate grieving? To turn the tide? Or to enjoy this moment of waking awareness, aching consciousness? Or to observe, or reflect, or interpret, or decide about what? To be aware of words, thoughts, feelings, perceptions, perspectives, values, other ways of knowing? Or to rest in wonder and gratitude? Or all of it? Or none of it? What? Time to check in with social media. Time for morning meditation. For feeding the cat. For breakfast and tea. For greeting the beloved. For taking a hot shower. For planning the day. For meeting my brother. For errands and thoughts and feelings. And what? What SHOULD I BE DOING? I will write and edit and design a retreat. But how do I save life on Earth?

How do I help catalyze a compassionate civilization this day, this instant of penetrating the creative vortex, becoming one with the explosive unfolding? Such gratitude, ineffable gratitude for knowing-doing-being. Yes!

Creativity, Grief, and Gratitude

in Lockdown: My 2020 Report

(December 2020, Swannanoa, North Carolina)

Compassionate Civilization Press

My major work of 2020 was publishing three books: in January, *Serving People & Planet: In Mystery, Love, and Gratitude*, an autobiography; in July, *Earthling Love: Living Poems 1965 - 2020*; and in October, *The Critical Decade 2020 – 2029: Calls for Ecological, Compassionate Leadership*, twelve "calls to action" given around the world in 2010 – 2019. All three books can be ordered through local bookshops as well as online including Amazon, IngramSpark, Lulu, and Bookdepository. Most of the marketing of the books was carried out on Facebook, LinkedIn, Twitter, and email.

The *Black Mountain News* in North Carolina published an article with photographs for the launch of each book. Two of the books were carried in the Oklahoma State University (OSU) student union store in Stillwater, Oklahoma, and Sassafras on Sutton bookstore in Black Mountain, North Carolina. Each book was sent by request to the Association of Former International Civil Servants (AFICS) Library in New York City, the Library of Congress in Washington, D.C., the

ICA Social Research Center Library in Chicago, the Black Mountain Library, and the Durant High School Library in Durant, Oklahoma. Also, by request, two of the books were sent to the University of Oxford Bodleian Library in London for a UN staff project collection. For the three books, there were a total of twenty-three published endorsements and thirteen reviews on Amazon and Lulu.

Work in Ukraine led by Svitlana Salamatova continued on a Ukrainian language edition of *A Compassionate Civilization*. I created a new website for my publications and continued posting blogs on the "Compassionate Civilization" blogsite. My article on innovative leadership was published in the online *Integral Leadership Review*.

As requested, I wrote reviews and endorsements for several important new books by authors Dr. Larry Ward (*America's Racial Karma*), Chic Dambach (*Exhaust the Limits*), Ricardo Neves (*Sensemaking*), Martin Gilbraith (*Power of Facilitation*), Dr. Shabbir Cheema (*Democratic Local Governance*), Rich Flanders (MS for "Under the Great Elm"), and Dr. Nikhil Chandavarkar (two historical novels).

Other Professional Activities

At the request of Ms Ishu Subba, executive director of ICA Nepal, I became an adviser to their educational and school support program. And at the invitation of Richard Henry Whitehurst, I became an advisor to Planetary Human, and Overview Earth. I advised director Maureen Connolly on preparations for the UN 75th anniversary global governance online forum. I participated in Extinction Rebellion's global call on the movement of movements (MoM.) I participated in the ICA Social Research Center online meeting and hosted a Zoom conversation on the MoM. I received an invitation to assist the University of Oxford's research project on the MoM. I was invited by Blue Ridge Consulting director Dr. Ameena Zia to be an online lecturer in the UN Experiential Fellowship program. I had an online conversation with Dr. Herman Green of the Center of Ecozoic Studies. I was invited to speak in an international conference at Harvard but declined to attend because of the pandemic.

Personal/Family Activities

I was deeply saddened by the death of dear friends due to COVID-19: Maria Gitta, the loving wife of my consulting partner, Dr. Cosmas Gitta, and John Giancola, of my OSU days. I supported progressive issues and helped get out the vote for Democratic party candidates. Adding to my daily practice of meditation, I learned desk-yoga from colleague Tina Spencer on Zoom from Australia. Cataract surgery greatly improved my vision. My younger brother Duncan continued his journey with Parkinson's. My colleague Rev. Dr. Kang Byoung Hoon called me from Seoul. I celebrated the publication of two books by my wife Bonnie Myotai Treace: *A Year of Zen* (#1 in Zen Spirituality for several months) and *Zen Meditation for Beginners*. Bonnie's profound new podcast "A Year of Zen" had fifty episodes and was heard in twenty-two countries. Bonnie's lockdown haircuts were as good as my professional barber! I participated in Zoom memorials for several old friends. I was amazed at the creativity of our two grandchildren, ten and twelve – composing music, building a computer, learning programming code language, and singing beautifully. Their weekly visits-at-a-distance along with their parents in our front garden kept GrandBonnie and Grandpa Rob happy throughout the year.

Gratitude. May all beings everywhere realize peace, happiness, compassion, and understanding.

THEME

Awareness and Identity

What follows are a few essays written in 2004 – 2021 concerning transformations of awareness, relationships, reflection, and identity.

Awareness of What?

(November 2004, Garrison, New York)

Embodiment in flesh and blood. Embodiment in awareness-itself. Emergent from 13 billion years. Full of anxiety, angst, suffering, desire, drives, needs, wants, pleasures, joys. What is at the center of this conglomeration? Is there a center? Is there an "I". Certainly, there is not an independent "I". Thrown in space-time-energy. Waking up to "this". What is it? Where is it? What is going on? What is called for? Besides survival? Or is that it? Just getting by, day by day, until the days end.

But this is not what I wanted to write tonight. I wanted to write about Mary. I wanted to write about God. Or is this not what I am writing about?

Mary, you appeared in my life. Remember, when we were sitting on a bench on the campus of the University of Chicago, I called you an "angel." Then after you have gone, sixteen months ago, thirty-five years after that day on the bench, I realized that you really were and are an Angel.

You came into my life and gave me so much joy and hope and comfort and support and challenge. And now you are nowhere to be seen. Except in memory. Except in my two sons. Except in my heart. Except in this house. Except in your journals. Except in your words and deeds. Except in all the people you touched with your care and compassion and intelligence. Except in the Galactic Resource Center. Except in your next incarnation.

Well, it seems that I was quite wrong! You are very much to be found but not in the way you were with me and for me. Now, I must forge ahead with you but without you in the same way. But it was never the same. It was always changing. Why did I think that the changing would stop and not go on changing and changing? Well, it did not stop. It kept changing and here we are – together yet apart. Separated, yet united.

My love, I miss you so much in your former form. I now must learn to love you in your formless form or your trans-formed form, until we are reunited both in our formless form, in the eternal now.

And God? Was this not what I was writing about? Am writing about? The Ultimate Mystery. The One-without-a-second. The waking up to it all. And trying to make sense of it all. And doing something. And living a life. And dying a death. And trying to be useful in the process. Trying to be my being. Trying to give my uniqueness as a gift to the Universe.

Possibilities from the Landmark Forum

(24 November 2005, Garrison, New York)

Today is Thanksgiving. My son Benjamin came to my house and prepared a wonderful dinner that we had together. I am so thankful for my life.

Landmark Forum Review:
Landmark Forum was utterly amazing. I have a new sense of radical possibility for my life. I am aware of my rackets and strong suits. I invented and declared the possibility for myself and my life to be courageous, accepting, generous, and compassionate and to create a world that works for everyone. I relearned the power of putting things into language and bringing the future into the present. I relearned the power of choosing based on my own freedom rather than making decisions justified by reasons. I want to be a powerful, self-expressed, happy, loving person with great relationships with others.

I choose to live an authentic life and to let go of my inauthenticity. I can tell my inauthenticity when I experience a loss of power, freedom, and self-expression. I know that I need to choose UNDP or my template for the next eight months. I know that I need to choose to stay in my Garrison house or to move. I know that I need to let go of Mary's ashes as part of the way of completing my Earthly relationship with her. I know that I need to be more self-expressive with other people and especially those I love.

I choose my current reality; it then "disappears" and a clearing for the future appears. I choose the way life is. The world of possibility is present. If I stand in "nothing", all is possible. The constraints the past imposes on my view of life disappear and a new view of life emerges. New possibilities for being call me powerfully into being. New openings for action call me powerfully into action. The experience of being alive transforms me. I base my life on my word rather than my feelings. I create love from nothing, then I declare it. If I declare my being, my love, then I will do and have love. I declare who I am, my being. What is the type of extraordinary life I am up to? This is an art. I need to retrain people to relate to me as the new me. I need a powerful future to keep the past from filling my future. I identify with my stories about myself, others, and the world. Love arises as a presence when I accept another person as who they are and are not. When I stop trying to be right and to change people, then I can love them. I must practice giving up something in love.

People think of money as scarce. I got what I have, and I do not have what I do not have. It means nothing. I can create possibilities in the arena of money. I can create the possibility of abundance of money.

What games can I create for my life that will move, touch, and inspire other people? Such as Decentralizing the MDGs through Innovative Leadership (DMIL.)

The space of responsibility is a "stand." Who am I being when others are upset with me?

Integrity has to do with honoring my word. Do what I said I would do by when I said it and when I do not, clean it up and make new promises and keep them.

Being racket-free is to give up being right as soon as I notice and even when I know I am right.

Being powerful is to be straight in my communication and take what I get. Make five promises and five unreasonable requests each day.

Being courageous is to acknowledge my fear and then act.

Being peaceful is to give up the interpretation "there is something wrong here."

Being charismatic is to give up "in order to" and trying to get somewhere. Do what I am doing when I am doing it.

Being enrolled is to share my new possibilities in such a way that others are touched, moved, and inspired by that possibility.

Being extraordinary is to be unreasonable, to demand the most of people.

I need to talk in an authentic way with the people I love.

A breakdown is a gap between the possibility I have invented and my current experience. A conversation on what is wrong is not helpful. Just stand in your possibility. Breakdowns can be managed into breakthroughs. All that is going on are rackets and strong suits until I declare a possibility for myself and my life. The old me is powerfully in existence. A danger sign is when something is wrong. Breakdowns are good because I can then see that I am not living in the new possibility. The five-year old I was originally created my life. Now I must keep in existence my new possibility so that I create my life.

Promise that by next Tuesday at 10:45 pm, I will have made an unreasonable promise. Without a commitment, I let circumstances decide for me. But I am bigger than my circumstances. Choose yes or no. Honor and respect my and others' choices. Do not worry about myself. Do not worry about myself. Make sure everyone else is happy!

Everything is whole, complete, and perfect! Remember that I am a powerful person because everyone in the world is trying to "look good" for me.

Reflection on the Forum, etc.

I choose to go to Maputo and Stockholm. I choose to continue working with UNDP on DMIL, LIFE, training, facilitation, and coaching. I choose to continue living in Garrison. I choose to be who and what I am. I choose to have my cat Boots. I choose to have my two sons. I choose my aliveness! My life is whole, complete, and perfect! *The possibility I invent for myself and my life is the possibility of being courageous, self-expressed, generous, accepting, powerful, and compassionate and to create a world that works for everyone.*

What about my template – meditation, horn, dance, writing, publishing, leading retreats, consulting? I choose to meditate each day, play my horn occasionally now and more later, dance whenever possible now and more later, continue my journal writing for now and more extensive writing and publishing later, attend retreats now and design and lead retreats later, continue my UNDP work with an increase of training, facilitation and coaching now and later to do more consulting in these areas with UNDP and other organizations such as the Garrison Institute and Abbey North.

The challenge will be to be authentic in being and doing all the above. Not to do it half-heartedly or to make excuses because of circumstances, reasons, feelings, and judgments. I choose to accept UNDP just as it is. I choose to accept myself just as I am. I choose to accept life just as it is. I choose to accept each being just as it is.

Will I take the Landmark Advanced Course and if so, when? I would like to take it in January or February. Review the calendar and call them tomorrow and let Mounir Tabet know.

What have I noticed since the Forum? I do not have headaches and take Advil. My eyesight is better. I am not as tired. I am positive about my life and about life in general. I am accepting of myself and others. I have chosen to give myself unreservedly to my current commitments, e.g., UNDP, DMIL, family. I have chosen to live in a World of Possibility that is the future emerging in the present. I am aware when I am being inauthentic. I want to be authentic. Yes.

Reflections on the Eight Gates of the Second Half of Life by Angeles Arrien

(15 September 2005, Garrison, New York)

This essay is a reflection on the first two gates in Angeles Arrien's wonderful book.

*T*he SILVER Gate:
Reflective – curiosity – trust – flexibility – experiencing the new, the unknown – exploring the unexplored – adventurous – fresh innocence – beginning anew – every month celebrate birthday and do something new – listen deeply to what I am longing for – reconnect with what inspires me.

What am I doing that is new? Living alone. Taking dance class. Doing *sesshin*. Preparing Mary's poetry for publication.

What am exploring? Other living places – Cold Spring, Mt. Vernon, Yonkers, Riverdale, Asheville, the Philippines. New relationships.

What am I curious about? Experiencing other relationships.

Where have I been adventurous? Doing DMIL workshops with Jean Houston!

Where am I listening to what inspires me? My template of horn playing, dancing, writing, study, meditation, consulting, leading retreats.

Where am I being reflective? Daily meditation. Daily journal writing.

Where do I need to take the next step into the unknown? Deciding about my living place. Deciding about when to leave UNDP. Exploring new relationships.

Where do I need to trust? My ability to maneuver through UNDP these next months. That I will decide when the time is right about my housing and relationships.

What am I longing for? Happiness. Aliveness. Meaning. Giving myself to others.

Where do I experience the spirit of fluency (like a river flows) in my life? When I am dancing, playing my horn, writing, reading, talking with someone I care about.

Where do I experience symptoms of soul loss with inertia, apathy, emptiness, numbness, confusion, futility, discontent, anxiety? Encountering the UN bureaucracy from the inside, thinking about the misguided US administration, worrying about DMIL, DGP, BMZ, Sida, worrying about moving, worrying about being alone.

How do I renew and regenerate myself? Meditating, horn playing, dancing, being with people I love, writing, reading, being in other cultures, helping other people through training and facilitation.

What does fire (vision, heart, creativity, soul) reveal to me about my dreams, work, health, relationships, creativity, and soul's desire currently in my life? Life is about expenditure, burning oneself up, not saving oneself. Giving myself to my vision, following my heart, being my unique creative self without judgment or comparisons, caring for my soul and the souls of all beings. Dance it! Be it! Love it! Do not look back!

Tracking my work with curiosity and discernment but without judgment: Where am I being called in my work? To let go of my role, office, status, salary, power, identity. To help my colleagues on their journeys. To let go of pride and judgment of my colleagues and the organization and myself. To fill full the template of my soul's work.

What am I searching for in my work? To be recognized. But I need to let go of that desire. To have autonomy. But I need to let go of that as well. To provide the organization with new ways of doing development more effectively. Do I need to let go of that also? Perhaps what I am searching for is outside of being a UNDP staff member, and I need to be a loyal staff member until I leave and then pursue other interests rather than trying to force my agenda on UNDP.

In what ways is my workplace struggling? The organization is suffering from public scrutiny and criticism of our leader. BDP is becoming even more bureaucratic.

What breakthrough do I want to create in my work that would lead to a major advance for the organization in the next three months? To help the organization learn new ways of thinking, planning, and working as per DMIL.

What do I want to return to that I have found effective in my work? My sense of loyalty to and love of the organization. A sense of freshness, hope, optimism on the organization's role and potential, rather than cynicism and negativity.

The WHITE PICKET Gate
Changing identities, discovering one's true face, beyond our roles, masks and expertise, awakening to our essence, wisdom and radiance, five essential faces: child, youth, adult, elder, and essence; destroying the peace found in one's roles, beyond the ego's FACE (Fear, Attachment, Control, and Entitlement), embracing curiosity, letting go, trust and humility; realizing the authentic self, continuing to learn; self-acceptance; beyond external acceptance and approval.

What is my face as a child (0 – 13)? Son, brother, innocent, naïve, self-conscious, shy, cute, needing glasses to see, straightening of teeth, reflective, solitary.

As a youth (14 – 24)? Acne, artistic, musical, smart, narcissistic, poetic, philosophical, student, religious.

My adult face (24 – 60)? Married, husband, missional, corporate, vows, under assignment, responsible, father, NGO director, community and organizational developer, facilitator, project manager, global bureaucrat, decentralized governance expert, social choreographer, impresario.

My elder face (60 –)? Handsome, widower, dancer, meditator, writer, student, hermit, poet, philosopher.

My essence face? Impermanent/eternal, empty/full, suffering/nirvana, compassion, understanding, peace, happiness.

Which of the above faces are calling to be developed and integrated? My elder face, my essence face, my youth face.

What has the FACE (see above) of the ego taught me? fear of failure and being different, attachment to roles and social identity, controlled by the corporate, controlling of others, entitlement to leadership, going to Joseph Mathews' funeral, to being special (a no. 4).

How do I abandon my true nature for other's approval and acceptance? Being a good bureaucrat, being my colleagues' "powerful" friend, pleasing my mother and sons.

How do I perform, pretend, and hide because of my egoic preferences to be seen in a desired way? Perform as a bureaucrat.

What roles, masks and identities are difficult for me to release? Being responsible, missional, messianic, special, appreciated, recognized, respected, liked.

What illusory peace that I do not want to disturb may prevent my growth? Just staying in this house; staying in New York (?), being respectable, being a "good" person, being a Christian.

How do I currently embody the wisdom gifts of curiosity, flexibility, and self-acceptance? Through daily meditation, dancing, writing, study, photography, traveling, accepting leaving UNDP, accepting leaving this house, accepting my emotions, desire to play horn, and desire to lead retreats and to consult.

Only Intimacy

(2008, Garrison, New York)

Having married my beloved Bonnie in September, becoming a first-time granddad in January, consulting with the UN, preparing to teach grad school next year, helping my eighty-seven-year-old mother make a joyful transition to assisted living, writing, and meditating, my reflection is as follows: There is no separation. No inner, no outer. No self, no other. Only intimacy. Not two, only one.

O Mystery, O One-without-a-Second, who propels us into being and yanks us out of being, (or so it seems) we know that we are Thine and Thine alone. We are the unknown unknown even as Thou art the Unknown Unknown, the Endless Mystery. Thank You for the undeserved gift of life. World without end. Amen.

All phenomena manifest suffering, impermanence, and non-self which reveal that all is good, the no-self is accepted, the past approved, and the future open.

May all beings be happy. May all beings be at peace. May all beings be compassionate. May all beings be wise.

May we affirm life, be giving, honor the body, manifest truth, proceed clearly, see the perfection, realize self and other as one, give generously, actualize harmony, and experience the intimacy of things.

An Early Morning Playful, Prayerful, Philosophical, Prosaic Piece

(12 February 2021, Swannanoa, NC)

Conspire to breathe together to agree together to plot together inspire aspire poetry download Ulysses and James Joyce mind dump all one the algorithm is the key to it all one verse universe one consciousness logos The Word Made Flesh these fingers moving yes yes yes it is all good our valuation of reality mystery unknownedness this is it gratitude for this and all all is one a perfect mind mindful of all gratitude for this perfection line by line the observer affects the observation mind moving over the chaos ordering by observing and naming with words the greatest power letters syllables words phrases sentences paragraphs pages chapters books collections libraries the ancient Alexandria library was destroyed how many lives minds gone or is that true a new way of writing thinking being and Bonnie woke up and asked me what I am doing I told her I am mind dumping and Chickabee rubbed my legs and I rubbed his belly so fluffy and soft such perfection of fluffiness how long can I do this can this help anyone what about punctuation marks should I go back and put them in I do want to publish my essays and reflections as part of my sharing of this life how do I speak to the 7.6 billion of us humans and all the

other creatures we are all conscious empathic compassionate
Buddha was so right gratitude for knowing him/it/them/us
the light of the screen the white light put on my lens that filter
out that which can keep me awake but I am awake and I call all
beings everywhere to awaken to their perfection and consciousness and love and truth no room for hate even the sad ones
but we are each a sad one so limited and so powerful and so
connected and so disconnected can I go on like this and write
a book question mark yet I can write the punctuation mark
but how to transform the world can words do that of course
they always have yes transformation I want to touch every life
I want to bless every being blessings to all of you may you and
all beings realize happiness peace understanding and compassion the words keep flowing line by line letter by letter word by
word it is now six fifty-two in the morning on Friday the twelfth
of February 2021 shall I continue to capitalize or not necessary
this is it the perfect way to pass the time to create a new world
to love all beings to address all beings everywhere in this space
in this time in this way of perfection a perfect mind a perfect
message a perfect understanding awake awake awake now here
everywhere one place the uni-verse this one place this one time
all time NOW present flowing only change only appearing and
disappearing but no birth and no death simply this and all and
now and good and yes and please may it all be okay shall I go
back to bed now I will continue to do this later I have shown
what it is like what it is gratitude so grateful full of words and
ideas and consciousness and yes and yes and yes I have only
done this my whole life been consciousness shared words and
deeds as we each do is this a poem a stream of consciousness
exercise or is this the truth forged by particular observation
suppositions values how can we expose that as human beings
it is all about agreed upon valuation the value of a tie of a life
or a cat or a country or a civilization or money nothing but
agreed valuation which is everything for us humans or is it so is
there not something more something deeper something truer
something ultimate birth life death again and again in a poem

it doesn't have to flow it doesn't have to make sense it is not expository it is flowing it is the mind playing with other minds batting words around hey look at this hey you I love you look at this word this idea this feeling what do you think what are you feeling can we create a new civilization of compassion for all creatures big and small can we wake up from the nightmare of separateness can we sing together play together create together I am slowing down shall I go back to bed yes let us go then to lie down and give thanks for this new exercise of word play of prayer of philosophy of poetry yes but first I want to say that I want to speak to everyone I have ever loved ever encountered and also to everyone all seven billion six hundred million of us I love you all I love you each please be okay you are already perfect help is on the way we are waking up we can create an ecological compassionate community and civilization to care for all beings everywhere yes we can yes we will I love you . . . it is all okay and I am up again and awake and typing and the words flow and it is all good and the grass is turning green spring is coming soon gratitude for life on Earth and in this mysterious cosmos yes one mind one internet one world wide web one cosmos wide web of consciousness we are all thinking together Q-anon and the Dalai Lama and Chickabee the Cat and the bug-eyed bald buzzard-beaked billionaire all of us one here now thinking together no one is right we are all wrong cosmic consciousness alone is right feeling calm here now grateful yes flowing line by line all at once yes insane sanity let's create a new world now that cares for all that celebrates each that enables everyone to realize his/her/their full potential in this flickering life moment yes

THEME

Being and Presence

The Confessions of a Reflective Bureaucrat

(1997, New York)

> *Before joining the UN, I had always had great admiration for*
> *the institution. When I joined, I was ecstatic to be a UN world*
> *server. But after my first seven years, I realized I had somewhat*
> *lost my way and had to find it again which I did. To this day in*
> *2021, I have great respect for the UN as an essential institution*
> *of world service.*

I began my stint as a bureaucrat seven years ago full of hope, optimism, and commitment to the goals of sustainable and people-centered development. Somewhere along the line, I have become cynical, despairing, in mental anguish about my life and my work. What has happened to me? What can/should I do about it?

What has happened to me?

I have become a pampered, perfumed Lord of Poverty rather than a servant of the people.

I have become a paper-pusher rather than a person of action and impact.

I have become wedded to status and privilege rather than a humble worker for justice and peace.

I have become proud, elitist rather than a humble servant.

I have lost touch with the people I am to serve.

I have become afraid of losing my salary and status.

I have focused on gaining power within the bureaucracy rather than in making an impact in the world.

I have become busy – rather than effective.

I have become de-skilled rather than further refining and building my skills.

I have become obedient to the chain-of-command rather than speaking out in truth, clarity, conviction, and creativity.

I have become satisfied with the routine rather than risking new ideas and approaches to my work.

I have become cynical about my work, believing that it has no positive effect but is rather cosmetic, dull, and uninspiring.

I have become cynical about the entire organization believing that it never touches down in positive action in the lives of the poor, but stays afloat in paper, international commitments, words, meetings, and self-promotion and delusion.

I have become despairing about my own soul, that I have lost my way, that I have lost my original inspiration and commitment to justice and peace.

I have become awakened that not only I but my colleagues within the bureaucracy are suffering under this weight of despair and delusion, that I/we must break loose either within or without the organization to be authentic human beings.

I have become brain-dead, as I repeat the party-line, the jargon, the formulas of the bureaucracy, rather than thinking new thoughts, proposing creative solutions, risking my own ideas.

What can/should I do about this?
I must first acknowledge what has happened/is happening to me. I have begun to do this as in the above declarations. This must be done in compassion for myself and my colleagues, not in more cynicism or self-hatred. I am a worthy being. My colleagues are worthy beings. I/we can change. I/we can change my/our situation for the better.

I must also acknowledge what I/we are doing that is of value:
We are a symbol to the world of the possibility of humanity's cooperation to improve the lives of all people everywhere, to care for the environment in view of the next ten generations not only the present moment.

We are international civil servants with a tradition stemming from such spiritually awakened people as Dag Hammarskjold and U Thant. We are the servants of the people of planet earth, bringing cutting-edge knowledge to the remote comers of the world.

We are networkers, bringing disparate peoples together to listen, to learn, to cooperate in building a better world.

We are thinkers and communicators helping articulate state-of-the-art knowledge concerning how to improve human lives and the environment.

We are a global community/team that represents the possibility of people of different nationalities, cultures, religions, races, politics, and personalities to work together for the common good.

We are peacemakers, bringing opposing factions together to rebuild their society.

We are program practitioners, helping design and implement needed programs at community, municipal, national, regional, and global levels.

We are facilitators, bringing people together to brainstorm, analyze design, evaluate, and exchange knowledge, which is needed at the local level.

What can I do to bring my life and work into alignment with my authentic vocation as an international civil servant?
I can share my own feelings and analysis of my current despair and suffering.

I can share my own vision of what the organization is and can be.

I can speak out of my own insights, depth, and commitment and risk my ideas and contributions within the corporate dialogue.

I can rededicate myself to my profound sense of vocation as an international civil servant, with the emphasis on being a servant of the people.

I can remind myself daily of those whom I attempt to serve, through decor in my office, books I read, people I meet.

When. I am in the field, I can stay in touch with the poor by visiting the slums and squatter settlements and rural villages on every mission rather than staying only in hotels and office buildings.

I can keep a journal to write down my reflections about my work to keep myself honest about my experiences, feelings, and actions.

I can talk with my colleagues about how I feel and what I am attempting to do and ask them about their feelings, hopes, challenges, and plans.

I can maintain outside interests to keep myself fresh, open. learning, growing, as a person.

I can ensure adequate time for my family and friends to keep myself grounded in my closest circle of relationships of care.

I can advance my own knowledge and skills through outside reading, study, new experiences, and-challenges.

I can focus my energy on the few, key activities which I believe will have the most positive effect for the most people whom I serve.

I can support my colleagues rather than trying to put them down.

I can cooperate with my colleagues rather than competing with them for a little more status with the organization.

I can think about other things I could be doing with my life, so I do not feel trapped inside this one organization.

I can be grateful for my current opportunity to be an international civil servant with all the expectations for the quality of my service to others that it brings.

I can revisit my original inspiration and stay in touch with my original vision and hopes and goals.

I can politely challenge my superiors with new ideas, alternatives, and improvements in a way that honors them and in which they can see new options and possibilities.

I can avoid participating in cynical comments about the organization and negative gossip about my colleagues.

I can stay in touch with my own depth awareness of my life and death through my religious life and spiritual practices.

In Peace and War; in Sickness and Health

(2003, Garrison, New York)

At noon today, I lit a candle for peace along with hundreds of other UN staff members. The occasion was a ceremony for peace at the UN so staffers could express their personal views. The event was brief and objective but filled me with emotion. Even while violence and hatred have their day within the world and within each one of us, may we also "wage peace" as the antidote to war. As soon as the ceremony ended, I walked back to Grand Central Terminal and caught a train to return to my wife's hospital bed where she is "waging healing" amid cancer and infections.

Because of the effects of the most recent chemotherapy, her white blood count had been extremely low. This allowed her to contract a mysterious infectious disease. After enduring four days of powerful medications and painkiller, and now being off most of them, she was feeling much better when I walked into her room this morning. I had also sought out the prayers and positive energy of Jean Houston and some of the other most powerful healers Mary and I know. Her white blood count doubled each day strengthening her own immune system.

When I mentioned that there was going to be a peace vigil at the UN today, she said "Rob, you must go. I am fine. Come back and tell me about it." Mary is such a beautiful, precious person. I am filled with gratitude for living my life with her for these thirty-four years.

Mary makes me wild as I try to understand her, care for her, and love her. She drives me crazy with her mysterious words, illnesses, and compassion. She is for me an embodiment of the Bodhisattva Kwan Yin, the Buddha of Compassion.

The matrix of nodules in her lungs and the fractal pattern of sores on her skin are sacred wounds through which primordial light emerges from primordial darkness. In her words in a recent poem:

True Darkness
Light Resurrected
Eternal Now.

My Angle on Creation

True Darkness
Light Resurrects Me
Eternal Now.

May this process result in her own healing as she brings peace and healing to the world.

May all sentient beings know peace and happiness, wisdom, and compassion.

I Am So Grateful for My Life

(December 2003, Garrison, New York)

On 18 July 2003, at 3:40 pm, Mary Elizabeth Avery Work, surrounded by her loving family, took her last breath, and united her being with the Endlessness of Mystery. While her essence moved to the Other World amid This World, mine remained primarily in This World. After a thirty-five-year partnership and journey on this Earth, my wife's dramatic transformation launched me on an emotional roller coaster of grief as a finite being in a world of finite beings. It has been devastating and disorienting. Why is something so natural and expected, experienced as so unreal, shocking, and painful?

Mary was a practical mystic. She conducted village meetings, made sure the cars were in running order, kept the household going smoothly, ensured that our two sons were moving forward in their lives, and cared for her parents and husband in myriad ways. She was also deeply devoted to God the Father, Son and Holy Spirit, and especially to Mary, the Mother of God, and to Kwan Yin, the Bodhisattva of Compassion. Mary regularly wrote powerful poetry and profound reflections in her journals. Her meditations were full of light and life. She developed an energy model showing the flows, transitions, and intersections of energy in one's life. She tried to cherish and enliven everyone she encountered.

She came to accept her cancer as "a need to be kicked into/ onto a higher level, an evolutionary leap." Five days before passing over, she made the decision to let go of this life. We reaffirmed our marriage vows before priest, family, and friends. Three days later, Mary lay down before God and let go of her life in trust, humility, and gratitude. How could she do this? What was she showing me, teaching all of us?

Since her trans-substantiation, I cry, write her letters (she writes back), read her journals, talk with my sons, receive messages of comfort from friends and family, attend Episcopal mass, visit a nearby Buddhist monastery, participate in Mystery School, and go on with my life. I am so grateful for having encountered this angel of love named Mary, married her, and lived with her – what an incredible gift to know someone so precious. Our partnership continues but in new ways. We spent thirty-five years trying to "save the world," living and working in villages and slums in Asia and the Caribbean, and we continue this mission together. It is not so easy, however, to be helpful. The world does not always want to be saved or in the ways I think that it needs to be. What does it really mean to "save all sentient beings?"

I continue my work as a policy adviser with the United Nations Development Program. I give advice to countries on decentralized governance, prepare policy papers and tool kits, design new country programs, give speeches in international conferences, facilitate global dialogues and knowledge networks, and launch pilot projects testing innovative approaches such as emotional intelligence, social artistry, and whole system design. And I render it up to the Mystery. For me, life and death are utter mystery. That is all I know or have ever known. Who was it who said, "life is a mystery to be lived, not a problem to be solved"? What is the difference really?

And every day, I say, as Mary said five days before she died, "I am so grateful for my life." Soon enough I will join my beloved in the Endlessness of Mystery. For now, she has gone before me. Until that time we have much to do together on this beautiful, suffering Earth.

Everything Is New

(April 2004, Garrison, New York)

Please forgive the use of words rather than presence.
Please forgive the use of writing without speaking.
Please forgive email rather than a handwritten note.
Nevertheless, may there be a miracle of *commun*ication.

It is impossible to comprehend that it has been nine months since the disappearance of the physical body and presence of my beloved. What can be apprehended is the experience of pain and suffering that has ensued – of shock, denial, loss, confusion, guilt, nostalgia, longing, loneliness, lostness, and anger. Yes, all of these, and more.

And yet, there is more. With the magical disappearance of the physical body of my life partner, the awareness has emerged of her spiritual body and the spiritual body of the universe. Her thoughts, words, and actions are powerfully present and at work in the world and in my daily life. Her genetic continuation is present in her sons. Her spiritual continuation is present in her writings, words spoken, deeds done, gestures made, and values manifest. These are not locked up in the past or in memory. No, they are present in the Eternal Here and Now. And they will continue to be part of life, consciousness, history, and evolution forever.

There is no birth, no death
No coming, no going
Your beauty is still here
Your intelligence is still present
Your generosity and kindness are manifest everywhere
Not limited to time and space

And what of me? Who am I? What am I called to do with my life? I am the same yet irrevocably different. I am now single although I still wear a wedding band on my finger. I am alone yet grateful for solitude. I dwell in memories yet am wildly open to future possibilities. I completed my covenant of thirty-five years as a husband. Now I am free – to be what? What new roles await me? In twenty-eight months, I retire from the UN. What new engagements will challenge me? If I sell my beautiful home on the Hudson River, what new places beckon me? My sons are grown. What new relationships with them can be forged? The world is torn with suffering. What profound voice calls my name? Everything is new – open – terrifying – exciting – fresh – overwhelming.

Yes!

Suffering is the ground of happiness.
Separation is the condition for reunion and wholeness.

Turning Sixty

(31 July 2004, Garrison, New York)

I turned sixty today. What is the purpose of the rest of my life? It is not about security. It is not about status. It is not about stability. It is not about money.

It is about understanding everything. It is about compassion for all beings everywhere. It is about happiness for all beings. It is about peace for all beings. It is about transformation. It is about equity in the world. It is about a sustainable Earth. It is about participatory governance. It is about social artistry. It is about a daily spiritual practice. Be it so!

I am alive now! Yet I am dying every moment. Someday, I will die, and my body will be quite dead – cold, hard, still, silent, unmoving. What was my life about? What did I leave for this world? What were my thoughts, words, deeds, values, style, relationships, and creations? Was I generous? Was I loving? Did I make others happy?

Someday, everything that I love will pass away. Everyone I love will pass away. This is the nature of life. I must not succumb to fear, paranoia, clinging. I will be brave. I will be happy. I will love. I renounce guilt at this moment! I refuse to live out of guilt and fear. Be gone! Gone, gone, completely gone!

I am free, free to be this one – just this one – no other. It is good to be me. I can live my real, given life as a gift in gratitude and joy. Yes!

I renounce self-depreciation and self-doubt. I touch the Earth and stand my ground. I am awake. I am this one, no other, and it is good, accepted, received, and open to possibility. Yes!

Red Knight to Hermit Monk

(3 April 2005, Garrison, New York)

Oh, my, so much is happening, so much to share, but what to share briefly, helpfully? With twenty months behind me since my beloved wife was transformed into spirit and with seventeen months before me when I will leave our beloved UN as a staff member, who am I and who am I becoming? With a passion for both social and spiritual transformation, as well as artistic and intellectual creativity, who am I being called to be?

Every morning before I arrive at my office, I meditate, play my French horn, dance, write in my journal, and read spiritual literature. I then engage in the impossible mission of helping others respond to the problems of the world – harmful governance, poverty, HIV/AIDS, gender inequality, environmental degradation – after which, I return home, have dinner, go to bed, and start all over the next morning. Who am I becoming?

In Jungian terms, I have enjoyed being a Red Knight for over three decades trying to save the world. But the damsel is still in great distress and the dragon breathes even more fire than before. Therefore, I will change tactics and become a Hermit Monk. Then, I can truly save the world. At sixty, I choose a life of introspection – prayer, contemplation, and meditation. But never forget, the inner always contains the outer and the outer always contains the inner.

When I was a theology grad student, I got a phone call from Joe Mathews, "Will you and Mary go to Malaysia?" And off we went! It is now thirty-six years later. Mary is spirit and I want to practice spirituality as a major endeavor. The gift is that now I have thirty-six years of service in human development in fifty-three countries and thirty-five years of family life on which to reflect and with which to create something useful for others. As an introverted soul, I knew I needed real experience out in the world.

How is my life perfect now? I live alone, so can do solitary exercises, yet am connected to the whole world. I live in an isolated area, so can play my horn without bothering neighbors. I live in beautiful nature just one hour from Manhattan, the Capital of the World, and can write and read on the commuter train. My house has room to host retreats for up to seven overnight guests and twenty others. And I remember, if one person wakes up then all beings are awake, and yet, no one is saved until all are saved.

This moment is a wonderful moment – empty, therefore full of everything; impermanent, therefore eternal; and full of suffering, therefore full of the possibility of perfect happiness, peace, understanding, and compassion. For this I am deeply grateful.

Our Assisi

(11 November 2005, Garrison, New York)

After a lifetime of feeling that I am special and have a unique calling, increasingly I am aware that my life is very much like other people's lives. I experience my life as congested and busy; so do most other people. I experience loss and regret; so do many others. I plan and dream of possible futures; so do most other folks. I experience happiness and joy over small and big things in my life; so do all the others. I love my family and friends; so does virtually everyone. This awareness is a great relief. I am not strange or special. I am part of the great river of life, of human experience, flowing onward from generation to generation.

I am not a separate, independent, eternal entity. I am interdependent with all people and indeed all beings and all phenomena. I am also impermanent as this particular coming together of form, perceptions, feelings, conceptions, and consciousness in space-time. I experience suffering as do all beings; but I can also relieve this suffering. This is all a great relief. I do not have to, cannot, protect or even fully comprehend my own being as it is part of the great Mystery of Being and Nonbeing.

As part of my morning meditation, I am mindful, among others, of four realities: my teachers, compassion, my archetypes, and emptiness. Each day I am grateful for my spiritual teachers: Joseph Mathews, Jean Houston, Gehlek Rimpoche, Bonnie Myotai Treace, Sensei, and others. I am mindful of my decision to be compassion, to be love, to seek enlightenment for the sake of relieving the suffering of all beings. I am mindful that I embody my archetypes and spiritual essences – Jesus, Buddha, Mary the Mother of God, Kwan Yin, and others. And I am mindful that I, and indeed all beings and phenomena, are empty of a separate, independent, eternal self.

Without my wife of thirty-five years, I am a different being. Who am I? As I prepare to leave the UN this next summer after sixteen years, I will have new roles and opportunities. What am I to do? As I practice Buddhism in dialogue with Christianity, I am developing a new life understanding. How do I know my knowing? How do I take sixty-one years of intensified knowing-doing-being and actualize the fullest contribution and service possible? I want to shift more to the spiritual, artistic, and wisdom dimensions of societal transformation. How to do this? I should not be looking outward for my future – where to live, which house, when to leave UNDP, what plans, jobs, colleagues. I should be listening inward to my heart and soul. This is why my eyesight is blurry and why I am meditating and listening to so much music.

My intuition is that the world system requires a radical waking up. Saint Francis of Assisi comes to mind as an exemplar. He shocked his time awake with his authenticity. He stood naked before his father. He lived a life of poverty. He befriended animals and all people. He created a community of love. He danced. He sang. People thought he was mad. He was in ecstatic love with God, with the Mystery, with the Final Reality, with suffering humanity. What would this look like in the globalizing world of the 21st Century?

Why was Jessie Clements compelled to leave his comfortable retirement and go to Indonesia to build houses for the Tsunami victims? Why does he now want to go to the Gulf region to help the Katrina victims? Why does Louise Singleton leave the comfort of her home in Denver to go to Africa to teach villagers how to prevent HIV/AIDS? Why do Larry Ward and Peggy Rowe give Mindfulness Retreats when they could make a lot more money doing private sector consulting? Why does Jan Sanders risk her life amidst a Maoist uprising in rural Nepal to teach social artistry? Are these people mad? Or are they in love with the Mystery, with suffering humanity? How do you and I do this in our Assisi?

Sheer Possibility

(April 2007, Garrison, New York)

After retiring from the UN last summer and holding the *Dance of Life* celebration, I launched a one-year sabbatical to explore possible futures. Since then, I became engaged to beloved Bonnie Myotai Treace, conducted a UN consultancy designing a global urban poverty reduction program, conducted an ashes scattering ceremony in Phoenix, Arizona, for my wife Mary, gave a public talk at New York University (NYU), prepared a syllabus for an NYU grad course that I have been asked to teach, attended Jean Houston's Advanced Mystery School on the "Revolution of Consciousness" held at the Garrison Institute, traveled twice with Bonnie to Abbey North in Canada, to Asheville, North Carolina, to be with son Christopher, to Edmond, Oklahoma, to be with my mom, put my house on the market, hosted my family in my home for Thanksgiving and Christmas, continued to meditate and write daily in my journal, and took weekly dance classes – a full plate.

Before my sabbatical is over I will also conduct another UN consultancy preparing a paper on "participation" and training workshop facilitators at the Global Forum on Reinventing Government in Vienna, Austria, design my marriage journey and wedding liturgy, sell my house, take additional trips with Bonnie to Oklahoma; North Carolina; Vienna, Austria; Ithaca,

Greece; Whidbey Island, Washington; Ashland, Oregon; and Haliburton, Canada, and participate in another session of the Advanced Mystery School.

I have not yet been able to actualize as part of my sabbatical: playing my French horn, designing, and marketing a retreat, marketing other consultancies (e.g., the UN and the Garrison Institute), arranging additional teaching opportunities, participating in Abbey North's Africa work, designing the Hillside Institute, reading many more books, writing a book, and reading my journals of the past thirty-seven years.

The Transformation of Living and Dying

(30 March 2018, Garrison, New York)

This is the week of dying (again) and living (again). In fact, to live is to die, and to die is to live. There is no life without death; there is no true living unless we die to what has been and to our illusions about who we are. And what does this have to do with April in New York?

I have lived in New York state longer than anywhere else in the world, twenty-eight years. It is now time to let go and to be refashioned. I love New York for so many reasons. Thus, the grieving, at first gentle, and later perhaps stronger.

This is where we settled after living overseas almost two decades. After being with a nonprofit working in poor villages and slums, I was refashioned into a UN policy adviser in New York City, still traveling the globe. Oh, how I loved being an international civil servant those sixteen years. Well, it was also challenging, but I stuck with it and let go ("retirement".)

I was then transformed into a grad school professor, (who me?), very meaningful, and challenging. A new life as teacher, consultant, and writer.

Beginning on Manhattan's Lower East Side (Loisaida), we moved to the north bank of the Long Island Sound. Then further north on the east bank of the Hudson River. Then northward again, though still on the Hudson.

During this journey, we bought our first ever car and house. We got our sons through high school and university. After years of her courageous, insightful battle with cancer, my wife completed her life. Our youngest son got married. Then I, surprisingly and happily, married a most wonderful person. Then the first grandchild was born in North Carolina beginning nine years of trekking back and forth between New York and North Carolina twice a year. Then the second grandchild. Then buying a house in North Carolina. So much transformation.

And now, it is time again to die to the known and embrace a life unknown. Letting go is a little painful. I love the Hudson, the little river towns, the Garrison Institute, Chuang Yin Monastery, St. Mary's Episcopal Church, our St. Philip's cottage, family, friends, students, the greatest city in the world, iconic UN headquarters, the Washington Square NYU campus, the diversity, the crush of humanity.

What will our new life be? Will we be happy? Will we be healthy? Will we be able to serve locally, nationally, globally? How will our democracy fare? What about climate change? How will the mountains change us? How will we deal with aging? How can we inspire the grandkids? When and how will we leave this life altogether?

And then what? Our words and deeds will reverberate forever in new forms, speeches, buildings, books, communities, brains, institutions, mouths. Our DNA will perhaps flow onward. Our atoms and cells will refashion into flowers and trees and perhaps frogs and tigers and who knows what else.

Onward! We have more living and dying and living to do.

A Grateful Earthling: My Spiritual Journey

(31 March 2019, Swannanoa, North Carolina)

I was born a WASP – white, Anglo-Saxon, and protestant. My father had been a Baptist but at marriage joined my mother in the Christian Church, a Protestant denomination in the US in the Reformed tradition with historical ties to the Restoration Movement. We lived in Oklahoma most of my childhood, and I attended Sunday School and worship service including communion every Sunday. For many years I had perfect attendance in Sunday School and wore little colored enamel medals pinned and dangling from my jacket on my chest. After the ritual of my baptism by emersion my family told me that my feet stuck up out of the water when the pastor dunked me under.

We passed the communion trays down the aisles, and each ate a tiny hard wafer and drank grape juice from a little glass which we returned empty to its hole in the round metal tray. When I was old enough, I joined in serving the communion trays or the collection plates to the congregation. Our sanctuary had stained glass windows with pictures of Jesus. I listened to many sermons and learned that if I would be a good person and believed that Jesus was my savior, I would go to heaven when I died.

The year I went off to university, my dad sold his accounting business and left for theological seminary along with my mother and younger brother. Dad had felt called to be a pastor after his mother, my grandmother, passed away. Her death was also a crisis for me, the first death in our family. I wept loudly during her service and missed her so much. On campus I often attended the Wesley Foundation (Methodist) for discussion and music in the coffee house.

When I was a junior in college, a group of us students drove to Chicago and attended a weekend seminar at the Ecumenical Institute (EI) on the Theological Revolution of the 20th Century (RS-1). This was my first profound awakening.

In the seminar, we held group conversations, heard lectures, and studied papers by 20th century theologians including Rudolph Bultmann, Paul Tillich, Dietrich Bonhoeffer, and Richard Niebuhr. We learned that Christian symbols needed to be demythologized to be encountered and understood as life realities not just religious ideas. The universe had no second story. I realized that the verbal symbol "G-O-D" pointed to that mysterious power ("upagainstness") that drives us into life and cuts us off from life. I learned that the "Christ" was the word of possibility that enables one to live one's given life. The Word rang out: "All is Good. You are Accepted. The Past is Approved. The Future is Open." I learned that "Holy Spirit" was the freedom and obedience experienced in responsibility in the midst of that; and that "Church" was the group of social pioneers who lived between the no-longer and the not-yet laying down their lives to create a better world on behalf of all people.

I had a profound experience of being accepted just as I am and realized that I wanted to live my life on behalf of all people. When I returned to my college, I was so charged with energy and happiness that I sensed that I was levitating as I walked across campus. I became a campus activist for women's rights, civil rights, and peace. I wrote poetry and studied the existentialist philosophers and theologians. I felt that I was called to help create a world in which everyone could realize her or his full potential. When I would return home to visit my family, I would sometimes argue with my dad who had become a pastor in a local church. I realized that I did not always agree with his views of Christianity and about life.

After graduating from Oklahoma State University, I attended graduate school at Indiana University and then Chicago Theological Seminary (CTS). I did not want to become a minister but to study the journey of the Ultimate in history. While at CTS, I became a sojourner at the Ecumenical Institute (EI) in the westside African American ghetto. Early every morning we participated in our liturgical service, the Daily Office, followed by collegium (group discussion) and breakfast. At the core of the EI was an ecumenical, secular-religious, experimental family order, the Order Ecumenical (OE.) As Order members, we made three vows: poverty, living on a small stipend; obedience, being assignable anywhere in the world; and chastity, willing one's life to be about one thing, service on behalf of all.

After marrying my sweetheart from CTS who was also sojourning at EI, we travelled around the world in a one-month Global Odyssey with a group of EI colleagues to experience an intensification of global humanness. Thus, I fell in love with planet Earth and her people. After this we began a twenty-two-year journey of serving the least, the lost, and the last, in Malaysia, South Korea, USA, Jamaica, and Venezuela. During that time, the EI evolved into a secular organization, the Institute of Cultural Affairs (ICA.)

We lived in urban slums and poor rural villages and helped the local people improve their lives and create models that other communities could follow. In Malaysia, I encountered Islam and experienced other ways of being human that were sustaining. In South Korea, we had two sons, one by adoption, one by birth, and were changed by the deep collective wisdom of a Confucian-Buddhist-Christian culture. In Jamaica, I met Rastafarianism, learned to dance reggae, and trekked in the Blue Mountains. In Venezuela, I learned Spanish and encountered a Catholic culture and the vitality of Latin America. Around the world were many deep wells of meaning, symbols, and traditions, but they all seemed to connect to one vast reservoir of mystery, truth, and love. Being a self-conscious Earthling in a 13.7-billion-year-old universe was mysterious enough.

Over these many years as our staff came from different religious traditions, the ICA developed secular forms of spirituality – Profound Humanness, and the Other World amidst This World – experiences of mystery, consciousness, care, and tranquility.

In between our Jamaican and Venezuelan assignments, I woke up to Buddhist wisdom and meditation through Ken Wilber's book *No Boundaries*, and in an ICA summer global research assembly that began to change my spiritual orientation. Soon I started to meditate daily and to read Buddhist literature.

When we returned to the US, I worked with UNDP as a global policy adviser in local governance and later taught innovative leadership to graduate students at NYU Wagner. We joined the Episcopal Church (oh, how I loved the mass, processions, incense, and all), participated in Jean Houston's transformative Mystery Schools (filled with sensory, psychological, mythic, and unitive processes), and attended Buddhist retreats in the Zen and Tibetan traditions. I so appreciated that Buddhism was a philosophy and a practice for living rather than a religion.

In one Buddhist retreat in my native Oklahoma, I received the dharma name "Ancient Treasure of the Heart." I was grateful for the helpful practices of Buddhist precepts, mantras, and sitting meditation. I took vows to relieve the suffering of all sentient beings. When I experienced the death of my wife of thirty-five years after a long battle with cancer at only sixty, I was devastated, grieved hard, and did not plan to remarry; but life had other plans, and I fell deeply in love with an amazing woman who was a Zen teacher and writer, and happily did just that.

Two years ago, I published *A Compassionate Civilization* providing vision, actions, leadership methods, and selfcare practices for creating a sustainable, just, compassionate society that enables each person to realize her/his full potential. In that book, I wrote that ours is the most critical time in human history. We are facing multiple crises of climate chaos and ecosystem degradation, patriarchy and misogyny, systemic poverty and social deprivation, plutocracy and corporatocracy, racism and xenophobia, and perpetual warfare. If we are to survive and thrive, we must pivot to environmental sustainability, gender equality, socioeconomic justice, participatory governance, cultural tolerance, and peace and nonviolence. We must become mindful activists for sustainable development as members of a movement of movements (MOM.) This is our great calling today on planet Earth.

These days to nurture and make manifest my mind and heart, I meditate and say mantras, keep a journal, attend periodic Buddhist retreats, speak at conferences, do some consulting, engage in social and political activism, care for my family, walk in nature, and prepare for the completion of this brief incarnation.

My spiritual journey began in a traditional protestant denomination, evolved into demythologized ecumenical Christianity, to secular spirituality and global profound humanness, to the recovery of the ancient mystery schools, to Episcopalian liturgy, to Zen and Tibetan Buddhist practice, to my unique blend of spirituality of consciousness, mystery, gratitude, compassion, and wisdom.

I am so deeply grateful for life itself and for my life and am in the process of writing my autobiography – *Serving People & Planet* – which I hope to publish later this year for my seventy-fifth birthday. May it serve to inspire and guide others on their journey.

What for you is the meaning of life? What is the purpose of your life? What is your unique path? How are you being guided by love and truth?

May you realize peace, happiness, understanding, and compassion!

Acknowledgements

Gratitude to David D. Elliott (Vietnam) for reading the manuscript before publication and writing the Foreword.

Gratitude to those who read the manuscript before publication and wrote advance reviews including Professor Harold Nelson, PhD, Tina Spencer (Australia), Charles F. "Chic" Dambach, Elsa Javines Batica, and Kathleen Callahan.

Gratitude to friends around the world on LinkedIn and Facebook who shared their advice and encouragement on the formulation of the book during the first half of 2021 including Nikhil Chandavarkar, Mohammed Hosain, Osha Belle Hayden, Omoruyi Aigbe, Kathleen Callahan, John Cock, Pratibha Mehta, Jacqueline Priseman, Fayyaz Baqir, Nancy Trask, Jo Nelson, Lisi Ha Vinh, Kay Dambach, Resa Alboher, Mounir Tabet, Steve Rhea, Toni Wells, Kelly Jane, Sharon Fisher, Rebecca Oliveira, Brian Griffith, Michael Burns, Harold Nelson, Chic Dambach, Monica Bourgeau, Kevin Guyan, Jan Loubser, Matthew Lindberg-Work, Peter Palmeri, Kerry Christopher Dugan, Aatu Koskensilta, Mary Ann Bennett Rosburg, Ishu Subba, Pauline Apilado, Janet Sanders, John O'Neill, Hank Hankla, Kelli Brooke Haney, Henning Karcher, Ronnie Seagren, Debra Harris-Watson, Margaret Scott, Isobel Bishop, Cynthia Leonard, Jonas Chabroka Fadweck, Larry Ward, Pat Webb, Puthrika Moonesinghe, Elsa Javines Batica, Nu Nu Win, Carrie Crandall, Andrea Cassidy, Anjela Dale,

Gino Vrolijk, Myo Myint, Melanie Daniels, Julie Miesen, Lara Morrison, Pat Druckenmiller, Judi White, Amy Smith, Addi Batica, Dale Lature, Ayana Mustapha Salifu, Voice Vingo, Laura J. Bauer, John B. Hoag, Hiraman Gavai, Francielle Lacle, Diana Hartel, Bruce Robertson, David Elliott, Lisa Lindberg, David Treace, Blase Sands, and Johnny Andrews.

Gratitude to Amnet (India) for their help with cover design and interior layout, and to Kindle Direct Publishing (KDP) and IngramSpark for their assistance in printing, distribution, and marketing.

And special thanks to my wife Bonnie Myotai Treace for her insightful advice and kind encouragement for my writing and publishing.

Appendix

Author's Videos, Podcasts, Websites, and Books

Author's Online Resources:

Videos of author's speeches:

Chicago. ICA USA International Development Think Tank Keynote. 2010: https://www.youtube.com/user/bergdall2

Seoul. UN Forum Workshop Presentation. 2014: https://www.youtube.com/watch?v=KQ3E1AZqFgw

Oklahoma City. OCU Peace Symposium Keynote. 2014: https://vimeo.com/89274462

Fairfield, Iowa. World's Fairfield Peace Symposium Keynote. 2018: https://www.youtube.com/watch?v=hSI5cHwS4TY&feature=youtu.be

Colquitt, Georgia. Building Creative Communities Conference Keynote. 2019: https://www.youtube.com/channel/UCf6RHm5Hy-KT63DDsb9Ymlg/

Chicago. ICA USA Archives Collegium Presentation. 2019: https://www.facebook.com/icaukraine/videos/283358729261479/UzpfSTEzNzI4NDg1NjU6MTAyMTg3Mzc1MzM0NTQxMTM/

Zoom. Presentation to International e-Conference on Research and Development in South Asia. 2021: https://drive.google.com/file/d/1720s4vV26Nlt5YdBr7RMuVDyQaGwq3kE/view

347

Zoom/podcast. Presentation to UN Experiential Fellows. 2021: https://podcasts.apple.com/nl/podcast/blueridgespeak-ers-talk-by-robertson-work-blueridgefellows/id1543099064?i=1000510088481&l=en

Podcasts of radio interviews with author:
North Carolina. *Thinking of Travel.* 2017: http://speakingoftravel.net.buzzsprout.com/18461/603428-robertson-work-shares-how-to-become-a-global-local-citizen
Arizona. *Democratic Perspectives* #1. 2018: http://verdevalleyindependentdemocrats.org/2018/01/17/creating-more-compassionate-communities/
Arizona. *Democratic Perspectives* #2. 2018: http://verdevalley-independentdemocrats.org/2018/04/03/robertson-work-interview-podcast-april-2-2018/
California. *Aspire with Osha.* 2021: https://oshahayden.com/podcast/compassionate-civilization-a-conversation-with-robertson-work/

Websites with author's interviews, articles, or book excerpts:
Buddhadoor website author interview. 2018: https://www.buddhistdoor.net/features/creating-a-compassionate-civiliza-tion-an-interview-with-robertson-work
Garrison Institute website excerpt of ACC. 2017: https://www.garrisoninstitute.org/blog/catalyzing-empathic-engaged-citizens/
ICA International website excerpt of ACC. 2017: http://www.ica-international.org/2017/08/14/compassionate-civiliza-tion-urgency-sustainable-development-mindful-activism-reflections-recommendations-rob-work/
American Buddhist Perspectives website excerpt of ACC. 2018: https://www.patheos.com/blogs/americanbuddhist/2018/02/burn-never-guide-compassionate-mindful-activism.html
Progressive Buddhism website excerpt of ACC. 2018: https://progressivebuddhism.blogspot.com/2018/02/how-can-we-build-coalitions-in-this.html

NYU Wagner website article on ACC. 2017: https://wagner.nyu.
   edu/news/story/prof-robertson-work-out-book-compas-
   sionate-civilization-urgency-sustainable-development
Author's Social Media Sites:
A Compassionate Civilization (ACC):
Amazon: https://www.amazon.com/dp/1546972617
Blogsite: https://compassionatecivilization.blogspot.com/
Facebook page: https://www.facebook.com/compassiona
   tecivilization/
Movement of Movements (MOM) Facebook page: https://www.
   facebook.com/movementofmovementsMOM/
Robertson Work:
Facebook page: https://www.facebook.com/robertson.work
LinkedIn page: https://www.linkedin.com/in/robertsonwork/
   Twitter page: https://twitter.com/robertsonwork
Amazon author's page: https://www.amazon.com/Robertson-
   Work/e/B075612GBF%3Fref=dbs_a_mng_rwt_scns_share
Author's website: https://www.robertsonwork.com/

Author's Publications:
Work, Robertson. 2020. *The Critical Decade 2020 – 2029: Calls
   for Ecological, Compassionate Leadership.* Swannanoa NC:
   Compassionate Civilization Press.
_____. 2020. *Earthling Love: Living Poems.* Swannanoa
   NC: Compassionate Civilization Press.
_____. 2020. *Serving People & Planet: In Mystery,
   Love, and Gratitude.* Morrisville NC: Lulu Press.
_____. 2017. *A Compassionate Civilization: The Urgency
   of Sustainable Development and Mindful Activism – Reflections
   and Recommendations.* Swannanoa NC: Compassionate
   Civilization Collaborative (C3).
_____. 2010. "Civil Society Innovations in Gover-
   nance Leadership: International Demonstrations of Integral Development, the Technology of Participation (ToP),
   and Social Artistry". pages 112 – 130. *Engaging Civil Society:
   Emerging Trends in Democratic Governance.* editors Cheema,

G. Shabbir, and Popovski, Vesselin. Tokyo: UN University Press.

_____. 2001. "Decentralization, Governance, and Sustainable Regional Development". pages 21 – 34. *New Regional Development Paradigms, Vol. 3, Decentralization, Governance, and the New Planning for Local-Level Development*. editors, Stohr, Walter B., et al. Westport CT: Greenwood Press.

_____. 2003. "Decentralizing Governance: Participation and Partnership in Service Delivery to the Poor". pages 195 – 218. *Reinventing Government for the Twenty-First Center: State Capacity in a Globalizing Society*. Editors. Rondinelli, Dennis A., and Cheema, G. Shabbir. Bloomfield CT: Kumarian Press.

_____. 2003. "Overview of Decentralization Worldwide: A Steppingstone to Improved Governance and Human Development". pages 3 – 24. *Decentralization & Power Shift: An Imperative for Good Governance – A Sourcebook on Decentralization and Federalism Experiences, Vol. 11: Federalism: The Future of Decentralizing States*. Editors. Brillantes, Jr., Alex B, et al. Manila: Asian Resource Center for Decentralization/ UNDP Philippines.

_____. Editor. 1997. *Participatory Local Governance: LIFE's Method and Experience 1992 – 1997*. New York: UNDP.

_____. Editor. 2005. *Pro-Poor Urban Governance: Lessons from LIFE 1992 – 2005*. New York: UNDP.

_____. 1998. "The Role of Development Assistance in the Area of Decentralization". pages 51 – 56. *International Symposium on Local Development and the Role of Government: New Perspectives on Development Assistance*. JICA. Tokyo: IIC/ JICA

_____. 1995. "LIFE". pages 90 – 91. *Public Sector Management, Governance, and Sustainable Human Development*. MDGD/BPPS/UNDP. New York: UNDP.

_____. 2007. "The Global Citizen: A Love Story," pages 50 – 56, *Life Lessons for Loving the Way You Live: 7 Essential Ingredients for Finding Balance and Serenity.* Hawthorne, Jennifer Read. Deerfield Beach FL: Health Communications.

_____. 2009. "Strengthening Governance and Public Administration Capacities for Development: A UN ECOSOC Background Paper." New York: UN.

_____. 1993, *LIFE Mission Reports: Jamaica, Brazil, Pakistan, Thailand, Senegal, Tanzania, Egypt, Morocco.* New York: UNDP.

_____. 1994. *LIFE Report on the Global Advisory Committee and Donor Workshop, Stockholm: First Year Review and Strategic Planning.* New York: UNDP.

_____. 1995. *LIFE Report of the Second Annual Global Advisory Committee Workshop, Cairo: Phase 1 Assessment and Phase 2 Strategies.* New York: UNDP.

Recommended Reading

Publications

Berry, Thomas, and Brian Swimme.1994. *The Universe Story*. San Francisco: Harper One.

Bregman, Rutger. 2020. *Humankind: A Hopeful History*. New York: Little, Brown and Co.

_____. 2016. *Utopia for Realists*. Amsterdam: The Correspondent.

Canfield, Jack, Mark Victor Hansen, and Jennifer Read Hawthorne. 2007. *Life Lessons for Loving the Way You Live*. Deerfield Beach: Health Communications.

Cheema, G. Shabbir, ed. 2003. *Reinventing Government for the Twenty-First Century*. Boulder: Kumarian.

Cheema, G. Shabbir, and Vesselin Popovski, eds.2010. *Engaging Civil Society*. Tokyo: UN University Press.

Cooperrider, David L. 2005. *Appreciative Inquiry*. San Francisco: Berrett-Koehler.

Dalai Lama, 14th.2001. *Ethics for the New Millennium*. New York: Riverhead Books.

Eisenstein, Charles. 2011. *Sacred Economics*. Berkeley: Evolver Editions.

Emmott, Stephen. 2013. *Ten Billion*. New York: Vintage.

Gandhi, Mohandas. 1993. *Gandhi: An Autobiography—The Story of My Experiment with Truth*. New York: Beacon.

Goleman, Daniel. 2005. *Emotional Intelligence*. New York: Bantam.

Hansen, James. 2009. *Storms of My Grandchildren*. New York: Bloomsbury

Harman, Willis. 1990. *Global Mind Change*. New York: Grand Central.

Hock, Dee. 2000. *Birth of the Chaordic Age*. Oakland: Berrett-Koehler.

Houston, Jean. 2004. *Jump Time*. Boulder: Sentient Publications
_____. 1982. *The Possible Human*. Los Angeles: J. P. Tarcher.

King, Martin Luther, Jr. 2010. *Strength to Love*. Minneapolis: Fortress.

Klein, Naomi. 2017. *No Is Not Enough*. Chicago: Haymarket Books.

_____2014. *This Changes Everything: Capitalism vs. the Climate*. New York: Simon & Schuster Paperbacks.

Kolbert, Elizabeth. 2014. *The Sixth Extinction: An Unnatural History*. New York: Henry Holt.

Korten, David C. 1995. *When Corporations Rule the World*. Boulder: Kumarian and Berrett-Koehler.

Lawrence, D. H. 1959. *Selected Poems*. New York: Viking Compass.

Mandela, Nelson. 1995. *Long Walk to Freedom*. New York: Back Bay Books.

McKibben, Bill. 2011. *Eaarth: Making a Life on a Tough New Planet*. New York: St. Martin's Griffin.

Nelson, Harold. 2014. *The Design Way*. Boston: MIT Press.

Nhat Hanh, Thich. 1998. *The Heart of the Buddha's Teachings*. Berkeley: Parallax.

Owen, Harrison. 2008. *Open Space Technology*. San Francisco: Berrett-Koehler.

Ray, Paul H. 2000. *The Cultural Creatives*. New York: Three Rivers Press.

Reich, Robert B. 2016. *Saving Capitalism*. New York: Vintage.

Rifkin, Jeremy. 2009. *The Empathic Civilization*. New York: J. P. Tarcher/Penguin.

Rilke, Rainer Maria. 1986. *Letters to a Young Poet*. New York: Vintage.

Sanders, Bernie. 2016. *Our Revolution*. New York: Thomas Dunne Books.

Shantideva. 2003. *The Way of the Bodhisattva*. Boston: Shambhala

Stanfield, R. Brian. 2000. *The Art of Focused Conversation*. Toronto: The Canadian Institute of Cultural Affairs.

_____. 2012. *The Courage to Care*. 2nd Edition. Toronto: The Canadian Institute of Cultural Affairs.

_____ . 2002. *The Workshop Book*. Toronto: The Canadian Institute of Cultural Affairs.

Staples, Bill. 2012. *Transformational Strategy*. Toronto: Canadian Institute of Cultural Affairs.

Teilhard de Chardin, Pierre. 1959. *The Phenomenon of Man*. New York: Harper Colophon Books.

Thunberg, Greta. 2019. *No One Is Too Small To Make A Difference*. New York: Penguin Books.

Timsina, Tatwa. 2012. *Changing Lives, Changing Societies*. Kathmandu: ICA Nepal.

United Nations Development Programme. 2012. *Human Development Report 2011*. New York: Palgrave Macmillan/ United Nations.

Ward, Larry. 2020. *America's Racial Karma: An Invitation to Heal*. Westminster MD: Parallax.

Warren, Elizabeth. 2014. *A Fighting Chance*. Metropolitan Books, New York.

Wilber, Ken. 2001. *A Brief History of Everything*. Boulder: Shambhala.

_____. 2007. *The Integral Vision*. Boulder: Shambhala.

Williams, R. Bruce. 2006. *More Than 50 Ways to Build Team Consensus*. Thousand Oaks: Corwin.

Work, Robertson. 2007. "Strengthening Governance and Public Administration Capacities for Development: A UN Background Paper." New York: United Nations.

Yousafzai, Malala. 2015. *I Am Malala*. New York: Back Bay Books.

Websites
350.org

ACLU, www.aclu.org

A Compassionate Civilization (blog,) http://compassionatecivilization.blogspot.com/

Big History Project, www.bighistoryproject.com/home

Building Creative Communities Conference https://www.bc3-colquittga.com

Charter for Compassion, www.charterforcompassion.org

Democracy Now, www.democracynow.org/

Democracy Spring, www.democracyspring.org

Disruption, watchdisruption.com

Emberling, Dennis. 2005. "Stages of [Leadership] Development." www.developmentalconsulting.com/pdfs/Stages_of_Development_vA.pdf

Greenpeace, www.greenpeace.org/international/en

Gross National Happiness, http://www.gnhcentrebhutan.org/what-is-gnh/

Horace Mann School (NYC) https://www.horacemann.org/

Human Rights Watch, www.hrw.org

ICA Social Research Center/Archives: www.icaglobalarchives.org

IndivisibleGuide.com, www.indivisibleguide.com

Institute of Cultural Affairs (ICA) International, www.ica-international.org

Institute of Cultural Affairs USA www.ica-usa.org

Integral Institute, in.integralinstitute.org/integral.aspx

International Association of Facilitators (IAF), www.iaf-world.org/site

Kosmos, www.kosmosjournal.org

New York University (NYU) Wagner Graduate School of Public Service, wagner.nyu.edu

Oklahoma City University https://www.okcu.edu

One World House, oneworldhouse.net

Our Revolution, ourrevolution.com

Pale Blue Dot, www.youtube.com/watch?v=p86BPM1GV8M

Peoples Climate, peoplesclimate.org

People's Summit, www.thepeoplessummit.org

Social Artistry, www.jeanhouston.org/Social-Artistry/social-artistry.html

Story Bridge https://www.storybridge.space/

Swamp Gravy https://swampgravy.com/

Technology of Participation (ToP) Network, icausa.member-clicks.net

"The Story of Solutions", www.youtube.com/watch?v=cpkRvc-sOKk

Transition Towns, www.transitionus.org/transition-towns

UN Department of Economic and Social Affairs (UNDESA), www.un.org/development/desa/en

UNDESA Public Service Awards and Global Forum https://publicadministration.un.org/en/UNPSA

UN-Habitat, unhabitat.org

UN Intergovernmental Panel on Climate Change www.ipcc.ch

United Nations Development Programme, www.undp.org

United Nations Millennium Development Goals https://www.un.org/millenniumgoals/

United Nations Sustainable Development Goals, www.un.org/sustainabledevelopment/sustainable-development-goals

Universal Declaration of Human Rights, www.un.org/en/universal-declaration-human-rights/

World Fair Field International Festival https://worldfairfield.org/

About the Author

Moorman Robertson Work, Jr. is a nonfiction author, ecosystems/justice activist, and adviser to the Blue Ridge UN experiential fellowship program, the ICA Nepal educational support program, Planetary Human, and Overview Earth. He has published four previous books – a manifesto/handbook, autobiography, poetry, and speeches – and contributed to eleven others.

He has worked in over fifty countries for over fifty years as United Nations Development Program (UNDP) principal policy adviser for decentralized governance, New York University (NYU) Wagner Graduate School of Public Service adjunct professor of innovative leadership for sustainable development, and Institute of Cultural Affairs (ICA) executive-director of national offices in Malaysia, the Republic of Korea, Jamaica, and Venezuela, and regional offices in Dallas, Texas, and Indiahoma, Oklahoma, conducting community, organizational, and leadership development initiatives.

Robertson has also been a group facilitator, Fulbright senior specialist, UN consultant, and conference speaker. His graduate studies were at Indiana University and Chicago Theological Seminary, with undergraduate studies at Oklahoma State University which honored him in 2003 with the Distinguished Alumnus Award.

He lives with his wife in Swannanoa, North Carolina, near family and friends, the Blue Ridge Mountains, and the Great Smoky Mountains. Each day, he does what he can to help catalyze an ecological, compassionate community and civilization, and can be reached at: robertsonwork100@gmail.com.

Other books by the author available on Amazon.com, IngramSpark, Lulu, etc., and through local bookshops.

Made in the USA
Columbia, SC
05 October 2021

46770142R00211